Riddles and Wonders: Defining Humanity in Anglo-Saxon England

Riddles and Wonders: Defining Humanity in Anglo-Saxon England

Volume 31

Edited by

María José Álvarez-Faedo
Andrew Monnickendam
Beatriz Penas-Ibáñez

Jasmine Bria

Riddles and Wonders: Defining Humanity in Anglo-Saxon England

PETER LANG

Lausanne · Berlin · Bruxelles · Chennai · New York · Oxford

Bibliographic information published by the Deutsche Nationalbibliothek
The Deutsche Nationalbibliothek collects this publication in the Deutsche Nationalbibliografie.
Nationalbibliografie; detailed bibliographic data is available on the Internet at http://dnb.d-nb.de..

Library of Congress Cataloging-in-Publication
This book has been requested for registration in the Library of Congress
CIP catalog
of the Library of Congres
Cover illustration:
© Linnaea Mallette / publicdomainpictures.net
The publication of this book has been financed by the University Extension and Publications Commission of the Department of Modern Philology of the University of Alcalá.

ISSN 2297-4628
ISBN 978-3-0343-4504-0 (Print)
E-ISBN 978-3-0343-4772-3 (E-PDF)
E-ISBN 978-3-0343-4773-0 (E-PUB)
DOI 10.3726/b21170

© Peter Lang Group AG
International academic publishers
Bern 2023

All rights reserved.
This publication may not be reproduced, in whole or in part, or recorded or transmitted by any information retrieval system, in any form or by any means, whether mechanical, photochemical, electronic, magnetic, electro-optical
in or transmitted by any information retrieval system, in any form or by any means, mechanical, photochemical, electronic, magnetic, electro-optical, photocopying, or otherwise, without the prior written permission of the publisher.
written permission of the publisher.

This publication has been peer-reviewed.
www.peterlang.com

Contents

Acknowledgements 7

Preface 9

Introduction 11

1. The *Exeter Book* Collection and the Riddle Tradition 33
   1.1 The evolution of the riddle genre 35
   1.2 Riddle and metaphor 39

2. Prosopopoeia, Anthropomorphism and Empathy 47
   2.1 *#15/13:* Fight like a man 54
   2.2 *#77/74:* Eat like an animal 64
   2.3 *#72/70:* Slave away like an ox 71

3. Riddles and Metamorphosis 83
   3.1 *#26/24*: From animal to book 87

4. *Wonders of the East*: Men, Animals and In-Between 101
   4.1 Origin and circulation of the texts: From the *Letter of Pharasmanes* to *Wonders of the East* 102
   4.2 Structure and organization of *Wonders of the East* 108

5. Uncertain Humanity Denied Humanity 119
   5.1 Doubtful men: Cynocephali, ichthyophagi and onocentaurs 120
   5.2 The dehumanization of the hybrid women 134

6. Alien and Familiar 145
   6.1 Anthropomorphizing the animal: Lion-headed giants and Donestres 145
   6.2 Monstrosity: A Necessary Otherness 161

Conclusions 165

References 169

Acknowledgements

There are a number of people I would like to thank for helping me produce this book.

I am greatly indebted to Professor Carla Riviello for being a rigorous scholar and an excellent mentor; she gave me so much of her time over the last few years and helped me to sharpen and direct my ideas from the very beginning.

A special thank you goes out to Doctor Megan Cavell who welcomed me to the University of Birmingham, where I conducted part of my research, and was of enormous help to me both personally and scientifically.

I would also like to acknowledge with my gratitude the members of the Department of Humanities at University of Calabria. I am very obliged towards Professor Raffaele Perrelli and Professor Annafrancesca Naccarato for their ongoing support and encouragement; sincere thanks go also to Doctor Federica Vercillo, for her patience and expertise.

I wish also to thank Ulrike Döring at Peter Lang for her tireless assistance. I am also grateful to the series editors, whose comments and suggestions have been so valuable in the book's development. This volume would have never seen the light of day if it had not been for their insightful comments.

The biggest thank you is reserved for my family and friends, because so much of their love came to be part of my determination to complete this research.

Preface

Jasmine Bria's work offers an articulated analysis of the ways in which the human-animal relationship was represented in Anglo-Saxon literary documentation between the eighth and the eleventh centuries, focusing specifically on animal's portrayals in the *Exeter Book Riddles* and on the monstrous depictions in the teratological treatise known as *Wonders of the East*.

The author attempts to explore spaces of Anglo-Saxon thought in which animality and humanity appear to meet, thus providing an original reading about specific aspects regarding Early Medieval England, through the analysis of different but complementary works, appropriately contextualized in the relative cultural context.

The volume assesses the *Riddles* and the *Wonders of the East* in their entirety before focusing the study on the rhetorical strategies directed to the subjects' specific depictions. The work introduces and critically illustrates the origin and evolution of the enigmatographic and the teratological traditions, as well as the influences exerted on the composition of the works analysed; through a careful examination of the sources, the author reconstructs the genesis of the *Riddles* and the *Wonders* in their own manuscript tradition.

The author's main contribution is the attempt to examine in depth, from a philological-literary standpoint, both the numerous riddle-poems centred on animal figures, reproduced through highly anthropomorphic rhetorical strategies, and the catalogue of bestial characters and monstrous peoples depicted in the *Wonders of the East*, allowing the complexity of the correlations between man, animal and intermediate beings to emerge.

The study reveals the diverse but correlated modalities through which the creatures described in the *Wonders* and the *Riddles* defy categorization. The *Riddles*' metaphorical and metamorphic portrayals expose a universe made up of protean figures, a world of stories and entities that are always changing through time, where conceptual categories are continuously trespasses. In the *Wonders*, on the other hand, hybrid creatures reproduce a world of intrinsically multifaced differences, where conflicting and incompatible categories are forced to coexist.

Conducted with methodological clarity and sharp criticism, this path of textual interpretation therefore reveals the existence of a sometimes-contradictory relationship between the definitions of animality and humanity, a relationship in which the claims of a radical alteration of animal subjects are called into question. Although far from constituting an accurate reproduction of reality, the heterogeneous and complex representations analysed show that there was a manifold vision on non-human animals in Anglo-Saxon society. This work let emerge what can be considered affinity between species and a kind of concern for all that can be called different.

Carla Riviello

Introduction

The definition of an animal and its relationship to humans have been hotly contested topics throughout human culture's history. Human societies have made numerous and varied attempts to distinguish themselves from other animal species while, more often than not, acknowledging an instinctive connection.[1] This discussion has evolved over time, involving not only the law and social life but also finding expression in the arts and literature.

The most archaic pre-Christian cultures seemed to have perceived the boundary between humans and other animals as potentially permeable.[2] To some extent, remnants of this perspective can be seen in various Germanic cultures; for instance, the Nordic berserker tradition suggests that for Norse people the bodily matters of men and animals could somehow merge in order for the animal to protect and sustain the man.[3]

---

1   For instance, in the Western philosophical tradition on human nature – stretching from Plato and Aristotle through Plutarch, Polybius and even Machiavelli – it was understood that humans may have descended from animal ancestors who lacked language and civilization. Nonetheless, this same philosophical tradition, formed on Plato's idea of the soul as consisting of three parts – appetites, spirits, and reasons – frequently failed to acknowledge to animals the use of reason. See Masters, 113.

2   In south-western France, the cave paintings of the underground complex of Trois Frères (thirteenth millennium BCE) might be considered as evidence testifying this close link between the earlier human societies and animals, which were probably charged with a magic-religious value. In the cave, the partially engraved and partially painted figure of a deer-man – assisted by two smaller bison-men – dominates a series of other animal figures fighting each other. For a detailed reconstruction of animal representations in rock art see Klingender, 3–27. In the earliest evolution phases of humanity, the perceived closeness between species might have indicated the absence of a self-consciousness able to recognize itself as completely human: the first hunter-gatherer societies probably had a sense of being, *das Daseingefühl*, strictly connected to the animal kingdom; see Maag, 7–18 and Honegeer, 5–7.

3   As known, in the *Ynglinga Saga* Snorri Sturluson (*Heimskringla*, VI) designated these men as warriors at the service of Odin, who wore the furs of bears, wolves or reindeers and, just before entering the battlefield, went into a state of trance or rage, called *berserkrsgangr*; this condition of rapture made them strong, ferocious

Furthermore, the material culture dating back to the earlier centuries of Anglo-Saxon rule in England is rich in zoomorphic representations: jewels, caskets, weapons and armours often depict animals; thus, giving evidence to the idea that the image of an animal could transfer its own abilities to the man or the woman who wore it or carried it on. One might consider, for example, the intertwined snakes on the Sutton Hoo brooch, or the boar-crested helmets from Benty Grange and Wollostan,[4] both of which might have had an intended use reminding of the protective helm described in *Beowulf* (lines 303b–306a), when a handful of Geats arrive in Denmark:[5]

303   Eoforlic scionon
    ofer hleorber[g]an   gehroden golde,
    fah ond fyrheard,   ferhwearde heold
306 guþmod grimmon.[6]

[The images of boars shone on the cheek-guard, adorned with gold, coloured and hardened by fire, they kept guard on the life of the fierce men ready to battle.][7]

In the subsequent centuries, Latin written tradition and Christian models add to the idea of this dynamic relationship another mindset which, based on the pre-eminence of rationality, instead, sees humans and animals as innately distinct from one another. Derived from natural philosophy[8] and

---

and wild just as the beasts whose skin they wore. See Liberman, 401–411 and Merkelbach, 83–105.
4   Zoomorphic decoration-motives have been identified in the filigrees of many objects found in Staffordshire in 2009; see Leahy and Webster, 121–125. On the discoveries made in Sutton Hoo, Benty Granger and Wollaston see Bruce-Mitford, Carver – Evans et al., and Meadows, 17–26.
5   On the Early Germanic animal imagery see North, 151–175 and Glosecki, 3–23.
6   *Beowulf*'s text is quoted from *Klaeber's Beowulf*, fourth edition by Fulk et al.
7   All translations from Old English are mine, unless otherwise stated.
8   While Ancient Greece created various tales that expressed a belief in the intimate connection among humans and animals (see Tilley, 96–98), following a shift from a predominantly narrative discourse towards a philosophical one, natural philosophers used to consider nature and animals from a higher degree of detachment in comparison with any religious approach. Pythagoras (570–495 BCE) initiates a debate on the inner nature of animals; then, although considering man to be a

Late Ancient patristics, this perspective denies the presence of any intellectual faculty in animals other than humans, considering them as inferior living beings in a qualitative sense.[9]

Drawing on Augustine's commentary on the *Genesis*[10] (*De Genesi contra Manicheos*, II, 11, 16), referring to the well-known biblical

---

part of the animal world and influenced by Plato (428–348 BCE)'s model of the soul – divided into appetite, spirit, and reason – Aristotle (383–322 BCE) rejects the assumption that animals and human are equal in rationality. Subsequently, on the basis of this rational absence, the Stoics (300 BCE) assume that animals do not have any access to justice or to the pursuit of virtue; they regard them as designed in function of humanity. This perspective is similarly manifested in the Bible and, thus, profoundly influences later Judeo-Christian authors who wanted to clearly differentiate themselves from the Greco-Roman religion. See Klingender, 82–83; Salisbury, 3–4; Masters, 113.

9 For instance, arguing against the after-death transmigration of the human soul in the body of an animal, Ambrose denies any affinity between the species; the use of intellect and reasoning by humans is seen as an insurmountable qualitative difference (*De Excessu Fratris*, II, 127–129). In *De Civitate Dei* (XVI, viii) Augustine defines man as a rational mortal animal, 'animal rationale mortale', thus epitomizing what he had already longer discussed in *De Libero Arbitrio* (I, viii, xviii). Here, the bishop of Hippo lists the sensory (smell, taste, touch) and physical (feeding, growing, reproducing) characteristics that humans have in common with other living beings and, specifically, with other animals, eventually, recognizing how rational judgement is the discriminating element: the possibility of achieving happiness for the human being is, as a point in fact, determined by the ability to moderate desires and needs, a disposition that animals do not possess. The fundamental element of discrepancy is, therefore, the possession of a rational capacity which can mitigate the dependence on appetites and instincts. For a broader discussion on the modalities in which the claims of domination over animals become an additional element of differentiation, see Steel, 'How to Make a Human', 3–27. See, also, among others, Yamamoto and Crane.

10 In catechetical teachings, the first book of the Bible was used to compare the Christian notions of the universe with heathen visions. *Genesis* helped to answer questions concerning the human condition, the origin of evil and the promise of redemption. As a result, any event narrated in the *Genesis* was continuously retold, until they became the most popular biblical stories, as confirmed also by the exploitation of these episodes in the visual arts. On the popularity and importance of *Genesis* in the earlier centuries of the Middle Ages, see, among others, O'Loughlin, 2–8; with particular reference to the Anglo-Saxon context, see also Bremmer Jr., 156–157.

passage in which God invites the newly created man to impose a name on every creature (*Genesis*, 2:19), Bede writes:

> Causa autem adducendi ad Adam cuncta animantia terrae et volatilia caeli, ut videret quid ea vocaret, et eis nomina imponeret, haec est, ut sic demonstraret deus hominis quanto melior esset omnibus irrationabilibus animantibus. Ex hoc enim apparet ipsa ratione hominem meliorem esse quam pecora, quod distinguere et nominatim ea discernere non nisi ratio potest quae melior est (Bede, *Comm. in Genesin*, I, 2).

> [The reason for bringing all the animals of the earth and the birds of the air to Adam, so that he could see what he would call them and give them names, is that God would thus show man how much better he was than all irrational animals. From this it becomes clear that man is better than cattle precisely by virtue of reason itself, because only reason, which is better, can distinguish and set them apart by name.][11]

Similarly, centuries later, in *Interrogationes Sigewulfi in Genesim* (XXXII, 205), a translation in Old English of Alcuin's *Quaestiones in Genesim*, Ælfric expounds an analogous idea:

> Hwi wolde god þæt seman adam eallu nytenum naman gesceape? Þæt se man þurh þæt undergeate hu mycele betera he wæs þurh his gesceadwisnyssa þonne ða nytenu. ⁊ þæt he þæs þe swiþor his scyppend lufode þe hine swylcne geworhte.

> [Why did God want Adam to impose a name on every animal of the Creation? Because, as a result of this, man might have understood that, by virtue of his rationality, he was much better than any other animal. And, therefore, he would have loved more his Creator who made him as such.]

The dominion over the whole creation was given to man by the divine will and it is, therefore, linked to the possession of rationality, an ability that makes humans 'much better' ('mycele betera') than any other creature. Bede, Alcuin and Ælfric presume a qualitative distinction among the species and participate in the belief that animals were inferior. Human beings are considered the only creatures with the capacity to choose a name for other animals and, consequently, to recognize them; therefore, they are the only ones retaining the ability to recognize themselves.

In his homiletic works, Ælfric often argues on the nature of animals:

---

[11] All translations from Latin are mine, unless otherwise stated.

Ða gesceafta þe þæs an scyppend gesceop synden mænigfealde and mislices hiwes and ungelice farað [...]. Sume syndan creopende on eorðan mid eallum lichoman, swa swa wurmas doð. Sume gað on twam fotum, sume on feower fotum. Sume fleoð mid fyðerum, sume on flodum swimmað, and hi ealle swaþæh alotene beoð to þære eorðan weard and þider wilniað oððe þæs þe him lyst oððe þæs þe hi beþurfon; ac se man ana gæð uprihte (Ælfric, *Lives of Saints*, I, 49–57).[12]

[The creatures created by the only Creator are manifold, of many and different shapes [...]. Some creep on the earth with all their body, as snakes do. Some walk on two feet, others on four. Some fly with their wings, others swim in the waves, and they all are bent down towards the earth and they tend thither because it gives them pleasure or because they are obliged to; only man walks upright.]

According to the bishop of Eynsham, the proximity all animals have with the ground is particularly relevant, it implies a primitive existence, linked to instincts and to needs of a lower level. Moreover, their posture turned towards the ground might be explained by the lack of a superior intelligence; animals miss a particular piece of soul which would allow them to aspire towards higher and more spiritual purposes. Accordingly, on this matter, accepting the Platonic theory of the tripartite soul (Masters, 113), Ælfric comments thus:

Uþwytan sæcgað þæt þære sawle gecynd is ðryfeald: an dæl is on hire gewylnigendlic, oðer yrsigendlic, þrydde gesceadwislic. Twægen þissera dæla habbað deor and nytenu mid us, þæt is gewylnunge and yrre. Se man ana hæfð gescead and ræd and andgit (Ælfric, *Lives of Saints*, I, 96–100).

[The philosophers say that the nature of the soul is threefold: one part is capable of desire, another is capable of anger, a third is capable of reason. Wild and domestic animals share two of these parts with us, that is desire and anger. Only man has reason and intelligence and the ability to understand.]

Ælfric seems to follow a notion that ascribes to non-human beings only a limited percentage of soul, precisely that portion allowing them to feel desire and anger. They are excluded from possessing any intellectual faculty. Thus, in the didactic fiction of the *Colloquy* (249–251), written as a form of practising the Latin language, pupils promptly retort to their

---

12 All quotations from Ælfric's *Homilies* and *Lives of Saints* are taken from the Early English Text Society editions of the texts.

teacher's question that their interest for learning stems from the desire to distinguish themselves from animals:

> *M.*: Ic ahsiʒe eop, forhpi spa ʒeornlice leorni ʒe?
> *D.*: Forþam þe nellaþ pesan spa stunte nytenu, þa nan þinʒ pitaþ, buton ʒærs ⁊ pæter.
>
> *M.*: Interrogo uos, cur tam diligenter discitis?
> *D.*: Quia nolumus esse sicut bruta animalia, quae nihil sciunt nisi herbam et acquam.
>
> [*M:* I ask you, why do you learn so diligently?
> *D:* Because we do not want to be like the dumb animals that know nothing but grass and water.]

In this passage, Old English *stunt* 'dumb, foolish, stupid' translates the Latin *brūtus*.[13] Assigned indiscriminately to every non-human animal, this condition of foolishness ensues from the observation of their behaviour: they exclusively mind their own business, exemplified by the grass to eat or the water to drink; animals are seen as victims of their own needs and instincts.

---

13 Beyond the first meaning of 'heavy, unwieldy, immovable', *brūtus* can often indicate that somebody or something is 'dull, stupid' or 'unreasonable', especially when associated with animals, as it can be noted already in Pliny the Elder's *Naturalis Historia* (XI, 183): 'Bruta existimantur animalium, quibus cor durum riget; audacia, quibus parvum est; pavida, quibus praegrande' ('Among those animals believed to be irrational, that have a hard, rigid heart, the ones who have it small are courageous, and those who have it very large are timid'). Moreover, this second meaning comes out more frequently in medieval Latin, particularly in Anglo-Latin sources. Aside from Ælfric's usage in the *Colloquy*, it can be noted, for instance, in Aldhelm's *De virginitate*, line 2429: 'expertem sensu cum bruta mente vagando' ('wandering with irrational mind, lacking understanding'). See the *Lexicon Totius Latinate* by Forcellini (*Forcellini Lex*), and the Lewis-Short's *Latin Dictionary* (*ALD*) s.v. 'brūtus'. The meaning of Old English *stunt* seems to have gone through a similar direction; it appears as a gloss for *stultus* and *fătŭus*, with the meaning of 'foolish, stupid', in connection with both animals and human beings. However, occasionally, when referring to an animal, *nyten*, as opposed to a human being, it can also mean 'irrational'. As it can be seen in Wulfstan's *Sermo bone praedicatio* 'hi faraŏ fram wife to wife, eallswa stunte nytenu doŏ' ('They go from woman to woman, as irrational animals do'); or in Ælfric's 'Circumsion', *Catholic Homilies I*: 'he is for ŏi wiŏmeten stuntum nytenum' ('therefore he is compared to irrational animals'). See *Anglo-Saxon Dictionary (ASD)*, s.v. 'stunt'.

Thus, it seems, that this point of view posits Early English intellectuals in the wake of an ancient tradition in Western philosophy. Placing humans on one side and every other animal on the other, this anthropocentric perspective is based on the idea that the 'human' is good, the pinnacle of life on Earth, the highest stage of evolution, or, for Christians, the being closest to God; according to this belief, humanity cannot be defined simply by a series of biological features: humans contain something within themselves that distinguishes and elevates them above other living beings.

This anthropocentrism leads towards an instrumental vision of animals, which emphasises on their utility: a material utility and an allegorical utility. In Early Medieval England, a society which was primarily agrarian, the daily life of many people involved the constant presence of numerous animals, both as an aid in work activities or as raw material in clothing, food and the production of an indefinite number of objects.[14] This material and instrumental existence is rarely found in written records. Yet, the previously mentioned Ælfrician *Colloquy* (22-27) partly represents the instrumental role of many domestic animals. The pupils, exploring the daily routine of farmers, shepherds, herders, hunters, fowlers, etc., describe a situation where oxen, sheep, wild boar, deer and other animals are seen as a material resource:

> M.: Hpæt sæʒest þu, yrþlinʒe? Hu beʒæst þu peore þin?
> P.: Eala, leof hlaford, þearle ic deorfe. Ic ʒa ut on dæʒræd þypende oxon to felda, ⁊ iuʒie hiʒ to syl; nys hit spa stearc pinter þæt ic durre lutian æt ham for eʒe hlafordes mines, ac ʒeiukodan oxan, ⁊ ʒefæstnodon sceare ⁊ cultre mit þære syl, ælce dæʒ ic sceal erian fulne æcer oþþe mare.
>
> M.: Quid dicis tu, arator ? Quomodo exerces opus tuum ?
> P.: O, mi domine, nimium laboro. Exeo diluculo, minando boues ad campum, et iungo eos ad aratrum: non est tam aspera hiems ut audeam latere domi pro timore domini mei, sed iunctis bobus, et confirmato uomere et cultro aratro, omni die debeo arare integrum agrum aut plus.
>
> [M: What are you saying, ploughman? How do you do your work?
> P: Alas, dear lord, I have to work very hard. I go out at daybreak to drive the oxen to the field and yoke them to the plough; not even in the stark winter would I dare to

---

14   For a more detailed discussion on the argument see Salisbury, 10–59 and Frantzen, *Anglo-Saxon Keywords*, 15–19.

stay at home for fear of my lord, but, once yoked up the oxen and fastened coulter and ploughshare to the plough, then I must plough a whole field or more for the whole day.]

Animals in Anglo-Saxon literature, however, are most visible through the symbolic register. If animals retain only a mechanical form of life, then their behaviour must be caused by something else, by a divine hand, that had designed them to balance the world and to serve as a model for human beings. Animals – and the whole nature – are, therefore, to be observed thoroughly because they function as a fundamental help in understanding the human condition and the place occupied by humanity in the divine plan. An allegorical meaning is assigned to each of them, even the most ordinary. The tradition of the *Physiologus* and subsequent bestiaries is emblematic of this situation.[15] Ælfric, in his homilies, depicts various animal figures to provide examples in the specification of a given argument, as a term of behavioural comparison, or as a metaphor for the figure of Christ. Thus, the animal becomes an *exemplum* taking on either a positive or a negative value. The wolf is similar to the thief who lives by robbery (*Lives of Saints*, XIX, 160) or it could represent the devil who tries to induce men into sinning (*Catholic Homilies* I, XVII); fish can indicate both Christ (*Catholic Homilies II*, XVI, 86–199) and the devil himself (*Catholic Homilies I*, XIV, 172).

Nonetheless, even if systematically theorized in the Christian concept of the *liber naturae*, the symbolic representation of the animal is not an exclusively Christian characteristic. At times, even the literary production not immediately influenced by religion belies a symbolic outlook limiting the consideration on non-human beings: a case in point might be the formulaic theme of 'the beasts of battle', where eagles, ravens and wolves are more often than not introduced without any particular attention to their own individual peculiarity, they are interchangeable with each other.[16] Just as in the moral lesson sought after by Ælfric's *exempla*,

---

15 On animal symbolism see Ziolkowski, 1–23. For a discussion on the *Physiologus'* tradition in Germanic languages see, Dolcetti Corazza.

16 As noted by Estes, 132: 'they appear within the narratives not out of intrinsic interest in their presence but in structural and/or metaphorical relationships to human actors within the poems.'

the presence of 'beasts of battle' in the formulaic framework of Old English poetry has only a superficial relationship with the occurrence in nature of these animals on the battlefields. Wolves, eagles, ravens or vultures act, in these cases, as terms of an implicit comparison with the warriors preparing to slaughter other men.

In this context, it may appear that animality and humanity operate as opposed poles; their connection to one another might be defined as a dualistic relationship of domination/subordination, as articulated by Plumwood (47–48):

> Dualism is a relation of separation and domination inscribed and naturalised in culture and characterised by radical exclusion, distancing and opposition between orders constructed as systematically higher and lower, as inferior and superior, as ruler and ruled, which treats the division as part of the natures of beings construed not merely as different but as belonging to radically different orders or kinds, and hence as not open to change.

Within this system, all traits that humans share with nature and animals, that is, those features connected to sexuality, reproduction, affectivity (correlatively also connected to the feminine), and the material aspects of life, are rejected as not pertaining to the best expression of human life. This way of thinking places a strong emphasis on reason, which is thought to separate men from the natural sphere, as seen in Ælfric's works. This mindset could therefore help to explain why animals – and the natural aspects present in human life – are relegated to the background as mere resources rather than being considered creatures with intrinsic value.[17] However, in so doing, a form of discontinuity is established not only with respect to nature but also within the human psyche, since everything

---

17 According to Plumwood (58–65), a dualistic thinking uses several strategies to enact itself. Through *backgrounding* (or *denial*), the dominant side makes use of the other and, at the same time, denies its dependence on it, considering the other as inessential; *radical exclusion* (or *hyperseparation*) amplifies, emphasizes and maximizes the number and importance of the differences between dominated and dominant; through *incorporation* (or *relational definition*), the subordinated part of the pair is defined as something that is missing, a minus sign, a negativity, and the dominated is not recognized as having an independent identity. With *radical exclusion* and *incorporation* come two important corollaries, *instrumentalism* (or *objectification*) and *homogenization* (or *stereotyping*).

that is perceived as irrational, and therefore animal, must be removed. Thus, this discontinuity leads, in Freudian terms, to the resurfacing of the rejected aspects. In other words, an easily established distinction among rational humans and irrational animals is actually impossible and leads to unavoidable complications.

In order to investigate how generally a society deals with its marginal aspects (i.e. all those figures labelled as inferior, degraded, or deviant) Stallybrass and White similarly use a dichotomic pattern, with the two opposing concepts of 'high' and 'low', and employ the Freudian model of the peripheral returning to trouble the individual consciousness. According to their argument, any manifestations of the lower strata of society, while theoretically excluded, reappears in symbolic form, as the outcome of the effort in defining boundaries:

> What starts as a *simple* repulsion or rejection of symbolic matter foreign to the self inaugurates a process of introjection and negation which is always *complex* in its effects. [...] The point is that the *exclusion* necessary to the formation of social identity at level one is simultaneously a *production* at the level of the Imaginary and a production, what is more, of a complex hybrid fantasy emerging out of the very attempt to demarcate boundaries, to unite and purify the social collectivity. (Stallybrass-White, 193)

As a result, the 'high' is always in active dialogue with the 'low': in fact, it can only preserve its identity through such activity. The relations between 'high' and 'low' – the Self and the Other – end up being characterized by a dynamic instability.

Similar observations were transferred to the Medieval setting by Yamamoto (2–5), who noted that 'high' and 'low' have obvious embodiment in a hierarchical society such as twelfth-century England, like the one described in John of Salisbury's *Policraticus*, where the metaphor of the body defines society as a whole, and the ruler is imagined as the 'head', while the peasants are its 'feet'. Analogous considerations can be drawn for the social structure of the earlier Anglo-Saxon England. According to the worldview expressed in Ælfric's or Bede's works, all humans occupy a central position merely by virtue of being human, yet humans themselves can also be grouped based on their proximity to, or distance from, the centres of power.[18]

---

18 An analogous situation is described by DuBois, in relation to fourth-century BCE Greece. DuBois analyses how the discourse about difference evolved in Greece. In

The structure in early Anglo-Saxon society reflected a rank system based on a threefold class division among nobles (*eorlas* in Kent, *gesiþas* in Wessex, *þegnas* from the tenth century onwards), freemen (*ceorlas*) and slaves (*þeowas, esnas*), establishing a legal basis for the perceived differences among humans.[19] The main indicator dividing one rank from the other in the eyes of the law was the *wergild*, the amount of money to be paid in recompense for the murder of one of its members (Whitelock, 84). In Britain, the employment of slaves was fairly common under both Romans and Celts. From the fifth century onwards, when the Germanic

---

    the fifth century BCE, with the norm defined as Greek male human, difference is expressed in terms of the alien, the monstrous and the female: 'The "other" is seen as bestial, irrational, chaotic, subject to desire, hostile to marriage and exchange, enslaved' (122), furthermore, 'Centaurs, Amazons, and the barbarians, animals and females for whom they are emblematic, mark the boundaries of the self and the city, composed of equals. Analogy unites the citizens in their *isonomia*; they are in a relationship of polarized opposition to the "others", who are themselves linked in a pattern of analogy' (123). However, while flexible enough to accommodate various historical moments, these pattern of polarity and analogy starts to break down in the fourth century BCE: 'The Greeks can no longer sustain a description of themselves which makes identity rest on language, on one's common Hellenism, since within the body of the Hellenes there is division and war. The barbarian is within' (123). In the face of war, fourth-century philosophers did not broaden their notion of the human subject to embrace all kinds. Instead, a new rationalisation of social interactions arose in an attempt to fix the structure of the city. If the city's elite were comfortable with certain attributes, they were considered natural, and then articulated in terms of a 'hierarchy of difference' (133). Thus, for instance, DuBois sees a clear rupture with the past in the myth of metals in Plato's *Republic*: 'The great chain of being is beginning to take the place of a circle with man at its center. There is an articulated, natural, eternal hierarchy even among citizens' (135). Therefore, this system saw man (i.e. male, adult, Greek, free) at the top of this hierarchy as the centre of power. From that, based on a supposed deficiency in rationality, women, foreigners were ranked on a lower level, gradually distanced from the centre; finally, slaves were placed at the most remote periphery. Thus, the slave turned up to be considered as bordering on the animal universe.

19   Additionally, Æthelbert of Kent's law code (26) includes the *læt*, who might have been semi-free people or manumitted slaves. These social classes also had significant internal distinction, and mobility within and between them was not wholly impossible. For instance, Æthelbert's legislation (11–26) classified unfree and semi-free people into three sub-classes, whilst the nobility was divided into four. In Wessex, Ine's legal code (VI.3) cites free peasants of lower standing. See Pelteret, 294–295; Härke, 141.

elites gradually displaced the Romano-British ones, the institution of slavery remained an accepted part of ordinary life; trading and holding slaves continued to be a common practice at least until the twelfth century.[20] In this social system, slaves had no *wergild*, they were possessions, assets, belongings. Thus, being their master's personal and material property, slaves were deemed as fitting to a group akin to that of domestic animals.

The seven centuries of Anglo-Saxon dominion in England should not be treated as a monolithic cultural unity without allowing for the inevitable change in time and space,[21] yet slavery remained highly relevant as an integral part of everyday life, with the continuous conflicts providing a steady supply of slaves for centuries. As observed by Cavell (*Weaving Words*, 157):

> As an ever present economic institution, slavery needed to continually replenish itself; thus, the making of free people into slaves was integral to is survival. [...] There were a number of ways new slaves could be acquired, but in the early Anglo-Saxon period the greatest proportion of the slave population were victims of warfare and foreign conquest.

These practices might have been at the origin of the conceptual shifts that associate the slave with the foreigner, as the evolution of the term *wealh* might also suggest.[22] Slavery imagery was extremely present in Anglo-Saxon literary documents[23] and ultimately, the easily related notions of

---

20 Indeed, as Wyatt (5) points out, all communities in medieval Britain traded in and employed slaves. In 1086, at least 10 per cent of the population in England was still unfree. See also Pelteret, 41–47 and Cavell, *Weaving Words*, 157–159.
21 From the seventh century onwards, the introduction of land charters transformed the position of the freemen, altering the meaning of 'freedom' from the right to be protected by law to the faculty to leave an estate. See Pelteret, 251 and Härke, 142. Furthermore, with time, unfree people obtained some rights. For instance, slaves could earn their own money during their spare time. Under Alfred's legislation (43), they were allowed the four Wednesdays in the Ember weeks to sell what was gifted to them and what they have been able to earn otherwise. Wulfstan, in his *Sermo Lupi ad Anglos*, among the many reasons behind the sinful state of England, laments the purposeful disregard slaves' rights. On this, see Whitelock, 109 and Dutchak, 36.
22 On this see Pelteret, 248; see also chapter 3, n. 123.
23 As suggested by Pelteret (41), Christian writers contributed to this by using a rhetoric connected to it to describe human relationships with both God and the devil.

slave and animal connect to the almost as easily related ideas of slave and foreigner.[24] As a result, it seemed that the social structure of Early Medieval England provided the opportunity to establish categories of humanity that were viewed as 'less than', entities that may be understood as in-between, elements of conjunction born out of the attempt to create 'higher' and 'lower' humans, who could easily be associated with the animal 'Other'.

Thus, while man (i.e. free human male) is positioned as the higher stand in the Medieval hierarchical society, he cannot completely separate himself from the lower orders, 'for it is his degree of difference *from* them that constitutes his identity' (Yamamoto, 8). As a matter of fact, the definition of this 'purified' humanity necessitates the establishment of distinctions in terms of comparison: the animal, the alien, the monster, and the female are used to express contrast and, furthermore, 'the relation between high and low, centre and periphery, must always be characterized by a dynamic instability, as bodies of various kinds intermingle, trade features or try to articulate their ascendency' (Yamamoto, 8–9).

Therefore, it is not surprising that, on the side-line of the philosophico-theological framework evicted from Ælfric's and Bede's works, Early Medieval England produced also literary depictions which exploit the association between animals and all the 'marginal' categories of humans – exiles, slaves, foreigners, women, outsiders of all sorts –, thus reflecting a more dynamic relationship among men and animal and escaping any pretence of a clear-cut dichotomy. The collection of riddles preserved in the *Exeter Book* and the teratological prose text conventionally known as *Wonders of the East* permit us to explore a side of Anglo-Saxon society that does not often find a place in epic poetry or religious literature: among the *Riddles*, several poems focus on a particular animal

---

[24] In the Classical world, these association gave rise, through a conceptual shift, to the category of bestial men or monstrous men (Volpato, ch. 1); Anglo-Saxon literature shows a great interest for these creatures and generally for 'Otherness'. While the exploration of alterity is the main theme of texts like *Wonders of the East* and *Letter from Alexander to Aristotle*, the fear of the foreigner and distrust for the Other is a commonly occurring subject in many other surviving texts. In this sense, Amodio (376–377) notes that the figure of Grendel in *Beowulf* might be seen as 'something of a poster-boy' for this theme, because his aim to replace human society with a different kind similar to him poses a far larger threat than his cannibalism.

23

as the main subject to be guessed, often giving them a chance to speak in their own voice; whilst, as a catalogue for bestial creatures and monstrous people, *Wonders of the East* can be seen as the epitome for the complexity of the connection among humans, animals and in-between creatures. As a result of the richness of these collections, numerous elements of the interrelationships between animal and human creatures can be investigated.

Since they are vastly apart in time and space, the two pieces retain substantial differences. The Old English riddles display evident connections with Anglo-Latin riddles, filtered and re-elaborated according to metric and stylistic characteristics affiliated to the Germanic poetic tradition; on the other hand, *Wonders of the East* is an imported cultural product, derived from a Hellenistic and Late Antique context. The riddles are a brilliant sample of alliterative poetry, rich in variation, kennings and daring metaphors, while the treatise is written in a sparse prose, made up by short descriptions, in a paratactic and redundant style. The riddles portray some of the most common, even if diversified, features of Anglo-Saxon society; *Wonders of the East* uses illustrations and a small portion of text to show a peculiar universe, deliberately placed on the edge of the known world, as far as possible from the daily life of Anglo-Saxon people.

Nevertheless, it is possible to consider both works as collections of creatures to observe and discover, creatures that will induce in their audience an impression of wonder and curiosity.[25] The *Exeter Book* collection inspires a state of surprise while describing familiar objects, things and ideas by means of a highly metaphorical language and through an unusual point of view; *Wonders of the East* pursues a reaction of amazement looking out of the boundaries of the British Isles. The treatise imagines

---

25   Many subjects described in the riddles are qualified as *wrætlīc* or *wundorlīc* (in twenty-eight cases): #18/16, #20/18, #21/19, #23/21, #24/22, #25/23, #26/24, #29/27, #31/29, #33/31, #36/34, #39/37, #40/38, #42/40, #44/42, #47/45, #50/48, #51/49, #55/53, #59/57, #60/58, #67/65, #68–69/66, #70.1–4/67, #70.5–6/68, #83/79, #84/80, #87/83, #88/84. As per convention the Old English riddles are here mentioned according to the numeration proposed by Krapp and Dobbie in *The Anglo-Saxon Poetic Records* (hereafter, *ASPR*), followed, however, by the numeration proposed by Williamson in *The Old English Riddles of the Exeter Book*. All quotations are taken from Williamson's edition.

a world of the Other, made up by extreme places, a world filled with strange and dangerous people.[26] In fact, both collections produce amazement and wonder because they purposefully defy expectations, disturb habits, and destabilize the known world. The entities in both collections allow us to delve into the issue of identity; that is to say, many of the main subjects face the possibility that an entity might be or become something different. As suggested by Yamamoto, the inevitability of change is a key problematic feature when dealing with how human beings perceive their position towards animals. Focusing on the body as a guarantor for identity, she highlights the impossibility for this guarantee to work: because if no single body remains unchanged, how can it authentically reflect identity?

> The body is perpetually the site of tensions, of competing discourses. On the one hand, it is the basic building block of any social structure, on the other it is potentially aberrant, rebellious, the playground of Freud's Id. It is also our expressive medium par excellence, and as such partakes of a dangerous lability. If men stand upright and beasts crawl on all fours, what are we to make of a man who copies a beast's posture? If he starts to live like an animal, does he forfeit his humanity? (Yamamoto, 8)

The *Wonders of the East* and the *Exeter Book* riddles both depict creatures posing similar questions, but the two collections do so by using two fundamentally different – yet related – images or rhetorical strategies: metamorphosis and hybridity.

As highlighted by Bynum, hybridity and metamorphosis can be understood to be ways of representing a world fatally subjected to change; violating all sorts of boundaries both images induce a sense of horror and wonder. In other words, the reality imagined through hybridity and metamorphosis manifests the disorder and the fluidity characterizing the universe, both in the process and in the instant.[27]

---

26 Daily (466–469) argues that in a literary work such as *Wonders of the East*, that places its characters in a context considered completely Other, the main purpose of the text is inducing in the audience a state of wonder. Conversely, the *Riddles* use their poetic style in order to trigger a reaction of wonder and surprise. The *Exeter Book* collection explores things that may be considered ordinary but, when transposed into the enigmatic form, become *wrǣtlīc*; it's the poetic language that provides the mind with a new way to feel and read these figures.

27 See the pivotal work by C. W. Bynum, *Metamorphosis and Identity*.

The creatures represented in the *Exeter Book* riddles often have an ambivalent or metamorphic nature. This can be seen as a consequence of the role assumed by the metaphor in the structure of the enigmatic form. The riddle, as a literary game challenging its audience, can contemporarily disclose and hide the true nature of the depicted entity. As eloquently put by Williamson, 'riddles and metaphors disguise one creature in the garb of another' (Williamson, *A Feast for Creatures*, 26). In other words, in the enigmatic game, each creature assumes the appearance of another, in order to complicate and confuse the ways to identify the solution; thus, inviting its audience to think about the idea of mutability.

Therefore, the metaphoric structure underlying the description of any enigmatic subject can be compared to a metamorphic process.[28] Moreover, the rhetorical figure of prosopopoeia, widely present in the collection, ascribes to each enigmatic subject the ability to speak. In particular, amongst the gallery of animals on display in the collection,[29] prosopopoeia and other anthropomorphic strategies facilitate the process of mimesis with the speaking character. It can be said that it activates an

---

28 See Williamson, *A Feast for Creatures*, 38: 'Beyond the dead world of literate truth [a riddle] liberates us from the prison of reified perception and recalls the metamorphic flow.'

29 A first group of 'animal riddles' is focused on portraying birds: they are the main subjects in #7/5 ('swan', OE *swan/swon*), #8/6 ('nightingale', OE *nihtegale*), #9/7 ('cuckoo', OE *geāc*), #10/8 ('barnacle goose', OE *byrnete*). To this compact group, located at the beginning of the collection, it can be added #24/22, where runes are used to form the name OE *higoræ*, 'jay', and #57/55 which describes some small black birds difficult to identify, perhaps swallows (OE *swealwe*) or ravens (OE *crāwan*). #13/11 and #42/40, respectively, describe the birth of ten chicks, OE *tēn cicenu*, and the sexual intercourse between rooster and hen, OE *hana ond hæn*. #12/10, #38/36 and #72/70 portray the beast of burden that in Old English is called *oxa*, through their whole life experience, including their 'after-death': from young calf, to draft animal, to leather exploited for the manufacture of various objects. #15/13 describes a small quadruped, identified alternately as fox (OE *fox*), badger (OE *brocc*), porcupine or hedgehog (OE *igil*); #77/74 portrays an oyster (OE *ostre*) at the moment of being devoured; #47/45 exploits the paradox of that creature who devours books but learns nothing, the 'bookworm', OE *maþa*, while #85/81 takes up the Symphosian theme of the fish in the river. Some other riddles might or might not portray animals, e.g.: #75–76/73 could be a pun on dog and doe, OE *hund und hind*, #78/75 probably describes an aquatic animal, lamprey or crab, OE *crabba*. In this regard, see Niles, *Old English Enigmatic Poems*, 99.

empathic connection between the depicted animal and the human who is reading the text (Williamson, *A Feast for Creatures*, 25–40).

Moreover, the metaphorical game does not represent the only way through which the *Exeter Book* collection discloses its metamorphic vocation; several riddle-poems represent a creature undergoing an actual change. Indeed, the whole collection demonstrates thoroughly how many objects and tools in common use are usually animal derived. Thus, the Old English riddles let emerge a universe made by mutable and interconnected beings. As shown in the following pages, *#26/24* can be considered emblematic of this: the twenty-nine lines riddle outlines the preparation of a handmade book. At the beginning of the poem, the speaking subject presents itself as a freshly skinned animal, a victim of the tanning treatment destined to become a parchment page, as part of an adorned Bible. The subject is only one but its 'biographical' journey forces it to change, to suffer a constant series of substitutions among multiple stages and multiple entities. In this case, the overlapping of identities is not caused by the metaphorical game, but by the evolution – natural or anthropogenic – of the subject. The riddle is placed in a narrative space depicting a process of change. Similarly, *#12/10* is built on the paradoxical comparison between the actions of an ox in life and the objects created with it after its death. The behaviour of the living creature and its uses after death are quite distinct, but, at the same time, the first-person narrative attests to a continuity of identity between the draft animal and its hide exploited in various ways. Because the metamorphosis is a movement from one being to another, this kind of riddle reveals an inherent duplicity in the solution.[30]

This interest for narrating the mutability of things ultimately leads to reveal the continuity between seemingly disconnected aspects of nature: metamorphosis becomes a rhetorical strategy that discloses the spaces of intersection among humanity and animality. At the same time, the reversal in perspectives, often used in the collection, implies

---

30   There is no metamorphosis at the beginning and at the end of the narrative, where there is no trace of the Otherness from which and towards which the process is heading. The transformative process can be seen only in the middle. Although the metamorphosis is centred on the process, it is in fact about unity, identity, left behind or approached. See Bynum, 30.

recognizing the other as a centre of needs and values, a being whose ends are independent.

Conversely, *Wonders of the East* seems to focus on the 'wonderful' variety of nature, the treatise and the images that accompany it tell of a universe as fluid and destabilizing as the one emerging in the *Exeter Book* collection. Among the abnormalities populating the text, monstrous peoples play a central role. These monstrous races, these less-than-human peoples, were born in Classical Greece and developed throughout Late Ancient and Medieval Europe out of Western ethnocentrism, enabling a conceptual juxtaposition between the ideas concerning animals, slaves, and foreigners (Volpato, ch. 1). Thus, in *Wonders*, these people are often depicted as mixed forms of animal and man, such as the dog-headed Cynocephali (§ 7), the lion-headed giants (§ 12), the onocentaurs, called Homodubii (§ 17), et al.

The concept of hybridity stems from the necessity to conceptualize all those natural subjects seen as in-between categories[31] – for example, the coral that looks like it might be part plant, part stone or the mule born from the union of a jack, a male donkey, and a mare, a female horse. The hybrid then becomes a rhetorical strategy to define multiple substances, put together through a paradox. Placed in an eternal present, the hybrid is an entity composed of distinct parts, two or more, which are in conversation with each other, because each part constitutes a comment on the other (Bynum, 30).

Human-animal hybrids such as those depicted in *Wonders of the East* force the human beings to a direct confrontation with all those aspects of human identity which are relegated to the territories of the irrational (and therefore of the animal): instincts, passions and everything that is related to body and sexuality. These monstrous peoples can be considered as transitional figures; they possess human and bestial characteristics not only from a physical point of view: at times, even habits and customs indicate if a creature can be categorized as belonging to humanity or, conversely, as belonging to an animal species; devouring raw food might be perceived as a sign of strong animality, as much as the presence of fangs or claws.

---

31 All those entities which Bynum, 29, calls *midpoints*.

The hybrids in *Wonders of the East* and the ever-changing creatures of the *Riddles* violate categorical distinctions in different ways. The metamorphic and metaphorical riddles reveal a world of stories, of things that flow; they destroy categories by overcoming them, invading them. The hybrid, on the other hand, reveals a world of differences, a world that is multiple, a world that forces contradictory and incompatible categories to coexist.

Overview of chapters

The book, therefore, progresses analysing characters and themes as explored in the *Exeter Book* collection and the *Wonders of the East*, looking for the *loci* where animality and humanity might overlap.

Chapter 1, 'The *Exeter Book* Collection and the Riddle Tradition', briefly surveys the evolution of the riddle genre in Late Antiquity and the influences it had on the composition of the *Exeter Book* collection; hence, in order to understand the metaphoric nature of the riddles, the chapter focuses on the role of metaphor in the formation of riddle as a poetic genre. The poems in the *Exeter Book* riddle-collection exploit completely the metaphoric nature of the genre: for the purpose of complicating the guessing game, they often describe a creature taking on the appearance of another, therefore, inviting to consider the possibility of change in the main subjects' identities.

In Chapter 2, 'Prosopopoeia, Anthropomorphism and Empathy', I investigate specifically how this mutability can be expressed in the riddlic representations of the perceived boundaries between humans and animals. Prosopopoeia, as a figure of speech, is extensively used in the collection, providing each enigmatic subject with the ability to speak for themselves. Such forms of anthropomorphism promote the understanding of the animal's perspective. Riddles such as *#15/13*, *#77/74* and *#72/ 70* establish an empathic connection between their speaking subjects and their audience; a close-reading of these poems enables us to discover the experimental nature of the collection with its different methods in depicting animals.

The *Exeter Book* riddles, as a whole, show great interest in depicting the continuity between the aspects of nature and, consequently, in the mutability of things: in Chapter 3, 'Riddles and Metamorphosis', I consider this particular aspect, focusing specifically on riddle *#26/24*, which describes the production process of a decorated manuscript. The poem's speaking subject is both the murdered animal and the valuable object made out of its skins, thus, thanks to the fictional nature of the riddle-game, both identities have the chance to speak with a unified voice, that is to say, to express the metamorphic nature of a single subject.

Furthermore, the idea that, in Early Medieval England, there are no clear dividing lines between humans and animals emerges also from the concern with monstrosity. In Chapter 4, '*Wonders of the East*: Men, Animals and In-Between', I examine the intricate textual tradition of *Wonders of the East*, in an attempt to highlight the significance assumed by hybridity in the structure of the entire treatise: born out of the conceptual shifts associating the foreign Other with the animal Other, monstrous men are usually represented as inhuman; thus, as elements of conjunction between animals and humans.

Consequently, Chapter 5, 'Uncertain Humanity Denied Humanity' analyses all the monstrous figures not directly classified as humans in the treatise. The first part of the chapter focuses on those creatures which clearly show divergences between their textual depiction, mainly concerned with their monstrous appearance, and the associated pictures illustrating their figure as humanoid. This category includes the dog-headed Conopoenas or Cynocephali and two monstrous races labelled as Homodubii, the first one is a race of ichthyophages and the second one is a population of onocentaurs. The second part of the chapter is aimed at describing, instead, another category of hybrids, showing the even more ambiguous position of the hybrid women, openly condemned and dehumanized in the text.

Chapter 6, 'Alien and Familiar' focuses, instead, on two other specific races: a population of lion-headed giants and the Donestre people. As represented in the *Wonders*, these creatures supposedly are humanoid hybrids, yet the textual traditions at the origin of these two chapters portrayed instead animal figures, hippos in the first instance, hyenas and crocodiles in the latter. In the course of textual transmission, these animals have undergone a process of anthropomorphization. Their original animal form, while lost in the transmission, is somehow kept in their interpretation as ambiguous species of humans, somehow both reassuring and dangerous. Their hybridity is a perfect representation of what is at the same time familiar and destructive: those hybrid bodies cannot be guarantors of identity, by enclosing both the Other and the Self constantly threatens boundaries of the Self.

Thus, *Riddles* and *Wonders* deal with fundamental questions on what it meant to be human for Early Medieval English society. Through these six chapters, I intend to provide a textual and thematic study of both works, as well as a thorough assessment of their literary tradition, in order to explore the ways in which the relationship between human and animal beings might have been perceived and elaborated in the Anglo-Saxon cultural universe between the eighth and eleventh centuries. My aim is to reveal the peculiar features of the Early Medieval English perspective in the definition of humanity with regard to animal and non-human figures, as well as to demonstrate that a strong anthropocentric vocation can coexist with an outlook that recognizes a close affinity among different species. The creatures depicted in the *Exeter Book* riddles and in the *Wonders of the East*, diverse and manifold, might, in fact, reveal a multifaceted view on both human and non-human animals.

1. The *Exeter Book* Collection and the Riddle Tradition

Weather phenomena, weapons, music instruments, nightingales, decorated chalices, horns, drafts animals, burning metals, and red-haired foxes: already defined as 'a mosaic of the actualities of daily experience' (Kennedy, 134), the Old English riddle-collection provides an uneven but detailed idea on how early medieval English society experienced the world. The *Exeter Book* (Exeter, Cathedral Library MS 3501) present these enigmatic poems without any title or solution, spread throughout several sections of the manuscript, covering also the variously damaged closing part of the codex.[32] The texts copied on folios 123v and 124r – *The Husband's Message* and *The Ruin* – have not been identified as riddles; nevertheless, on the basis of palaeographic and stylistic considerations, it can be suggested that the scribe might have associated them to the riddle genre; therefore, it is possible that, according to the intention of the compiler, the collection should have been formed by two macro-sections: from folio 101r to folio 115r and from folio 122v to the end of the codex.[33]

---

32 Various texts of different kind are copied between the sections containing the riddles. According to conventional titles, the sequence can be thus summarized: *Riddles* (from *#1-2-3/1* to *#59/57*) ff. 101r–f. 115r; *The Wife's Lament* ff. 115r–116r, *The Judgement Day I* ff. 116r–117v, *Resignation* (A) and (B) ff. 117v–119v, *The Descent into Hell* ff. 120r–121v, *Alms-Giving* ff. 121v–122r, *Pharaoh* f. 122r, *The Lord's Prayer I* f. 122r, *Homiletic Fragment II* ff. 122r–122v, *Riddles* #30/28b and #60/ 58 ff. 122v–123r, *The Husband's Message* ff. 122r–123v, *The Ruin* ff. 123v–124v, *Riddles* (from *#61/59* to *#95/91*), ff. 124v–130v. The last fourteen folia have been damaged by a diagonal burn, so that, at present, substantial parts of many riddles are illegible. For a detailed presentation of the codex see Muir. As a general convention, Old English poetic texts are referred according by the titles given by Krapp and Dobbie in *ASPR*. If not otherwise stated, citations of the Old English Poetic Corpus are from *ASPR*.

33 According to Muir (607), the layout of *The Husband's Message* displays a text divided into three parts, suggesting a distinction in three poems: 'each "poem" begins with a large capital, is followed by heavy punctuation, and uses blank

One of the characterizing features of the collection is having placed at the centre of the poetic creation the most diverse components of nature and of the material world, subjects often belonging to everyday life. Very few texts are devoted to concepts pertaining Christian doctrine (e.g. *#40/ 38* focuses on the theme of the creation, OE *gesceaft*, *#43/41* analyses the relationship between 'soul and body', OE *gǣst ond līc-hama*) or to refined objects (such as *#48/46* 'chalice', OE *calic* or *hūsel-fæt* and *#83/79* 'gold/ore' OE *ōra*). On the contrary, the instances where the text focuses on 'small things' are far more numerous; humble animals and trivial objects of everyday use are usually sketched in the few lines of the riddle and, viewed through an unusual perspective, transform an apparently unmistakable object into a strange and uncanny creature, a *wiht*[34] in Old English (Wilcox, 47).

As a literary product of highly refined formality, the *Exeter Book* riddles trace their roots both in the Latin riddle tradition, from which they draw themes and motives, and in orality, notably in the ways the enigmatic proposition is formed: a riddle is usually based on an interdependence between a literal solution and a metaphoric focalization, used to obscure the explanation (Murphy, 18).

---

    space in its final line to set it off from the following text, as is the scribe's custom'. Williamson (*The Old English Riddles*, 4) choses not to comment on this: 'it may be that the Anglo-Saxon notion of poetic order remains simply too far removed from our modern sensibilities to be comprehended'. More recently, however, Klinck (197) supposes that the compiler of the collection may have thought that the sections thus marked were riddle or 'riddle-like'. For Orchard, (*Reconstructing The Ruin*, 46) the scribe may have associated the two poems with riddles because of the presence of runes and the superficial similarity between the first lines (also considering the use of the adjective *wrǣtlic*).

34 *Wiht* is defined in *ASD* (s.v. 'wiht') as 'a wight, creature, being, created thing; a whit, thing'. The riddles use *wiht* to identify many different things: food, drink, animals, weapons, etc. Yet, it does not refer simply to material things but could be also used in a more abstract sense. As emphasised by Paz (10): 'The word *wiht* straddles the bounds between the abstract and tangible, immaterial and material, man-made and natural, living creature and dead artefact. The reoccurring use of *wiht* in the riddles further identifies these things as lively, resistant and elusive.'

1.1 The evolution of the riddle genre

Riddle practice is one of the primary expressions of an oral culture, so much that it is possible to find analogous structure, themes and motives in cultures and societies vastly distanced both in space and time. Just as the fable, the riddle can be considered as a wandering motif regarding the fundamental rites of passage in the life of a human being.[35]

Distinguishing between folk riddle, a text of oral and popular origin, and literary riddle is a primary concern. According to Taylor (12), the literary riddle differs from the folk riddle because it is composed by an artist animated by a conscious literary intent. The discriminating factor does not involve the structure of the enigmatic formulation, but rather the level of formal elaboration. Thus, Blauner (49) and Lendinara (*Aspetti della società germanica*, 9–10) map out the elements characterizing them: a folk riddle generally develops a single contradiction and is characterized by the absence of a descriptive framework, therefore by its brevity; a literary riddle, on the other hand, requires a formal elaboration with the involvement of abstract themes, prepares a surprising solution and is based on paradoxes and contradictions designed to outline a single meaningful discourse. In both cases, therefore, the riddle can be defined

---

35 Originally, it might have been that the enigmatic practice had a function similar to that of an initiation rite, they were associated with hidden wisdom. As explained by Borysławski (18), riddles participate in a playful quest for knowledge typical for archaic society: 'just as for children play is a way of learning about the world, archaic man was attempting to comprehend it through the forms of play which [...] possessed the deeper purpose of gaining knowledge about the world'. Because the answers to riddles are only discovered after careful deliberations associated with feelings of joy and anxiety, the knowledge thus gathered becomes sacred. The earliest sacred books begin with an explanation of cosmology presented in enigmatic form. Thus, in early civilisations, riddles served as repositories for this cosmologic knowledge, accessible only to those who could understand their code. Evidence from Ancient Greece and Vedic India suggests that for the most ancient peoples the solution of a riddle was connected to the question only in a conventional way. Originally, therefore, the enigmatic question was not intended to test the wit of the interlocutor, but their degree of knowledge about the shared tradition, an ability that would have proved their belonging to the same cultural community. On this, see also Tupper, xxvi; Caillois and Mehlman, 151; Meli, 41–49; Senderovich, 12.

as a proposition that invites the reader or listener to guess a concept, an object or a person.

In Western culture, literary riddles have had a long tradition: they must have been a symposium entertainment in Greece since the fifth century BCE. Extensive riddles collections can be found in the work of Athenaeus of Naucratis (second century CE) and in the *Palatine Anthology*. However, there is not much of a record in classical Latin literature: in book VI of *Noctes Atticae*, Aulus Gellius puts in writing one riddle by Varro, while in the *Satyricon* Petronius quotes some others.[36] The earliest organized collection of *aenigmata* dates back to Late Antiquity. The collection is ascribed to Symphosius, a writer of uncertain identity active probably in North Africa between the fourth and fifth century. His name might have been an allusive pseudonym to the convivial sphere, as suggested by the *praefatio* which places the composition in the context of the *Saturnalia* (Lapidge, 334 ; Lapidge and Rosier, 62). His work collects one hundred riddles, three-line poems composed in hexameters, whose solution is generally provided by the title preceding them. The *Aenigmata* by Symphosius deal with the most diverse topics; occasionally, the poems are connected according to a thematic criterion: the main subjects may be related to natural elements, animals, household objects, work tools, etc (Bergamin).

Symphosius' influence can be found scattered in the literary production of medieval Europe: some of the Symphosian texts are inserted in romances such as the *Historia Apollonii Regis Tyrii* (fifth century ca.)[37] or in didactic florilegia such as the eight century *Collectanea* previously attributed to Bede. Even the *Disputatio Pippini cum Albino*, a close exchange of witticisms between Alcuin (735–804) and his pupil, one of Charlemagne's sons, Pippin, combines wisdom literature with some prose rewritings of Symphosian riddles.

---

36   Interestingly, as noted by Orchard (*The Old English and Anglo-Latin Riddle Tradition*, ix–x), the Latin tongue borrowed the two main Greek words for 'riddle' (i.e. *aenigma* and *griphus*) and, as documented in Aulus Gellius, riddle contests were associated mainly with Saturnalian amusements in Athens.

37   The romance circulated in England in a vernacular version dating back to 1000 ca. Unfortunately, in the surviving codices the section containing Symphosius's *Aenigmata* is missing. See Bitterli, *Say What I Am Called*, 15.

The model established by Symphosius is then deliberately followed by numerous writers in Early Medieval England who took on the genre. Aldhelm (640–709), the most prominent exponent of Anglo-Latin riddle tradition,[38] inserts in his *Epistola ad Acircium* a 'century' of riddles, one hundred enigmatic poems ranging in length and written in hexameters, as *exempla* for his treatise on Latin metre. Aldhelm's collection builds on the Symphosian experience, however, themes and tones are clearly differentiated. Aldhelm's *aenigmata* have a manifest Christian drive: beyond the encyclopaedic aim, proved by the multiplicity of the objects portrayed, the main purpose of the entire collection seems to be the exploration of the divine creation compared with man-made work. Thus, the conclusive riddle of the collection is a reflection on the beauty and complexity of the universe, as the title *Creatura* suggests (Lapidge and Rosier, 3–6).

The riddle-poems by Tatwine (d. 734), archbishop of Canterbury, take inspiration from Aldhelm's example and, to a lesser extent, from the Symphosian influence. Tatwine wrote forty acrostics dealing with theological subjects, school objects, monsters, wonders and natural phenomena; his collection was thematically 'completed' by the sixty riddles, composed by Eusebius, probably Hwaetberht (d. 747), abbot of Wearmouth. Even Boniface (ca. 680–754) wrote twenty riddle-poems, focused on vices and virtues, whose solution was provided by an acrostic found in each text. Furthermore, the seventh-century sixty-three *Aenigmata Tullii*, known also as *Bern Riddles*, as well as the twelve *Lorsch Riddles*, written anonymously in hexameters in the eighth century, could reasonably be associated to Anglo-Saxon England (Orchard, *The Old English and Anglo-Latin Riddle Tradition*, xii–xv).

The *Exeter Book* riddles represent an additional contribution to this well-established Anglo-Latin tradition, a formally elaborated response in Old English (Bitterli, *Say What I Am Called*, 4). For a long time, the relationship between Anglo-Latin *aenigmata* and Old English riddles was reduced to a sterile opposition: on the one hand, because the Latin texts had the solution in the title, they were read as exclusively focused on didactic topics, nullifying the challenging element of the enigmatic genre, while the Old English poems, enhancing the playful side, portrayed

---

38 Anglo-Latin riddles are quoted from F. Glorie's edition.

everyday objects through unusual perspectives.[39] This distinction is now considered obsolete: the entire tradition is indistinctly characterized by a curiosity in studying both natural world and human creations, as well as a desire for etymological and linguistic games. Similarly, numerous rhetorical figures, stylistic and structural traits, such as personification and prosopopoeia, may be found in both traditions, as can opening and closing formulas that, while more common in the Anglo-Saxon collection, can also be found in the Latin texts (Orchard, *Enigma Variations*, 284–304). Furthermore, beyond any direct adaptation, such as riddles *#35/33* and *#40/38* – Old English versions of Aldhelm's *Lorica* (XXXIII)[40] and *Creatura* (C) – the two branches of the tradition are united by recurring subjects, motifs, and thematic links.[41]

The *Exeter Book* collection, on the other hand, has its own unique features: it is the earliest collection of enigmatic poems in a vernacular language and is marked by an eclecticism of themes and approaches.

---

39 As noted by Wilcox (47): 'Whereas the Anglo-Latin *enigmata* generally circulate with titles that name the object described, the Old English riddle highlight their playful challenge by lacking any stated solution.' Similarly, the lack of the challenging element in the Latin poems is strongly emphasized by Williamson (23–24) who, while acknowledging their influence on the *Exeter Book* collection, does not seem to judge the Latin texts in a positive light: 'Most of these Latin riddles are admittedly a far cry from the Old English.' He also writes about Symphosius's *aenigmata*: 'The construction is regular to the point of boredom,' while, otherwise, 'the Old English riddles [...] assumed distinct Old English qualities, namely imaginative portrayal and projection and the power of a dramatic literary game.'

40 Prior to this translation transcribed in the *Exeter Book* there is another Old English version known as *Leiden Riddle*. The poem is thus called because it is kept in Leiden, Bibliotheek der Rijksuniversiteit, Vossius Lat. 4° 106. The riddle, accompanying the Latin text from which it was translated, was probably copied in Fleury during the tenth century but has linguistic characteristics of the Northumbrian dialect, dating back to the eighth. See Parkes, 207–217.

41 There are several free adaptations of Symphosius' tristichs in the collection: *#16/14*, describing an anchor, *#47/45*, on the bookworm, *#85/81*, developing the theme of the fish in the river and, finally, *#86/82*, surprising the audience with its description of the one-eyed garlic seller; they are rewriting, respectively, LXI *Anchora*, XVI *Tinea*, XII *Flumen et piscis* and XCIV *Luscus alium vendens*. Moreover, the initial lines of *#26/24* clearly evoke the Tatwinian verses devoted to the parchment page in his *De Membrano*. See Bitterli, *Say What I Am Called*, 25–26; Orchard, *The Old English and Anglo-Latin Riddle Tradition*, xvi–xxix.

This diverse scope can be ascribed to the dialectic involving various cultural solicitations characteristic of the Old English poetic tradition.[42] The enigmatic genre is the ideal field to express a distinctive feature of Old English poetry, a propensity to identify an object not by simply designating it by name, but by emphasizing its quality, through the use of periphrases, variations, comparisons and appositions.[43] Finally, when compared to the Anglo-Latin *aenigmata*, the *Exeter Book* riddles demonstrate a greater affinity to the oral tradition[44] in their proclivity for extensive elaboration of metaphorical imagery. Indeed, the enigmatic proposition is frequently related not only to the concealed solution but also to an underlying metaphorical focus that organizes all of the text's obfuscation strategies.

1.2 Riddle and metaphor

Since Aristotle, the word αἴνιγμα has been used in rhetorical discourse as a semantic figure related to the field of analogy. The peripatetic philosopher recognized how this trope was dependent on the metaphor since he believed that good metaphors may be drawn from well-made riddles:[45]

---

42 As noted by Nelson (*The Rhetoric of the Exeter Book Riddles*, 421): '[T]he riddles enabled or compelled members of Anglo-Saxon audiences to draw upon several areas of knowledge to find their solutions. These areas involved the heroic, patristic, and erotic perspectives of the men in the mead halls and in the monasteries, and they reflected the multiple frames of reference which were the natural result of the fusion of cultures.'

43 See Manganella, 262–263. Moreover, on the taste for wordplay in Old English, see also Frank, 207–226.

44 Williamson (*The Old English Riddles*, 23) considered the influence of the oral tradition on the collection to be almost non-existent, he saw the presence of an Anglo-Saxon riddle tradition not attested in poetry nor in prose as unlikely. Nevertheless, as it happened throughout the rest of the world, it is reasonable to suppose an oral diffusion for the riddle genre even in Anglo-Saxon England (Lapidge and Rosier, 62).

45 'Καὶ ὅλως ἐκ τῶν εὖ ἠνιγμένων ἔστι μεταφορὰς λαβεῖν ἐπιεικεῖς· μεταφοραὶ γὰρ αἰνίττονται, ὥστε δῆλον ὅτι εὖ μετενήνεκται. καὶ ἀπὸ καλῶν' ('And, generally speaking, good metaphors could be drawn from well-made enigmas; for metaphor

riddles can connect things that should have been impossible to connect in the real world by using the metaphor.[46] According to Aristotle, the enigmatic formulation is a proposition that is 'badly' structured from a semantic standpoint, and thus it is a contradiction that requires the participation of the metaphor.[47]

Thereafter, taking on from the Aristotelian argument, the Latin scholars of rhetoric argue on the relationship between what they called *aenigma* and other metaphoric figures of speech: in *De Oratore*, Cicero (III, XLI, 166) compares the enigmatic proposition to the concept of allegory; in *Institutio Oratoria*, Quintilian (VI, III, 51) continues on the ideas of his predecessors and relates *aenigma* and *ambages*. Similarly, Donatus, in his *Ars Major* (III, 6), classifies *aenigma* as one of the seven kinds of allegory,[48] defining it thus:

> Aenigma est obscura sententia per occultam similitudinem rerum ut
> *Mater me genuit, eadem mox gignitur ex me*
> cum significet aquam in glaciem concrescere et ex eadem rursus effluere.

---

  is a kind of enigma, and consequently it is clear that the transference is well made') (Aristotle, *Rethoric*, 1405b).

46 'Αἰνίγματός τε γὰρ ἰδέα αὕτη ἐστί, τὸ λέγοντα ὑπάρχοντα ἀδύνατα συνάψαι· κατὰ μὲν οὖν τὴν τῶν <ἄλλων> ὀνομάτων σύνθεσιν οὐχ οἷόν τε τοῦτο ποιῆσαι, κατὰ δὲ τὴν μεταφορῶν ἐνδέχεται, οἷον 'ἄνδρ' εἶδον πυρὶ χαλκὸν ἐπ' ἀνέρι κολλήσαντα', καὶ τὰ τοιαῦτα' ('Indeed, the essence of the enigma consists of expressing a fact by combining words in an impossible way; this cannot be made by a mere combination of names, but it is made possible by the use of metaphors. For instance, "I saw a man weld bronze upon a man with fire" and so on') (Aristotle, *Poetics*: 22, 25–30).

47 As explained by Colli (56): 'Dato che per Aristotele collegare cose impossibili significa formulare una contraddizione, la sua definizione vuol dire che l'enigma è una contraddizione che designa qualcosa di reale, anziché indicare nulla, come di regola. Perché ciò avvenga, aggiunge Aristotele, non si possono collegare i nomi nel loro significato ordinario, ma bisogna far intervenire la metafora' ('Since for Aristotle combining impossible things means expressing a contradiction, according to his definition the enigma is a contradiction used to designate something real, rather than to indicate something that does not exist, as usual. In order for that to happen, Aristotle adds, nouns cannot be connected through their original meaning, but metaphor needs to intervene').

48 *Aenigma* was classified with irony, antiphrasis, euphemism (*charientismos*), paroemia or proverb, sarcasm (*sarcasmos*) and urbanity (*astismos*).

[Enigma is an expression that is obscure because of some hidden similarities between things, such as 'My mother bore me and soon was born out of me', which means that water solidify into ice and flows back out of it.]

The Late Antique rhetor clearly shows the mechanics of the trope by connecting the riddle to the similitude: as a trope, enigma reveals the similarities and affinities among apparently distant subjects, analogies that would otherwise be obscured. However, enigma and similitude relate these subjects in distinct ways: similitude is a direct association, but the enigmatic filter adds a dissociative aspect, a contradiction, a paradox. Water is compared to a creating mother, yet unlike any other, this mother is also generated by her son; whereas a simile concentrates on the two comparable parts, the enigma shifts the focus to those aspects that equate and separate the two entities (Cook, 40).

As a rhetorical figure, the juxtaposition of metaphor and enigma plays an important part in the composition of the riddle as a literary work. A riddle-poem is typically created by expanding on this basic framework: things, frequently belonging to different conceptual categories, are joined in a single meaningful discourse, up to the development of an insoluble paradox, which acts as a revealing clue. For instance, *Flumen et piscis*, riddle xII in the Symphosian collection reads:

> Est domus in terris, clara quae uoce resultat.
> Ipsa domus resonat, tacitus sed non sonat hospes.
> Ambo tamen currunt, hospes simul et domus una.
>
> [There is a house in the earth, whose clear voice echoes around. The house itself resounds, but the guest doesn't sound. Yet both run together, guest and house.]

This is a popular motif widely known:[49] the river is seen as a noisy house, while the fish, which dwells in it, is its silent guest. Coherently, the second line states the central paradox: the house resounds, 'resonat', while the guest keeps quiet; the crucial clue is expressed in the final verse: no house could run, *currere*.[50]

---

49 Tupper (225) has found influence of this theme even in Turkey.
50 The Symphosian model influences also Alcuin. In *Disputatio Pippini cum Albino*, young Pippin rather than giving a straight answer to the master's riddle, alludes to the fish with a metonymy: 'A. Vidi hospitem currentem cum domo sua, et ille

Thus, similarly in the *Exeter Book* riddles, the metaphoric aspect is essential. In order to define the riddle's structure, Williamson examines the relations among the elements of the enigmatic proposition, drawing from the definition of the metaphor proposed by Richards in 1936. According to this definition, a metaphor is the expression of an idea or a thought (*tenor*) through a term (*vehicle*) usually reserved to express another idea or thought. Just as the metaphor does, the riddle connects two apparently incompatible concepts in a single representation. In the structure of a riddle, the hidden creature – the main subject, the 'solution' – is the *tenor* of the metaphoric formulation, while the *vehicle* is being used as a disguise. What brings the two poles of the confrontation together is a common ground. Nevertheless, in order for the guessing game to work, the riddle cannot simply list all the analogous features, it needs also a negative element, i.e. one or more characteristics leading to an explicit paradox in the description of the subject, something that can immediately be recognized as illogic and, subsequently, can produce a distancing effect (Salvador-Bello, *Direct and Indirect Speech*, 17). For instance, riddle #70.1–4/67[51] reads:

    Wiht is wrætlic   þam þe hyre wisan ne conn:
    singeð þurh sidan;   is se sweora woh,
3   orþoncum geworht;   hafaþ eaxle tua,
    scearp on gescyldrum.   His gesceapo * * *

[The creature is wonderful, for those who don't know her habits: she sings through her sides, her neck is curved, skilfully shaped; she has two pointed shoulders above her back. Her destiny . . .]

---

    tacebat et domus sonabat. B. Para mihi rete, et pandam tibi' ('A: I saw a guest running with its own house, while it was silent, the house resonated. B: Set up a net for me, and I'll lead you to it').

51 Krapp and Dobbie count as one single poem, #70, two riddles that, according to Williamson's numeration, are instead #67 and #68. These two riddles had been studied and edited as a single text until Pope (615–622) discovered a missing folio in the codex between f. 125 and f. 126. Thus, the texts are to be studied as two distinct riddle-poems: the first one is missing the conclusion, while the second one is missing the initial lines. See also Williamson, *The Old English Riddles*, 336–337 and Muir, 711.

The central metaphor of this poem is based on the juxtaposition between a human figure who works as a *vehicle* and the hidden *tenor*, the lyre. Both creatures have two shoulders, a tapered neck and a melodious voice making sounds, however, when the riddle-poet suggests that the song is produced by the creature's sides or hips the comparison falters. 'Singeð þurh sidan' (line 2a), 'sings through her sides', is an immediate contradiction to the rest of the proposition: therefore, this information distances the creature to be guessed from the description suggested in the poem, it is an explicit paradox that Williamson labels as a 'metaphoric gap' (Williamson, *A Feast for Creatures*, 27).

In the economy of the enigmatic proposition, there might not be a single paradox, riddle-poems often multiply the small contradictions within the description and the more or less veiled reference to distance or proximity between *vehicle* and *tenor*. Elements of affinity and conflicting characteristics are juxtaposed with the aim to build up a pattern of obscuring and revealing clues so that the subject continuously challenges the ability to distinguish categories through rational perception. What are considered separated identities in a strictly logical universe become incoherent and ambiguous visions through the dreamlike perspective of the riddle-poet, a place where any entity could become something completely different. Indeed, the riddle deliberately ignores any kind of ontological taxonomy, and, actually, finds its *raison d'être* in questioning any conceptual categorization (Williamson, *A Feasts for Creatures*, 25–33).

According to Murphy (18), in the structure of the *Exeter Book* riddles, the associating and distancing features add up to form a cohesive discourse, an extended metaphor underlying the poem to provide it with coherence and consistency:

> The simple idea is that an Old English Riddle's proposition (the 'question' or description posed) may at times relate not only to an unnamed solution but also to what I call its 'focus', and underlying metaphor that lends coherence to the text's strategy of obfuscation.

Solving a riddle-poem, generally, does not simply consist in proposing a solution, and this is also true for the *Exeter Book* collection; understanding an enigmatic poem entails being able to recognize and explain all the obfuscation strategies or the semantic choices that deliberately aim to conceal the solution (Doane, 243). In other words, riddle-poems are not organized solely in relation to the creature to be guessed, they are also structured around an implicit metaphorical focus. Some aspects in the description may not be useful in directing towards the right answer, and yet these same aspects are crucial in revealing any double meaning, literal and metaphorical.[52] Associating and distancing features are used to produce ambiguity and are required in the obfuscation of the main subject. The elements of *common ground* and *metaphoric gap* in the Old English riddles are never chosen arbitrarily: the metaphorical focus of the riddle organizes the rest of the formulation, emphasizing or suppressing the primary subject's traits and proposing information about it that is generally attributed to the secondary subject (Murphy, 47). The metaphor underlying the riddle generally operates in an 'interactive' manner, as described by Black in *Models and Metaphor* (41–45): the metaphor's focus, which can be considered as equivalent to Richards' *vehicle*, implies a system of *topoi* or stereotypes that model and modify the understanding of the main subject. #34/32 is a good example of how any detail directly related to the metaphorical focus may alter one's perspective on the primary subject:

```
     Ic with geseah         in wera burgum
     seo þæt feoh fedeð.    Hafað fela toþa;
3    nebb biþ hyre æt nytte; niþerweard gongeð,
     hiþeð holdlice         ond to ham tyhð,
     wæþeð geond weallas,   wyrte seceð.
6    Aa heo þa findeð       þa þe fæst ne biþ;
     læteð hio þa wlitigan  wyrtum fæste,
     stille stondan         on staþolwonge,
9    beorthe blican,        blowan ond growan.
```

[I saw a creature in the town of men, she feeds the cattle. She has many teeth; her nose is useful; it goes pointing down, she plucks carefully and turns for home, she

---

52 As noted again by Murphy (18), understanding the popular influences on the collection is pivotal for interpreting not only themes and motifs, but also the methods used to structure these riddles: 'In fact, as the simple presence of "double-entendre" riddles in the collection suggests, the very modes of riddling in the *Exeter Book* are likely to be influenced by popular, as well as learned, enigmatic kinds.'

hunts along the walls, looks for plants. She always finds those not firmly rooted; she leaves alone the beautiful ones, held by their roots, quietly standing on its log, brightly shining, blowing and growing.]

The audience is led to believe that the speaking subject is a living creature, a dog, from the start of the riddle; the poem refers explicitly to nose (line 3a), teeth (line 2b) and to the act of following something along the wall. All these references are explained by the generally proposed solution – rake, OE *raca* – only after reading the final lines which describe the main ability of the character: uprooting weeds in order to save the best plants. Thus, the subject's final actions clarify its identity, while the earlier lines induce the audience to confuse dog and rake. The system of stereotypes associated to the dog has been juxtaposed to the system of stereotypes associated to the rake.

The core metaphor of the poem is expanded throughout a succession of interwoven variations, made up by concatenations of elements that, while not always in contradiction with one another, produce what Murphy (40–41) described as 'a pleasing sense of intricacy', a puzzle to be solved when the proper key is found.

Throughout the whole collection, the interplay between literal clues and metaphorical images is elaborated through a paratactic style which often implies any logical connective, such that the many connotations are simply juxtaposed.[53] This contributes to the impression of disharmony: even when the riddle subject can be guessed with a high degree of certainty, the element's irregular juxtaposition prevents the visualization of a fully formed overall picture. The riddle-poems in the collection are developed around contradictions and around the transitions from one state to another: from animate to inanimate, from life to death and from death to life, from happy childhood to a woeful adult life; creatures are

---

53   In line with the style of Old English poetry, as described by Robinson (15), a poetic style characterized by 'artfully congested syntax, the heavily nominal surface structure and the martialing of juxtapposition'. On this, Niles (*Old English Enigmatic Poems*, 45) also notes: 'in their style and form, the Exeter Book riddles are a quintessential example of the Anglo-Saxon *ars poetica* [. . .] their syntax is interlaced in the customary poetic manner, which differs so noticeably from that of prose; and their phrasing is densely impacted to the point of being difficult to understand, even when one knows the answers.'

wonderful – *wundorlīc* or *wrǣtlīc* – because they possess the ability to switch between different identities. Each creature is represented as itself but also as something else, the figures that populate the *Exeter Book* collection always appear as being double, multiple or metamorphic: behind the nightingale there is always the poet (#8/6), behind the garlic seller there is a monster (#86/82), behind the rake the dog can be glimpsed (#34/32), behind the fox remains, on the background, the human being (*#15/13*). It is in this sense that, despite the eclectic nature of the collection, it is possible to read within it an interest in the instability and fluidity of the subjects of the world, impossible to organize into specific categories.

2. Prosopopoeia, Anthropomorphism and Empathy

Already in 1910, Tupper (xc) noticed how, in the *Exeter Book* collection, creatures such as storms, shields, beers, bows, ostriches, oxen and all the others, assumed a dynamic mental state typically associated with human beings:

> in many riddles, the subject is quickened into full life. The riddler points to the living soul of his creatures, or else he follows the far more effective method of ascribing to beast or even to inanimate things the traits and passion of men.

The habit to confer to animals and to inanimate objects passions of men is a direct consequence of the metaphoric process which, as already seen, affects the structure of a riddle. Throughout the *Exeter Book* collection, personification is easily the most frequent obfuscation strategy.

More precisely, according to Williamson (*The Old English Riddles*, 25–26), all the poems in the collection can be classified according to two poles of perception: riddle subjects could be described by an external observer, speaking in the third person; otherwise, they could self-introduce themselves, speaking in the first person. In the so-called *third-person riddles of description*, the text usually begins with phrases such as *Ic seah, Ic gefrægn* and then continues to illustrate in detail the various paradoxical characteristics of the observed creature: the structure of the text is narrative, as well as descriptive, and while the external observer retains their own humanity, the creature, which rarely is a human being, is outlined in purely anthropomorphic terms. Conversely, in the approximately fifty *first-person riddles of personification*, the opening sentence, often *Ic eom* or *Ic wæs*, assigns to inanimate objects, animals or natural phenomena the ability to elaborate a speech, giving to the subjects the chance to show themselves as if they were endowed with will of action, emotions and experience.[54] These are prosopopoeic riddles.

---

54 For a more detailed explanation on the use of prosopopoeia in Old English literature in general and in the *Exeter Book* riddles in particular see Schlauch, 23–34; Nelson, *The Rhetoric of the Exeter Book Riddles*, 421–440; Orton, 1–15.

After all, personification is a figure of speech fairly present in Old English poetry.[55] The best-known case is probably the passion of Christ narrated by the cross, in *The Dream of the Rood*; similarly, in *The Husband's Message*, a poem copied in the *Exeter Book* among the riddles, the message itself describes part of its own journey.[56] Likewise, in the metric preface of Alfred's translation of the *Cura Pastoralis*, the speaking subject is Gregory's work itself, illustrating its fate in the land of the Anglo-Saxons. Moreover, the Cambridge manuscript, Corpus Christi College, MS 326 (tenth century), preserves a metric preface for Aldhem's prose text *De Virginate*, where the treatise itself pays homage to its author, introducing itself in a macaronic verse mixing Old English, Latin and some transliterated Greek.

Furthermore, such a widespread use of prosopopoeia[57] is also reflected in the ancient practice of engraving swords or other objects with statements indicating origins and belongings.[58] Inscriptions of a prosopopoeic nature in Old English range from simple declarations of production, as in the case of the ninth century *King's Alfred Jewel*, engraved with 'Ælfred mec heht gewyrcean' ('Alfred ordered me to be done'), to small epigrams like the one inscribed on the *Brussels Cross*:

---

55 This widespread interest for prosopopoeia might be explained by what Guerrieri (330) called 'gusto per la umanizzazione', a 'taste for humanization'. This is the reason why even monstrous creatures like Grendel and his mother 'demonstrate to have undoubted cognitive and emotional abilities', 'mostrano di possedere innegabili capacità cognitive ed emozionali'.

56 For a more detailed discussion on the *The Husband's Message* and the riddle preceding it in the codex, #60/58, see Klinck, 27, 56–60 and 199–208.

57 On this Knappe (*Classical Rhetoric*, 23) wrote: 'The lightest impact of Latin learning is to be expected in the most "Germanic" genre, which is heroic poetry. Here, the influence of structural figures is usually acknowledged in scholarship, whereas figurative diction such as personification and synecdoche [...] is often attributed to Germanic tradition.' On the knowledge of classical rhetoric in Anglo-Saxon England and on its use on Old English literary works, see again Knappe, *Traditionen der klassischen Rhetorik*, and, among others, J. Campbell; Gneuss; Steen.

58 Lois Bragg (*The Lyric Speaker*, 43–45) conveniently noted how these first-person epigraphs could represent the earliest form of writing for cultures not used to the practice. Therefore, in contexts where written documentation for transactions was not common, these inscriptions might have been used to give voice to the object because, unlike the people involved in the transaction, the object is a permanent element.

     Rod is min nama.   Geo ic ricne Cyning
     bær byfigynde,   blode bestemed.
3   Þas rode het æþlmær wyrican and Aþelwold hys beroþor
     Criste to lofe for ælfrices saule hyra beroþor[?].

[Rood is my name. In the past I carried a powerful king, while trembling, covered by blood. Æthelmær ordered for this rood to be made and Athelwold, his brother, for the love of Christ and for the soul of Ælfric, their brother.]

In situations such as this, the prosopopoeia's structure highlights the identity of the people fabricating the object or the people commissioning the work, with the clear aim to promote their notoriety.

The lyrical quality of the *Exeter Book* poems is placed very far from the simplicity of such inscriptions; as noted by Williamson, among the verses of the riddles, it is possible to recognize a mode to celebrate the non-human other, an *ante-litteram* version of *negative capability*, a way to represent in human and poetic terms a world which is not human at all.[59] This celebration of diversity coincides with an act of symbiosis or an act of mimesis where creature and human being use each other as a disguise, thus uniting and blurring their own identities.

Prosopopoeia is a crucial factor in this. Endowing the non-human subjects of the riddles with a form of speech calls into question one quality exclusive to humanity: the ability to use language. It is no coincidence that in Old English the inanimate being is designed with the present participle of the verb *cweðan* 'to speak, to say', prefixed with a negation: the inanimate is *uncweðende*, the 'un-speaking';[60] moreover, in *The Dream*

---

59   Williamson (*The Old English Riddles*, 26) noted: 'There is nothing in the classical tradition to explain the particular lyric quality – almost a celebration of the non-human Other – in the Old English poems'; while the concept of *negative capability* was developed by John Keats in a letter of the 22 December 1817, addressed to his brothers, George and Thomas (edited by Forman, 227): 'I mean Negative Capability, that is, when a man is capable of being in uncertainties, mysteries, doubts, without any irritable reaching after fact and reason.'

60   See the Old English translation of Boethius' *De Consolatione Philosophiae* (XXXIV): 'Hwæþer þu giet ongite þæt ða uncweðendan gesceafta wilnodon to bionne on ecnesse swa ilce swa men gif hi meahten?' ('Do you yet perceive that the inanimate creatures would like to exist for ever, as human beings do, if they were

of the Rood, (line 3a) the speaking subject defines men as those who carry speech, *reordberend*.[61] Conveniently, Hayes relates the *Exeter Book* riddles in the context of an oral performance[62] and draws attention on the vocal paradoxes intrinsic in prosopopoeia, paradoxes that might have led the audience to recognize the close connection between the voice of the performer and the written text.[63] Frequently in the riddles of personification, the object describing itself turns the situation around, asking to the public to say out loud the identity of the speaker: 'Saga hwæt ic hatte' ('Say what I am called'). This stratagem would seem to invite a critical reflection on the voice that the performer lends to the main subject of the riddle. This *performance*, that is the vocalization of the experience of the non-human creatures, could facilitate a process of mimesis and could push towards a re-evaluation of one's perceptual categories, often in an anthropomorphic direction (Hayes, 25–27).

Similarly, Bragg (*The Lyric Speaker*, 43–45) reads the riddles as a particular form of lyric poetry and recognizes that the processes of identification between the speaking character and the audience, made possible by prosopopoeia, are crucial for the comprehension of a riddle. The

---

able?'). Meaningfully, even Old Saxon refers to the inanimate being in a similar way: *unqueðandi*. See Guerrieri, 330.

61 This is a compound word derived from the present participle of *beran* 'to carry, to bear' (see *Dictionary of Old English – DOE*, s.v. 'beran') and *reord* 'speech, tongue, language, voice' (see *ASD*, s.v. 'reord').

62 Although it is not possible to establish with certainty the specific context for which the collection was composed, it would seem riddles would be performed in social contexts more than in exclusively didactic situations. Conversely, Aldhelm's, Eusebius', Tatwine's and Boniface's *aenigmata* were almost surely composed with the aim to be used in the schoolroom. According to Orchard the *Exeter Book* collection was aimed 'less for the classroom than for the wine hall' (Orchard, *Enigma Variations*, 284).

63 For instance, in #60/58, solved as *rūnstæf* (sometimes, indicated also as *hrēod*, 'reed' or 'quill'), the subject discloses the strangeness of its own situation: being a creature without a mouth, 'muðleas', who, nevertheless, is able to speak, 'sprecan', and to exchange words 'wordum wrixlan' (lines 9b–10a). The peculiarity of *#60/58* is to describe an object with an inscription. The presence of this kind of objects in the collection favours a reflection on the relationship between oral and written communication, since, as written by Hayes, these sort of objects 'reflect on the particular circumstances under which they acquire a voice: when the reader vocalizes the riddle's text' (Hayes, 26).

primary solution strategy is imagining the point of view of the subject to be guessed. Whether it is a tool, an animal or an abstract entity, any solver must try to understand the functioning of the creature, they must put themselves in the subject's shoes, in other words, they must experiment empathy.[64] Thus, *#88/84*, a riddle usually solved as 'inkwell' (OE *blæchorn*), develops the complex story of two brothers who lived happily in a forest, before being separated:

9	Ac ic uplong stod þær ic [....]x	
	ond min broþor – begen wæron hearde.	
	Eard wæs þy weorðra þe wit on stodan,	
12	hyrstum þy hyrra. Ful oft unc holt wrugon,	
	wudubeama helm wonnum nihtum,	
	scildon wið scurum. Unc gescop meotud.	
15	Nu unc mæran twam magas uncre	
	sculon æfter cuman, eard oðþringan	
	gingran broþor. Eom ic gumcynnes	
18	anga ofer eorþan. Is min innaþ blæc,	
	wonn ond wundorlic; ic on wuda stonde	
	bordes on ende. Nis min broþor her	
21	ac ic sceal broþorleas bordes on ende	
	staþol weardian, stondan fæste;	
	ne wat hwær min broþor on wera æhtum	
24	eorþan sceata eardian sceal,	
	se me ær be healfe heah eardade.	
	Wit wæron gesome sæcce to fremmanne;	
27	næfre uncer awþer, his ellen cyðde	
	swa wit þære beadwe begen ne onþungan.	
	Nu mec unsceafta innan slitað,	
30	wyrdaþ mec be wombe; ic gewendan ne mæg.	

---

64 Zaki and Ochsner (871) define empathy as 'the ability and tendency to share and understand others' internal states'. Empathy is not born out an intellectual effort, is, instead, part of the genetic makeup of the human species; it is a skill belonging to both the human and the animal experience. To be able to understand moods, frames of mind, mental conditions or the emotions of another person is, indeed, a mechanism for survival, and this is what could explain behaviours like schooling for fish. See Cavell, 'A Poetics of Empathy?: Non-human Experience in the Anglo-Saxon Bovine Riddles', forthcoming. I owe many thanks to Dr Megan Cavell who allowed me to read her essay before it was published.

[Yet I stood upright, where I ... ... and my brother – we both were hard. That place was worthier when we stood there, on top as ornaments. Often the forest concealed us, the helmet of trees, in the dark nights, shielded us from showers. The creator made us both. Now our kindred shall come after us, the illustrious pair, our younger brothers must drive us out of our home. I am alone, divided from my kind across the earth. My insides are black, dark and wonderful; I stand upon the wood, at the end of the board. My brother is not here, yet I must, brotherless, guard my place at the end of the board, standing fixed in place; I don't know where my brother is, among things owned by men, where he must dwell across the corners of the earth, he once stood high by my side. We banded together in order to give battle; neither of us showing off our value, unless we both were useful to the battle. Now ferocious beings tear me from inside, hurting me by the womb; I cannot change this situation.]

The choice to narrate in the first-person dual focuses attention on the figure of the absent brother, a metaphor and an essential clue because it implies that the speaking subject lives in pairs in the natural condition. As a result, brotherhood is a prominent motif in the poem, and it becomes a focal point in the audience's emotional response. The dual form[65] emphasises the idea of brotherhood, which serves as an analogy to explore the connection between human audience and the stolen antlers; however, the poem includes some aspects that cannot be associated to a human figure: the depiction of life in the woods (lines 11a–17a) resists any form of anthropocentrism. The protagonist cannot be human, but the subject establishes an empathic relationship with the audience through a tale that is strongly connected to the human experience of exile, forced removal from one's environment, and permanent separation from a beloved brother (Bragg, *The Lyric Speaker*, 49).

In a sense, the reaction induced by a riddle of this kind is analogous to what Orton theorises is created by the narration of the cross in *The Dream of the Rood*: an emotional inference provokes a feeling of

---

65 In Old English poetry, dual form for pronouns is not common. When used, it usually serves to emphasize the connection or the closeness between two subjects or beings; on the use of the dual from in *Genesis B* see Hall, 139–145, but also in *The Wife's Lament* and in *Soul and Body*, see Murphy, 21. The dual form is similarly used in other riddles of the collection: for example, *#95/91* (depicting again an inkhorn built out of antlers) and *#85/81* (focused on the symbiotic existence of fish and river, as already seen).

participating in the pain. The presence of the personal pronoun *ic* in association with verbs that evoke the painful experience, such as *slītan* 'to tear' or *wyrdan* 'to hurt, to wound',[66] may drive the audience to relate with the speaking subject; accepting the possibility that an animal could have its own personality and emotions, the public may feel compassion for its sufferings (Orton, 3–4).

Therefore, these anthropomorphizing techniques can support the autonomy of the speaking creature, which transforms from object to subject, as they prevent the non-human from being seen as an empty vessel to be filled with human desires and purposes. As written by Dale (68):

> Using anthropomorphism in this way, as a tool for exploring an intangible voice, makes the created world familiar to humanity as opposed to 'alien', whilst still preserving the living thing as a separate entity to humans, a non-intelligent being. It simultaneously allows humans to gain access to nature's perspective whilst also allowing nature to resist complete assimilation into the world of human beings.

This attitude, which affects most of the Old English riddles, is particularly evident when the main characters are animal figures.

---

66 For the meaning of *slītan* see *ASD*, s.v. 'slītan': 'to slit, to tear, to rend; to split'. The verb is used multiple times in the collection in reference to animated subjects. It normally means 'to slit, tear' but it can also imply 'to pluck, pull off with force'. See *#12/10*, line 1b: 'foldan slite' ('tearing up the fields'), referring to the ox working with the plough; *#13/11*, line 8: 'muþum slitan' ('lacerate with the mouth'), referring to the new-born chicks who break the shell with their beak; *#16/14*, line 6: 'ond mec slitende soma flymað' ('and uprooting me, they make me flee'), referring to the effect of the waves on the anchor. Moreover, it can also imply a figurative connotation such as 'to torment'; see, for instance, *The Seafarer*, lines 11–12: 'hungor innan slat merewerges mod' ('hunger tore from inside the soul weary by the sea'), and *Genesis B*, lines 802b–803a 'nu slit me hunger and þurst / bitre on breostum' ('now hunger and thirst brutally rip my breast'). For *wyrdan* see *ASD*, s.v. 'wyrdan' and 'wirdan': 'to injure, hurt, annoy'. See *Elene*, lines 902–904: 'Hwæt is þis, la, manna, þe minne eft / þurh fyrngeflit folgaþ wyrdeð, / iceð ealdne nið, æhta strudeð?' ('What sort of man is this, oh, who hurts my retinue through this ancient conflict, increases this old enmity, robs my possessions?'); and the Old English *De Consolatione Philosophiae* (XXXVI): 'Ða gnættas mid swyðe lytlum sticelum him deriað, and eac ða smalan wyrmas ðe ðone mon ægðer ge innan ge utan wyrdað' ('Gnats harm it with small stings, and every small reptile both inside and out hurts it').

Two significant examples of this process can be found in riddles *#15/13* and *#72/70*; the use of register and vocabulary drawn from other poetic genres,[67] usually reserved to human beings, can facilitate an empathic relationship. Additionally, personification sometimes acts in such a way as to completely alter the mutual positions of man and animal, as in *#77/74*. In each of these riddles, regardless of the particular strategies used to hide or reveal the identity of the main subject, the empathic connection established through the anthropomorphic metaphor allows us to assess the distinctions between human and animal with a greater sense of flexibility.

2.1 *#15/13:* Fight like a man

Counting twenty-nine lines, *#15/13* is one of the longest poems in the collection; it is undoubtedly the longest riddle among those that can be solved as an animal. The poem is characterized by its dynamic and narrative pace: not only does the text recast the challenging nature of the riddle genre through an original perspective, but it also depicts a comparison

---

[67] It should be noted that the notion of genre, which is always ambiguous and debatable in literature, has an even more complicated application in the context of Old English poetry, whose corpus is made up by a collection of mostly anonymous compositions, almost always attested in a single copy, the sources and origins of which are frequently debated. As written by Niles (*Old English Literature*, 222): 'genre customarily implies a conspiracy of expectations between authors and readers or, in the oral context, between performers and listeners'. It is difficult to determine whether the meanings given to Old English poetry by modern interpreters correlate to the expectations that the Anglo-Saxons had of these materials. Recognizing that the notion of a single genre is a historical construct rather than a foundational paradigm makes the usage of any modern terminology anachronistic (R. Cohen, 87–105). The majority of Old English poetry is made up by hybrid texts in which characteristics of different genres are combined. Nonetheless, with due caution, it is possible to discern a series of elements – in both tone and content – that unite some compositions and distinguish them from others. For example, in a study of traditional incipits, Battles has uncovered the traces of a purposeful differentiation among genres by Old English poets (Battles, 1–33).

between the situation of the animal who steadfastly protects its whelps and the audience made up of human beings who could have lived through similar circumstances.

```
        Hals is min hwit    ond heafod fealo,
        sidan swa some.   Swift ic eom on feþe,
3       beadowæpen bere.    Me on bæce standað
        her swylce swe on hleorum;   hlifiað tu
        earan ofer eagum.    Ordum ic steppe
6       in grene græs.   Me bið gyrn witod
        gif mec onhæle    an onfindeð
        wælgrim wiga    þær ic wic buge,
9       bold mid bearnum,    ond ic bide þær
        mid geoguðcnosle.    Hwonne gæst cume
        to durum minum,    him biþ deað witod;
12      forþon ic sceal of eðle    eaforan mine
        forhtmod fergan,    fleame nergan.
        Gif he me æfterweard    ealles weorþeð –
15      hine breost berað –    ic his bidan ne dear,
        reþes on geruman –    ne ic þæt ræd teale –
        ac ic sceal fromlice    feþemundum
18      þurh steapne beorg    stræte wyrcan.
        Eaþe ic mæg freora    feorh genergan
        gif ic mægburge mot    mine gelædan
21      on degolne weg    þurh dunþyrel
        swæse ond gesibbe;    ic me siþþan ne þearf
        wælhwelpes wig    wiht onsittan.
24      Gif se niðsceaþa    nearwe stige
        me on swaþe seceþ,    ne tosæleþ him
        on þam gegnpaþe    guþgemotes,
27      siþþan ic þurh hylles    hrof geræce
        ond þurh hest hrino    hildepilum
        laðgewinnan    þam þe ic longe fleah.
```

[My neck is white and my head is brown, as are my sides. I am swift of foot; I bear on me battle-weapons. Hair covers my back as well as my cheeks; two ears stand high above my eyes. I walk on my toes through the green grass. Grief is assured for me if a bloodthirsty warrior finds me hidden where I live, at home with my children, and there I stay with my young family. When this guest comes at my doors, death is assured for them; thus, I must lead my children far from home and save them, frightened fleeing. If that creature will follow me – it slithers on its belly – I dare not await that cruel being in my home – good sense does not suggest it – but I must build up a road through the steep hill strenuously with my forefeet. Then I will easily save the lives of my loved ones, if I can guide my relatives out by a secret way through a hole in the hill; after, I won't need to bother with the attack of the slaying dog. If this malignant foe still looks for me through that narrow pathway, he won't miss a battle-meeting on the hostile path; once I've reached the top of the hill and I will hit fiercely with my darts the hateful enemy from whom I long fled.]

The poem begins by describing the physical features of the main subject, focusing on the details rather than on the overall picture: alternate colours of the fur (lines 1–2a), swiftness of foot (line 2b), thick hair on the cheeks and on the back (lines 3b–4a), uptight ears, sitting over the eyes (lines 4b–5a), forefeet capable of digging long underground tunnels (lines 17–18). As noted by Bitterli (*Say What I Am Called*, 472), while describing its own physical appearance, the speaking subject provides information that is, at the same time, detailed and vague, because it may relate to any small quadruped mammal.

Some aspects in the description, such as the striped colouring of the fur on the back and on the sides of the animal and the ability to dig deep burrows in the ground (lines 17–22), have led some interpreters to identify the solution as a badger (OE *brocc*).[68] Therefore, the weapons of war, *beaduwǣpen* (lines 3a), carried by the main subject, could have easily referred to claws or sharp teeth. Others, however, assumed them to be the quills of a porcupine;[69] although not native to the British Isles, this animal was fairly known in Anglo-Saxon England, thanks to an extensive

---

68 This suggested solution was first proposed by Dietrich, 'Die Räthsel des Exeterbuchs' [1859], 465. Many scholars supported this idea: Tupper, 101–104, Trautmann, 75–76 and Nelson, 'Badger', 447–450.

69 Walz, 261–268, and, more recently, Bitterli, 'Exeter Book Riddle 15', 461–487, argued in favour of the solution 'porcupine'. Both consider the compound noun *hildepīl* as a clear reference to a special skill ascribed to the porcupine's quills: if necessary, they could apparently be thrown away at will.

literary tradition of classical and medieval texts.⁷⁰ The porcupine owns its name in Old English to its resemblance to the hedgehog:⁷¹ the Latin *hystrix* was, indeed, glossed *se māra igil*, while *ērīcīus* was glossed *se læssa igil*.⁷²

There is, however, a third and more plausible suggested solution: the thick cheeks covered with fur, the indication of a brownish fur on the sides⁷³ and white colouring on throat, belly and tip of the tail are

---

70   The porcupine was described in Aristotle's *History of Animals* (IX, 39, 623a), in Claudius Aelianus' *De Natura Animalium* (I, 31), in Oppianus's *Cynegetica* (III, 391–409) and in the poem *Hystrix* by the late Latin-Greek author Claudianus (fourth–fifth century). Pliny the Elder gives a long description in *Naturalis Historia* (VIII, 125); thus, it is mentioned also in Solinus' *Collectanea rerum memorabilium* (30, 38), a sort of summary of the Plinian encyclopaedia, so widespread in Late Antique and Early Medieval period that even Isidore of Seville uses it as source material (*Etymologies*, XII, ii, 35). On the circulation of Isidore's and Solinus' work in Anglo-Saxon England see Lapidge.

71   Orchard (*A Commentary*, 361) argues for the solution 'hedgehog', citing Isidore's description and most importantly the *Bestiaries* tradition 'which describes how the hedgehog has a burrow with two separate entrances, in case of danger' (see, for instance, one of the Bodleian Bestiaries: Oxford MS Bodley, 764, ff. 52v–53r).

72   Cavell ('The Igil', 206–210) sees this taxonomic separation as forced and unhistorical, she suggests the idea that the poet could have a composite imagine of what an *igil* was, joining the naturalistic observations on the hedgehog with the literary tradition on the porcupine. On this see also the glosses on Corpus Glossary section 5, line 303 and section 8, line 108 in Hessels; and glosses #3475 and #3477 in Stryker.

73   Words describing colours in Old English are notoriously difficult to define for contemporary interpreters. *Fealu* derives from Proto-Germanic **falwa-* (besides OE *fealu*, see also OS *falu* 'pale yellow', OHG *falo* 'pale, reddish yellow'. See Orel s.v. '*falwaz*'). Etymologically tied with ModE *fallow*, *fealu* suggests a very wide gradation of colours: from pale yellow to reddish, brownish and also grey. According to *DOE* (s.v. 'fealu'), among at least forty occurrences, there are several nuances of this particular colour in the Old English corpus: 'the corpus yields the most evidence for a colour basically yellow but variously tinted with shades of red, brown or grey, often pale but always unsaturated, i.e. not vivid; hence "tawny", "yellow(ed)", "yellowish-red", "yellowish-brown", "yellowish-grey" all appear as translations'. Moreover, Biggam (*Grey*, 44) noted how the concept of yellow and grey could juxtapose in Old English, *fealu* can designate both colours: 'The evidence for yellow and yellow-brown above, and also the fact that *fealu* can mean yellow as well as grey, suggest that these were related concepts for the Anglo-Saxons.' On the semantics of colour in Old English see, also, Barley, 15–28, Bragg, 'Color words in Beowulf', 47–55 and further works by Biggam, especially, 'The ambiguity of

characteristics of another small quadruped: the fox (OE *fox*).[74] The fox is a very lithe animal, its swift movements can be described as walking on tiptoes, exactly like the main character of the riddle does in lines 5b–6a; furthermore, foxes have triangular ears, mobile and pointed, which protrude above their eyes; a position well described by the Old English verb *hlīfian*.[75] Moreover, their sharp teeth could be considered as a weapon in the eternal battle against their natural enemies, who have always been dogs and wolves (Williamson, *The Old English Riddles*, 175). The compound word *wælhwelp* (line 23a) could refer to one or the other; this hapax associates the noun *hwelp*, usually used to indicate the puppies of a canid species, to the idea of destruction produced by war, *wæl*.[76]

Furthermore, this solution would seem to be confirmed by the behaviour of the speaking subject. Although the poem makes no explicit reference to the cunning abilities usually attributed to the fox, the creature's attitude in the riddle conforms both with the actual behaviour of the fox in nature and with the resourcefulness ascribed to them in their literary fame.[77] In the riddle, even though the animal runs away from

---

brightness', 171–187 and 'The development of the basic colour terms of English', 231–266.

74 The first scholar who proposed this solution was Brett (258–260); subsequently followed by many others: Williamson (*The Old English Riddles*, 173–174), Pinsker and Ziegler (172–176), Niles (*Old English Enigmatic Poems*, 141), Osborn (173–187). The solution 'wesle' ('weasel') suggested by Young (304–306) is akin to the fox solution. Weasels are swift and aggressive animals; they have a dark fur on the back and white hair on the stomach. However, they do not dig burrows on their own, but they use lairs abandoned by other animals. Furthermore, they have short and round ears. Young sees the cruel enemy, slithering on its breast, as a snake, but, as noted first by Williamson (*The Old English Riddles*, 175–176) and lately by Bitterli ('Exeter Book Riddle 15', 477), weasels are actually the ones preying on snakes.

75 See *DOE*, s.v. 'hlīfian': 'to stand high, to tower, to stand out prominently'.

76 *Wæl* designates 'in a collective sense, the slain, the dead, a number of slain, generally of death in battle' (*ASD*, s.v. 'wæl'), from Proto-Germanic *walaz: ON *valr*, OE *wæl*, OS *wal-dād*, OHG *wal*. See Orel, s.v. '*walaz'.

77 According to Bitterli ('Exeter Book Riddle 15', 475), an animal that runs away in a fearful state, 'forhtmod fergan' (line 13a), seems distant from the image of the sharp and deceiving fox usually represented in the classical and medieval literary tradition; as depicted, for instance, by Symphosius in his *aenigma* xxxiv, *Vulpes*: 'Exiguum corpus sed cor mihi corpore maius. / Sum versuta dolis, arguto callida sensu; / Et fera sum sapiens, sapiens fera si qua vocatur' ('I have a small

the fight, it does not do so out of cowardice; it hides its young family to protect them and actively looks for the best position to fight back at the most propitious moment. Even if scared, it is not just running away, but it is implementing a shrewd defence strategy, consistent with the idea of a fox that, at the slightest hint of danger, takes the children away from the lair (Lloyd, 120). In other words, the idea of postponing a fight until you are sure you can play on equal terms would not seem a choice unusual for the proverbial cunning fox (Osborn, 175–179).

Nevertheless, whether the riddle can be solved as *brocc*, *igil* or *fox*, there is no doubt about the anthropomorphic character of the representation. Following the first five lines where the speaking subjects describe their own physical appearance, the semi-verse 6b signals a clear change in approach: the descriptive structure typical of the riddle genre is given up in favour of a narrative that fully exploits the potential of mimesis of a first-person narration. Moreover, through kennings and metaphorical compounds associated mainly with the lexicon and the register of the heroic genre, this kind of narrative transfers to the little animal the whole system of *topoi* usually associated with the warrior (Tigges, 99). Therefore, after the first descriptive moment, the speaking subject imagines the possibility of a direct assault on its home by an unidentified predator and, assessing the option of waiting in secret, fears a tragic end (lines 6–11).

The definiteness of pain, expressed in line 6b ('Me bið gyrn witod'), echoes in the analogous sense of fatality stated in the following 11b ('him biþ dead witod').[78] The two lines, related in a circular structure, suggest how the dreaded sufferings must necessarily be correlated with the likelihood of death for the young cubs. Similarly, alliterations and variations seem to highlight a chain of connections between the cubs, the place that hosts them and should protect them, and the predator who threatens their integrity: in line 8, 'wælgrim wiga',[79] 'bloodthirsty warrior' alliterates

---

    body, but my heart is bigger than my body, I am skilful in deceit, expert in wittiness and I am a wise animal, if an animal can be called wise').

78 Similar formula is found in the final line of *#85/81*, used to express the inevitability of death for the fish which gets separated from water: 'gif wit unc gedælað, me bið dead witod' ('if we two are divided, death is assured for me'). See Orchard, *A Commentary*, 362.

79 The predator is designed as a warrior, *wiga*. This noun can be tied to the other noun *wig* 'fight, battle, war' and to the verb *wīgan* 'to fight' (from Proto-Germanic

meaningfully with 'wīc' 'dwelling-place, home'; an imagine evoked in variation by the following verse, where 'bold', 'building, dwelling house', is associated with the presence of offspring, 'mid bearnum'; similarly, on line 10, 'geoguðcnosle', 'young family', a compound word used to again designate the cubs,[80] alliterates with 'gæst', 'guest, stranger, enemy', another noun used to classify the predator as a menace.

With the aim to avoid this tragic destiny, the animal considers retreating out of the den as the only conceivable reaction. The urgency to act with courage, 'fromlice' (line 17b), overlaps the naturally frightened, 'forhtmod' (line 13a), frame of mind: to save the lives of their cubs, the animal is forced to envision an alternative situation to their helpless waiting, thus they dig a path through the hill (lines 18–21). Only at this point, with the cubs safe and sound, the protagonist can leave back any kind of fear (lines 21–22) and get ready for a direct confrontation with the enemy.

Riddle *#15/13* exploits motifs related to the heroic genre: while the main character is presented as a hero, the poem makes clear the presence of an enemy and a battlefield.[81] It is an ideal example of what Irving (199) writes on the possibility to 'play safely' in the *Exeter Book* collection:

> The Riddles occasionally furnish some authentic experience possibly not considered worthy of more serious treatment, expressed in facetious 'play' mode and therefore safely.

---

*wīxanan or *wīʒanan, see Goth. *weihan* 'to dispute, to fight', ON *vega* 'to fight', OHG *ubarwehan* 'to overcome'. It seems also to be connected with OIr. *fichim* 'to fight' and Lat. *vincō* 'to conquer'; see Orel, s.v. '*wīxanan'). The adjective qualifies the predator as *grim*, 'fierce, cruel' (see *DOE*, s.v. 'grim'), while the first element of the compound *wæl* 'the slain' is a noun that, as already noted, is reiterated on line 23b in the hapax legomena *wælhwelp*, referring again to the antagonist.

80 A compound word formed by the nouns *geōguþ* 'youth' and *cnōsl* 'progeny, offspring, descendants, family, kin' (see *DOE*, s.v. 'geōguþ' and 'cnōsl').

81 Just like any other riddle in the collection, *#15/13* addresses an audience who is able to partake in many areas of knowledge in order to guess the right solution: the affinity between the animal who is the main character and the human being relies on the ability of the Anglo-Saxon public to recognize a heroic frame of reference. See Nelson, 'The Rethoric', 421–422 and 'Old English Riddle 15', 449.

In other words, if the Old English riddles, on the whole, are characterized by a tendency to subvert perspectives, in the specific case of *#15/13*, the choice to use the point of view of the animal allows the riddle-poet to represent an experience of flight and fight in a positive light, which would not be allowed within the canon of the heroic genre.[82]

It is no coincidence that words related to the lexicon of war are recurrent throughout the poem. The battle between the two enemies is defined as 'guþgemot' (line 26), it is reached by a 'gegnpaþe' (line 26) 'a hostile path' or 'a path along which one goes to oppose another'.[83] Teeth, claws or quills are metaphorically referred to as *beaduwæpen* (line 4a), 'weapons of war', and *hildepīl*[84] ('war spears').[85] Even the dative 'ordum' (line 5a) which properly indicates the animal's habit of walking on their

---

82 Osborn (176) argues that if we choose to see as meaningful the feminine ending for the adjective 'onheale', 'hidden', we might find in it an indication on the gender of the speaking subject. Despite the fact that adjectives' endings are not always coherent in regard to gender (see, for instance, 'swift' on line 2b, which, however, might depend by 'wiht'), making the speaking subject a female animal could have been a deliberate choice by the riddle-poet, with the aim to undermine both the heroic genre and the custom of hunting, both usually associated exclusively with masculinity.

83 See *ASD* s.v. 'gegn-pæþ'. *DOE* (s.v. 'gēan-pæþ', 'gegn-pæþ') define it an 'hostile path, opposing road'. This hapax legomena has been glossed by Grein (253) with 'via hostilis' and afterwards variously read as indicating 'a narrow path' (Mackie, 107), 'hostile opposing road' (Williamson, *The Old English Riddles*, 176) 'opposing path' (Bitterli, 'Exeter Book Riddle 15', 468), 'facing path, opposing path' (Osborn, 181), 'hostile road' (Orchard, *The Old English and Anglo-Latin Riddle Tradition*, 319).

84 The second element *-pīl* has often been read as indicating a throwing weapon, because it is linked to Lat. *pĭlum* 'javellin, spear'. It seems it could indicate any object with a pointy end, as demonstrated by the use in *#21/19*, where it designates part of a plough, and in *#91/87*, where it is mentioned in regard to the tools used by a blacksmith. See Cavell, 'The Igil', 209.

85 These two compound words are used again in association in *#17/19*, lines 5b–9a: 'Frea þæt bihealdeð, / hu me of hrife fleogað hyldepilas. / Hwilum ic sweartum swelgan onginne / brunum beadowæpnum, bitrum ordum, / eglum attorsperum' ('The lord beholds how bolts flow from my stomach. Sometimes I begin to swallow brown battle-weapons, sharp points, loathsome poisoned spears'). This riddle has not been solved yet in a persuasive manner, it might depict a beehive, or a lion surrounded by bees; in any case, the image of bolts thrown away in battle might suggest a bee sting (see Osborn, 7–18; Cavell, 'The Igil', 208).

tiptoes, could allude to similar weapons because in the most frequent use it indicates the tip of a weapon, and, by metonymy, it could also designate spears or other pointed weapons.[86]

Moreover, the numerous variations to designate the predator and the cubs refer to an analogous lexical area. On line 8, the antagonist is firstly defined as a 'wælgrim wiga'; subsequently, the poet resort to three hapax legomena to characterize its aggressive and dangerous approach: the first one is *wælhwelp*, which, as seen, combines the image of a massacre with a reference to the natural behaviour of the creature – identifying the enemy as a canid; the other two compound nouns highlight instead the wicked, 'niðsceaþa',[87] and hostile, 'laðgewinna',[88] nature of such a fiend. As for the language referring to the cubs, *eafor*, 'offspring, child, descendant', *mǣg-burh*, 'kindred, family, relatives, tribe', and the already seen *geōguþ-cnōsl*, 'young family' have all elegiac and heroic connotations.

Therefore, these lexical choices seem to aim towards the expansion of the analogy between the fox and the human parent, posited in a heroic context. The anthropomorphic process on the main character is so pervasive that some interpreters have gone as far as to suggest 'human being' as a solution,[89] thus confusing the metaphoric focus around which the riddle is structured with the actual solution. However, a reading like this is symptomatic of how *#15/13* might lead the audience towards an almost complete mimesis with the little animal: for some scholars, the poem

---

86 'Seaxes ord', in *#60/58* on line 12 as well as in *#77/74* on line 6b, indicate the pointy end of a knife, used, in first case, to engrave a *rūnstæf*, and, in the latter instance, to open up an oyster. See *ASD*, s.v. 'ord'.

87 'A malignant foe' both in the translation made by Mackie (107) and according to the definition in *ASD* (s.v. 'nīþsceaða'), this compound word joins together the meanings of *nīþ* 'envy, hatred, enmity, rancour, spite' but also 'evil, wickedness, malice' (*ASD*, s.v. 'nīþ') (from Proto-Germanic **nīþan* or **nīþaz* 'envy, spite, hatred, enmity', see Goth. *neiþ*, ON *nīð*, OFris *nīth*, OS *nīth*, OHG *nīd*; *Orel*, s.v. '**nīþan*') and *sceaþa*, a noun usually reserved for dangerous warriors and enemies, such as Grendel and the dragon in *Beowulf* (lines 2278; 2093; 2689).

88 *Gewinna* is an enemy, a foe, a rival (see *ASD*, s.v. 'gewinna'), while *lāþ* is something that can cause pain and suffering (see *ASD*, s.v. 'lāþ'), from Proto-Germanic **laiþaz*, it is linked to the Greek verb ἀλιταίνω 'to transgress', must have designated something 'loathed' or 'hostile'; see Burg. **laips*, ON *leiðr*, OFr *lēth*, OS *lēth*, OHG *leid* (Orel, s.v. '**laiþaz*').

89 On this see the solution proposed by Jember, 54.

would seem to be based on this emotional connection between the animal and the human rather than on any enigmatic tension. The main character may have tawny hair and a tail, but its flight, its extreme need to protect its family, and the open confrontation with an enemy – who acts as an actual invader – is hugely similar to scenes of life that might have been very common in a country plagued by Viking invasions and continuous internal struggles, as was England between the ninth and tenth century. The frenetic style of the poem makes it possible for the audience to partake in the experience of fight and struggle. On this, Irving (204) argues in favour of a completely anthropocentric reading:

> Of course this riddle is not about an animal – how could it be? – but about people driven to act like animals and about how that would feel: women (and men) attacked mercilessly in their houses, hiding in forests or bogs, dragging their children, hands clapped over screaming mouths, out of the way of some marauder. It may not be action at the high and significant heroic level, but the riddle knows it is important action, to be viewed with empathy and respect. It is fighting any way we can for the survival of those we love.

Nonetheless, a completely metaphorical interpretation of the riddle is not entirely sustainable. The poem certainly evokes familiar emotions for an audience that must have known feelings of fear and dread caused by a sudden attack on their own home, but, as in the case of *#88/84*, numerous lines of *#15/13* oppose a complete anthropomorphization of the main character: the animal is described completely within a natural habitat and, as seen, in the text there is a decent level of literal fidelity to the behaviour of foxes in nature (Osborn, 176).

    Elegiac and heroic tones serve the purpose of the riddle, aiming to complicate the guessing game. The numerous metaphors serve to develop a constant movement between revealing information and obscuring clues. The poem clearly provides the speaking subject with a strong animal identity, nevertheless, the focus on the flight and on the fight between the characters uses anthropomorphic strategies. The communicative strength of *#15/13* lies in the poet's ability to remain close to a realistic and natural description, recreating the point of view of a fighting wild animal, while at the same time, giving them fears and reactions easy to understand from a human point of view, with empathy and respect. When the poem depicts the small animal while it cunningly awaits its enemy and protects with determination those it loves, the poet is recognizing all those aspects in the animal that bring it closer to the human audience. *#15/13* is posited in-between categories: it reveals how much of an animal there is in a human being and how much of a human there could be in an animal.

2.2 *#77/74:* Eat like an animal

Personification does not simply serve to establish a connection between audience and speaking subject, it is also a precious tool for a complete reversal in perspective. Riddle *#77/74* portrays the experience of a sea-creature that, once captured, is voraciously devoured. Despite being damaged at the end, the poem clearly evokes the image of an oyster (OE *ostre*).[90] The decision to leave the narration of the story to the creature's own voice not only heightens the dramatic tone of the passage – because the animal eaten alive is the one relating its experience – but it also highlights the role-play between man and shellfish. The riddle ascribes an animalistic behaviour to humans, entrusting them with the role of aggressor.

In Early Medieval England, oysters were a well-known and often consumed dish (Hagen, 169–170). In Ælfric's *Colloquy* (105–108), a pupil impersonating a fisherman counts oysters as part of the catch:

> M: Hpæt fehst þu on sæ?
> P: Hærincȝas ⁊ leaxas, merespyn ⁊ stirian, ostran ⁊ crabban, muslan, pinepinclan, sæcoccas, faȝc ⁊ floc ⁊ lopystran ⁊ fela spylces.
>
> M: Quid capis in mari?
> P: Alleces et isicios, delfinos et sturias, ostreas et cancros, muscolas, torniculi, neptigalli, platesia et platissa et polipodes et similia.

---

90 This solution was firstly proposed by Dietrich ('Die Räthsel des Exeterbuchs' [1859], 483) and was accepted by most commentators since. Preston (25–34) proposes 'flatfish' as a secondary solution used as way of obfuscation. See also Orchard, *A Commentary*, 462.

[M: What do you catch in the sea?
P: Herring and salmon, dolphins and sturgeon, oysters and crabs, mussels, cockles, flatfish and plaice and lobsters and other like that.]

As further proof of the food's popularity, the Old English version of the *Monasteriales Indicia* specifies all the movements required to silently indicate the wish to eat an oyster:[91]

> Gif þu ostran habban wylle þonne clæm þu þine wynstran hand ðam gemete þe þu ostran on handa hæbbe and do mid sexe oððe mid fingre swylce þu ostran scenan wyll.
>
> [If you want to have an oyster then you should close your left hand as if you have an oyster in it and with a knife or with a finger do just as you would to open the oyster.]

It is not unexpected, then, that oysters appear as a riddle subject in the *Exeter Book*.[92]

> Sæ mec fedde,   sundhelm þeahte,
> ond mec yþa wrugon   eorþan getenge,
> 3   feþelease;   oft ic flode ongean
> muð ontynde.   Nu wile monna sum
> min flæsc fretan ;   felles ne recceð,
> 6   siþþan he me of sidan   seaxes orde
> hyd arypeð,   [...]ec hr[.]þe siþþan
> iteð unsodene   ea[.................]d
>
> [The sea fed me, the water-helmet hid me, and the waves engulfed me against the ground, without feet; I often opened my mouth to the sea. Now a certain man wants to devour my flesh; he doesn't care about my skin when he tears my entrails with the point of a knife, [...] and then he eats me raw [...]]]

---

91   They were a fairly popular food in monastic refectories, as evidenced by the fact that, in addition to the sign denoting fish in general, there was a specific sign for eels and oysters in the sign language used by the monks to explain themselves during times when the rule of silence was in effect. See Banham, *Food and Drink*, 65.

92   Salvador-Bello considers Isidore's *Etymologies* as the primary source for thematic organization of the entire collection, and identifies the solution of the subsequent riddle as 'crab', thus she believes that the two animals were chosen because, as molluscs, they were placed side by side in the Isidorean encyclopaedia. See Salvador-Bello, *Isidorean Perception of Order*, 402–422.

The first four lines depict an oyster that feeds in complete harmony with the marine habitat, but it is a completely passive being (lines 1–2): the animal lacks feet ('feþelease', line 3a), so it cannot move or defend itself; additionally, the personal pronoun in the accusative 'mec' appears twice before the nominative 'ic' (line 3b), and this same subject pronoun does not reflect an action performed by the animal, but rather signals a moment of opening to the outside world: 'Oft ic flode ongean muð ontynde' ('I often opened my mouth towards the sea'). The sea is both the oyster's major source of sustenance and its only method of protection.[93]

An external character bursts into this perfect ecosystem upsetting its harmony. The adverb 'nu' ('now', line 4b) indicates a temporal caesura between the two contrasting moments. The man is immediately characterized as hostile: he acts carelessly ('felles ne recceð', lines 5b), and tears the internal flesh of the animal ('hyd arypeð')[94] with the tip of the knife ('seaxes orde'), thus, destroying the fragile defences of the speaking subject. After all, this protective layer is made up of a simple shell, which is designated in the poem as *fell* 'skin' rather than a more accurate *scill*. Presumably, the constraint of alliteration suggested the noun to the poet, although *fell* is a word that, when describing a protective outer layer, refers to the porous flexibility of the skin of a mammal rather than the rigidity of a shellfish. With *fell*, the poem appears to reaffirm the vulnerability of the helpless oyster, which is at the mercy of external forces (Cavell, *Weaving Words*, 87; Steel, *How Not to Make a Human*, 155).

The notion that the primary character is a defenceless creature emerges particularly in contrast to the human figure's impetuousness. The riddle exposes the person's impatience and greed through the specific

---

93 The marine habitat meets all of the shellfish's needs; the open mouth allows the oyster to be totally integrated with its ecosystem. As Steel (*How Not to Make a Human*, 154) suggests, line 4a, 'mu ontynde' ('I opened my mouth'), appears to be related in a circular pattern with the poem's first line, 'sae mec feede' ('Sea fed me'). The line might seal 'the loop on the opening to circulate the sea again and again through the oyster's cavernous body'.

94 The image here appears to echo a moment depicted in the Bible-riddle, *#26/24* (lines 5b–6a: 'Heard mec sian sna seaxses ecg' ['then the blade of the knife sliced me severely']) in which the human being is cast in an identical antagonistic position.

usage of the verb *fretan* (line 5a) in addition to stressing the brusque eagerness in cutting the oyster with a knife (line 5a).

Fretan typically designates a violent and impatient way of eating, which can also have metaphorical connotations[95] but more frequently suggests a behaviour deemed animalistic, uncivilized, or evil, even though it is rarely used in reference to human.[96] For instance, it might be useful to consider how *fretan* is used to represent the moth that consumes pages after pages of a parchment codex in riddle *#47/45*: 'Moððe word fræt' ('A moth devoured words', line 1a). Another example can be found in the *Old English Martyrology*; on 15 November (225), the bishop Minus, anticipating vengeance for his murderers, puts among the expected horrors for the two homicidal brothers several birds preparing to consume their flesh: 'and fugelas fretað incer flæsc' ('and birds will eat your flesh'). Occasionally *fretan* has been used to refer to humans. In *Solomon e Saturn II* (lines 224–226), the wise man is represented as swiftly consuming a piece of food that had fallen on the ground.[97]

---

95 In *Exodus* (line 147), for example, *fretan* denotes the broken pact between Israelites and Egyptians: 'wære fræton' ('they devoured the pact'); whereas in Psalms 52 of the *Paris Psalter* (lines 15–18), it is used to condemn the abuses of sinners on innocent and just people: 'Ac ge þæs ealle ne magon andgyt habban / þe unrihtes elne wyrcead and min folc fretad swa fælne hlaf/, ne hio god wyllad georne ciegan' ('But have you no comprehension, you who commit crimes and devour my people as if they were fine bread? Don't you want to invoke God eagerly?').

96 The action of eating is denoted by two verbs in Old English: *etan* and *fretan*. It has been proposed that there is a distinction between these two, comparable to that seen in modern German, which distinguishes *essen*, in regard to humans, from *fressen*, in reference to animals and beasts. However, in Old English, the definitions of *etan* and *fretan* overlap, and the distinction is not as apparent as in German: *etan* is employed in a broader sense; it can indistinctly include both men and animals as subjects, but *fretan*, while more commonly linked with animals, has no shortage of uses in regard to humans (see *DOE*, s.v. 'fretan'). Examining a variety of occurrences for *fretan*, Magennis (78) notes: '*Fretan* [...] has that sense of voracious, eager and complete eating'. Similarly, Page (13–14) mentions *fretan* in relation to numerous creatures or monsters: 'dogs, bears, snakes, maggots, drones, locusts, bookworms, and monster like Grendel, tearing at the bodies of men, or the Devil who consume mankind'.

97 It seems that the text here implies an underlying moral imperative to not waste even the smallest crumb that has fallen to the ground.

>   Ðonne snottrum men   snæd oððglideð
>   ða he be leohte gesihð,   luteð æfter,
> 226 gesegnað ond gesyfleð   ond him sylf fryteð

[When a wise man loses a bit of food, he sees it in the light, bends over it, blesses and seasons it, and eats it himself.]

Furthermore, *fretan* is frequently associated with humanoid beings who exhibit cannibalistic impulses. In *Beowulf*, it refers to Grendel when he attacks Hrothgar's Hall at night and devours fifteen sleeping men:

>   ac he hraþe wolde
>   Grendle forgyldan   guð-ræsa fela
> 1578   ðara þe he geworhte   to West-Denum
>   oftor micle   ðonne on ænne sið,
>   þonne he Hroðgares   heorð-geneatas
> 1581   sloh on sweofote,   slæpende fræt
>   folces Denigea   fyftyne men

[He wanted to immediately recompense Grendel for the countless battle assaults he had fought against the West Danes, many more times than the one in which he had slaughtered his companions in Hrothgar's Hall in their sleep, he had torn to pieces fifteen Danish men while they slept.]

In *Wonders of the East*, *fretan* analogously occurs in relation to the dietary habits of two monstrous people, which differ from the other creatures described in the treatise in that they are cannibals. The Hostes (§ 13), defined as being dark-skinned giants, are said to usually devour every person they meet: 'swa hwylcne mann swa hi gefoð, þonne fretað hi hine'.[98] Similarly, the Donestre[99] (§ 20), a people of hybrid fortune-tellers who can speak whatever language they hear, lure guests by replicating their language before devouring their entire body except the head: 'þænne æfter þan hi hine fretað ealne butan his heafde'. Even the scant details provided on the eating practices of the extraordinary people in *Wonders of the East* are meant to emphasize a deviation from what is considered the norm for humankind. The text mentions the food

---

98 Text cited from Orchard, *Appendix* to *Pride and Prodigies*, 173–203.
99 For a more detailed discussion on the peculiarities of this people, see section 6.1.

practices of two other populations: chapter § 28 depicts a people whose peculiarity is to live only on raw meat and honey ('þær syndon men ða be hreawan flæsce ⁊ be hunige lifigeað'), while chapter § 8 describes a lineage of men with long beards and long hair which stands out because they eat raw fish: 'Homodubii hi sindon hatene, þæt bioð twylice, ⁊ be hreawan fisceon hi libbað ⁊ þa etað' ('they are called Homodubii, that is, Doubtful-people, and they eat raw fish and live off it'). It seems that the latter's humanity is being questioned precisely because of the uniqueness of consuming raw food, a behaviour regarded as alien to the norms and beliefs of a civil society.[100]

The conduct of the man in #77/74 is clearly informed by this idea of incivility: the poem abruptly ends with a reference to the fact that oysters are typically served uncooked. Line 8a works as a significant clue for solving the riddle, but the term *ungesoden*, meaning 'raw, not cooked',[101] could also have been employed to convey further nuances of displeasure towards behaviour of the man.

As a result, the choice to use *fretan* in the narrative of a man who devours raw shellfish does not appear to be arbitrary; rather, it may have communicated to the Anglo-Saxon audience that that individual was eating like a beast. The Benedictine Reform's environment may have also affected the composition of #77/74: the negative depiction of the man could reflect a scathing condemnation of a clerical class unable to contain itself in the face of gluttonous temptations (Salvador-Bello, *Isidorean Perception*, 407–408). The description of the man's voracious appetite finds an explicit parallel in the conclusion of *The Seasons for Fasting*, a homiletical poem composed during the Reform[102] and primarily focused on the calculation of the dates for the *Quattro tempora*, the three days which the Church dedicated to fasting, abstinence, and prayer

---

100 Food preparation and consumption procedures have always been a source of prejudice and discrimination amongst peoples. Cooking meals is said to be one of the key milestones in the evolution of humanity. Lévi-Strauss (43–71) equates raw food with nature, from which man emerges with the invention of fire and cooking. See section 5.1 for a more in-depth discussion.
101 The word derives from the negation prefix *un-* and the participle preterite of *seōþan* 'to seethe, boil, cook in a liquid' (see *ASD*, s.v. 'seōþan').
102 The book was preserved in single copy in the British Library, Cotton Otho B XI, but the manuscript was destroyed in the Ashburnham House fire in 1731. Laurence Nowell made a copy in 1562, which is now kept in British Library, Ms Add. 43703.

in each season of the year.[103] The final sentences of the poem (lines 216-223) condemn the sinfulness of priests and monks who are unable to restrain their appetites, mentioning oysters as an example, because, as mollusc, they were considered as acceptable food even on the days of meat abstinence.

> 216 Hwæt! Hi leaslice   leogan ongynnað
> and þone tæppere   tyhtaþ gelome,
> secgaþ þæt he synleas   syllan mote
> 219 ostran to æte   and æþele wyn
> emb morgentyd;   þæs þe me þingað
> þæt hund and wulf   healdað þa ilcan
> 222 wisan on worulde   and ne wigliað
> hwænne hie to mose fon,   mæða bedæled.

> [Alas! They deceptively begin to lie and continuously urge the tapster, saying that he may, without sin, offer them oysters to eat and good wine at morning-tide; thus, it seems to me that a dog and a wolf live in the same way in the world and don't know when they consume food, lacking moderation.]

The monks' inability to curb their excessive appetites is thus brought to light by an animal metaphor: when man lacks moderation, he is reduced to the level of a dog or a wolf. The moralizing warnings of *The Seasons for Fasting* are a vivid example of how desires associated with the natural world are correlated with undesirable behaviour.[104]

Regardless of the merits of this suggestive interpretation, the riddle's overturning of perspectives is undeniable; the oyster assumes the role of helpless victim, while the human aggressor, on the other hand, is characterized by greed, a vice associating him with some species not entirely considered human.

---

103 See M. P. Richards for a detailed introduction of the poem.
104 When analysing Old English poetry, Magennis (78) noted that the portrayals of eating animals or monsters considerably outnumber the rare images of men sitting at the table. Only in the context of individuals who exhibit dishonourable and corrupt behaviour does Anglo-Saxon poetry depict the act of consuming food, and this is frequently done through a comparison with animals.

In #77/74, if the riddle's censure is primarily directed at men's failure to resist temptation, the sympathetic portrayal of the oyster protagonist is a corollary on the one hand, but a consequence on the other. To emphasize this sinful action the riddle-poet chose to use the perspective of the animal, which is thus shown as the defenceless victim of the man perceived as an enemy. This allows for a reassessment of the perspectives and promotes identification between the audience and the speaking oyster, even when considered in the playful context of the riddle.

2.3 #72/70: Slave away like an ox

In the Old English riddle corpus, there are at least two poems – #38/36, #72/70 – that devote their attention to the most commonly employed beast of burden in agricultural work in Early Medieval England. Oxen and cattle had a significant role in the Anglo-Saxon economic system.[105]

---

105 Raising a large animal such as a cow, an ox, or a bull to maturity was an expensive investment in Early Medieval England; yet, the possession of a beast of burden allowed a farmer to better manage their agricultural production and was a symbol of material prosperity. The economic worth of an ox was only slightly lower than the value of a horse, because even its skin was employed to make an unlimited variety of common goods. The greater importance that cattle enjoyed in comparison to the rest of the livestock appears to be supported by the definition of *feoh* and *ceāp*. *Feoh* had the double meaning of 'livestock, cattle, beasts of the field' and 'property, wealth, money' (see *DOE*, s.v. 'feoh'), it seems to be derived from the PIE root **pék̑-u-* 'to pluck; cattle', related to Skt. *pású* 'animal' and Lat. *pecū* 'cattle, animal', et al. Proto-Germanic **fexu* must have been used to designate both livestock and movable goods: Goth. *faihu*, ON *fē*, OE *feoh*, OFr. *fiā*, OS *fehu* OHG *fihu* (see Orel, s.v. '*fexu'). *Ceāp* mainly denoted a sale or a deal, but could be used to indicate 'movable property' and therefore it was sometimes used with the meaning of livestock. See *DOE*, s.v. 'ceāp': '1. purchase or sale, bargain, business transaction [...] 2. possessions, chattel, moveable property (including cattle)'. Proto-Germanic **kaupaz* probably denoted a purchase, a deal or a sale: ON -*kaup* (only in compound words), OE *ceāp*, OFr. *kāp*, OS *kōp*, OHG *kouf* (see Orel, s.v. '*kaupaz'). In Anglo-Saxon thought, the concepts of 'wealth' and 'cattle' were thus seen as interchangeable. For a more in-depth explanation of the monetary worth of cattle see Banham and Faith, 86–87.

A third riddle, *#12/10*, also describes an ox, but it spends more words to portray the applications of cowhide after the animal's earthly existence, distinguishing it from the other two riddles, which are more concentrated on the depiction of a living animal.[106]

Motifs involving oxen and cows can be found in the riddle tradition as early as Symphosius, in riddle LVI, *Caliga*:

> Maior eram longe quondam, dum uita manebat;
> at nunc exanimis, lacerata, ligata, reuulsa,
> 3   dedita sum terrae, tumulo sed condita non sum.

> [Once, I used to be bigger, when life remained; but now lifeless, torn apart, tied up and ripped, I am devoted to the earth, but not buried in a tomb.]

The triplet-poem focuses on the procedure transforming the animal's skin into the leather needed to make a booth. The riddle's central paradox is built on the conflict between the previous existence as an animal and the afterlife as an inanimate item. This contraposition has been employed also by Aldhelm in riddle LXXXIII, *Iuvencus*:

> Arida spumosis dissoluens faucibus ora
> bis binis bibulus potum de fontibus hausi.
> 3   Viuens nam terrae glebas cum stirpibus imis
> nisu uirtutis ualidae disrumpo feraces;
> at uero linquit dum spiritus algida membra,
> 6   nexibus horrendis homines constrigere possum.

---

106   Bitterli (*Say What I Am Called*, 27) sees in each of these riddles a different intertextual gateway to the Latin *aenigmata*, and considers them the most significant exemplification of the collection's experimental approach to rewriting the sources. Along these lines, Dale (70–76) proposes examining the so-called *ox riddles* – to which she adds *#4/2* and *#52/50*, otherwise considered to have an uncertain solution – as an enigmatic sub-genre, aimed at describing the master/servant's hierarchy, established in the relationship between man and working animals. In fact, the evolution of this specific sub-genre seems to move in the direction of a greater emphasis on the animal's pain.

[Thirsty, I sipped the drink from two fountains, satisfying my dry mouth with foamy jaws. Indeed, when living, I shatter the fertile clods of earth in the deepest roots, through the power of my great vigour; yet when the spirit abandons my freezing limbs, I can bind men with dreadful ropes.]

The abbot of Malmesbury composes his riddle on the ox by surveying three precise moments, allocated to the three couplets that, progressively, represent the three phases of life: childhood defined by nurturing, adulthood defined by work, and a third phase dedicated to life after death as an object. The first two lines depict the act of consuming milk from the mother's breasts, which are imagined as four springs or fountains 'bis binis bibilus' (line 2), from which the young animal drinks voraciously and vivaciously. This form of nourishment gives the animal its strength (*virtus valida*, line 4), which allows the newly grown ox to shatter (*disrumpere*, line 4) the ground furrowed in the act of ploughing. This same force will remain with the animal even after death, when its hide will be able to bind men.[107]

Aldhelm depicts a vigorous, robust animal, paying little attention to the creature's emotional state or to any experience that is not purely

---

107 A series of elements, already present in Aldhelm's riddle, will be developed in various ways in the following enigmatographic tradition: the opposition between the service performed by the living animal and the purposes of the inanimate item, the image of the four springs, and the motif of the broken earth from the ox's labour. Very similar to Aldhelm's poem are both Eusebius' *De uitulo* ('Post genitrix me quam peperit mea, spe solesco / Inter ab uno fonte riuos bis bibere binos / progredientes; et si uixero, rumpere colles / Incipiam; uiuos moriens aut alligo multos' 'After my mother gave birth to me, I got into the habit of drinking from two double streams out of a single source; and if I live on, I'll start breaking the hills; dying, however, I will bind many living people') and the poem *De tauro* from the *Lorsch* collection ('Quando fui iuuenis bis binis fontibus hausi, / Postquam consenui montes uallesque de imis / sedibus euertens naturae iura rescidi, / Post misero fato torpenti morte tabescens, / Mortuus horrende uiuorum stringo lucertos, / Necnon humanis praebens munimina plantis / Frigoris a rigigidis inlaesas reddo pruinis: / Sic mea diuersis uariantur fata sub annis' 'When I was young, I used to drink from double fountains. Then when I got older, I used to tear mountains and valleys from their deep roots. Then, consuming myself to death, in the miserable fate stopping me, dead I horribly clasp the arms of the living, and also, by providing protection for the soles of men's feet, I make them unharmed from the freezing winter frost. Thus my fates vary every year').

physical: in fact, the energy of the ox is remarked both while alive, when it allows it to tow the plough, to create furrows in the ground, and after death, when its skin and entrails are transformed into a tool for binding human beings. Similarly, the Old English riddle *#38/36* shows clearly the bovine's enduring strength:

>   Ic þa wiht geseah   wæpnedcynnes
>   geoguðmyrþe grædig: him on gafol forlet
> 3   ferðfriþende   feower wellan
>   scire sceotan,   on gesceap þeotan.
>   Mon maþelade,   se þe me gesægde:
> 6   'Seo wiht, gif hio gedygeð,   duna briceð;
>   gif he tobirsteð,   bindeð cwice.'

> [I saw a creature of the armed kind, greedy with youthful excitement; as a payment for him the giver of life let four clear fountains pour, sighing in delight. A man spoke, he said to me: 'If he lives, that creature breaks the hills; if he burst, he binds the living'.]

The bullock is characterized by its ravenous attitude in drinking and by a martial attire; it is called 'grædig' (line 2a) and it is qualified as belonging to a *wæpnedcynn*[108] (line 1b). Both qualifications are chosen to emphasize the youthful vibrancy and enthusiasm of the young animal. The poem appears to focus on the moment of nurture, comparable with another Latin source, Eusebius' riddle XIII, *De uacca:*

>   Sunt pecudes multae mihi, quas nutrire solebam;
>   meque premente fame non lacteque carneue uescor,
> 3   cumque cibis aliis et pascor aquis alienis;
>   ex me multi uiuunt, ex me et flumina currunt.

> [I have many cattle herds which I used to feed; and when I am overwhelmed by hunger, I do not eat milk nor meat; and when I feed on other food or graze on other people's waters; many live thanks to me and from me rivers run.]

---

108 This compound word is constituted by the noun *cyn* 'kind, race, lineage' and the adjective *wæpned* 'male, man', which is linked to the verb *wæpnian* 'to provide with weapons, to arm' (see *ASD*, s.v. 'cyn', 'wæpned', 'wæpnian'); thus, it literally means the 'armed kind', but metaphorically it alludes to the male gender.

The specifics about the brightness of the milk ('scire', line 4a) and the allusion to the sound made while nursing brings the situation to life, convey an impression of engagement in the audience, and accentuate the final paradox. Indeed, the calf's youthful energy is followed by a conclusion that re-proposes the dichotomy between the activities of the living creature and purposes of the dead materials.

The ultimate distinction between the Old English poem and the two Latin sources, however, is a shift in perspective. Aldhelm's and Eusebius's works are *first-person riddles of personification*; riddle *#38/36*, on the other hand, is a *third-person riddle of description*. The *Exeter Book* deprives the animal of the voice given to it by the Latin writers. The speaker is an external figure who describes the animal from the perspective of an observer, thus the final paradox that defines the creature is stated by a second voice.

Scholars have interpreted identity and purpose of this second character in the text in a variety of ways. According to Erbert (50), it might be an acknowledgement of the Latin sources, and *mon* could be referring to Aldhelm or Eusebius, a notion confirmed in part by Bitterli (*Say What I Am Called*, 30), who sees this poem as a kind of intertextual dialogue with the preceding Latin writers. Conversely, Williamson (*A Feast for Creatures*, 186; *The Old English Riddles*, 255) considers the introduction of direct speech as a way to emphasize the final paradox, and the man could simply be an insightful passer-by. Dale (72) has recently proposed the theory that the inclusion of the linguistic act in the riddle may aid to place the human being inside the animal universe:

> The Old English Riddles are particularly interested in how the human individual interacts with the world, and to use both spoken and visual observations in this riddle suggest a desire to comprehend the ox from the human perspective. Through the speech act, the ox riddle becomes a dialogue in which humans can participate.

Riddle *#72/70* depicts an ox once more, but unlike *#38/36*, the human presence is reduced to silence; the animal itself narrates its journey from innocent calf to beast of burden, using methods meant to elicit a deep empathic connection. In a way, the animal figure becomes a metaphorical exemplification of an existential condition:

```
        Ic wæs lytel [..........]
        fo [....................
3       .......]te geaf [............
        .......]þe  þe unc gemæne [.......
        ...........] sweostor min
6       fedde mec [......]   oft ic feower teah
        swæse broþor,    þara onsundran gehwylc
        dægtidum me    drincan sealde
9       þurh þyrel þearle.   Ic þæh on lust
        oþþæt ic wæs yldra    ond þæt anforlet
        sweartum hyrde;    siþade widdor,
12      mearcpaþas træd,   moras pæðde,
        bunden under beame,    beag hæfde on healse,
        wean on laste    weorc þrowade,
15      earfoða dæl.   Oft mec isern scod
        sare on sidan;    ic swigade,
        næfre meldade    monna ængum
18      gif me ordstæpe    egle wæron.
```

[I was little... gave ... in common to us two... my sister fed me... I often pulled four gentle brothers, where every day each of them separately gave me to drink through a hole. I grew up in pleasure, till I became older and gave that up for a dark herder; I travelled far and wide, I trod paths across borders, crossed moors, while bound under a beam, I wore a ring around my neck, I suffered pain on a path of misery, my share of hardships. Often the iron hit me hard on the side; I remained silent, I never accused anyone even if the pointed sticks were hateful to me.]

Although the beginning section of the poem is not completely legible, it is possible to detect the description of the speaking subject's first phase of life: the calf drinks from four dear brothers ('feower ... swæse broþor', lines 6b–7a) who metaphorically represent the mother's breasts. Even the mother is referred as 'sweostor' (lines 5b) with ironic and ambiguous intents.[109]

The anonymous author develops the riddle by establishing a clear contrast between the pleasant past and the present of pain, as seen by lines

---

[109] The four brothers metaphorically denote the four breasts of the mother, they represent one of the most innovative recasting of the theme on the four spring firstly exploited by Aldhelm. See Bitterli, *Say What I Am Called*, 33.

9b–10a: 'ic þæh on lust / oþþæt ic wæs yldra' ('I grew up in pleasure, till I became older'). The animal is forced to give up the pleasures of its early months of existence ('ond þæt anforlet' 'and gave that up', line 10b). The herdsman, 'hyrde' (line 11a), qualified as a *sweart*,[110] forces the now-grown ox into a perpetual effort from which it would never be able to harvest the reward. The mature life of the animal is dominated by an endless toil.[111] The herder may accompany it in this continuous commitment,[112] but, as Dale points out, the absence of references to the man's work seems significant;

---

110 According to Cavell (*Weaving Words*, 163), because *hirde* is a noun that does not provide explicit indications of social status but can metaphorically refer to both a 'keeper' and a 'guardian', the adjective *sweart* could provide an indication of social class. It might distinguish the members of the lower classes from the aristocracy, who had light hair. After all, the binary opposition – dark/light; black/white – can act as an organizing tool in the fields of experience and of ethics; in Anglo-Saxon literary documentation, the association of light and darkness with good and evil (as well as joy and sadness) is widely observed: Christ and the angels, for example, are frequently qualified by adjectives such as *scīr* or *beorht*, whereas demons, sin, and the infernal environment are always defined as *wann* or *sweart* (Barley, 17). Consider *Christ and Satan* where the contrast between good and evil is a central motif. From the beginning, Satan is described as 'black and sinful' 'swarte and synfulle' (line 52a), similarly, all his actions and his thoughts are formulaically considered obscure (line 370: 'þa Satanus swearte geþohte' ['Satan thought darkly']; lines 445/446a: 'þær nu Satanus swearte þingað / earm aglæca' ['there now Satan challenges them darkly, the wretched monster']; lines 577b/578: 'him þæt swearte forgeald / earm æglæca innon helle' ['the wretched monsters darkly demands this in hell']); whereas the angels are completely luminous, 'englas eallbeorhte' (line 521), and Christ is 'se torhta' ('the Bright One') who will lead humanity towards the kingdom of light (lines 293–297: 'Tæceð us se torhta trumlicne ham, / beorhte burhweallas. Beorhte scinað / gesælige sawle, sorgum bedælde' ['the Bright One will show us a safe home, the bright walls of the city. The holy souls shall shine brightly, freed from pain']).
111 Bitterli (*Say What I Am Called*, 34) describes this particular riddle as a 'mournful soliloquy [...] developed into a moving narrative, which boldly expands and ultimately obliterates traditional generic boundaries'.
112 On this, see, once again, what the pupils say about the work and fatigue of the farmer in Ælfric's *Colloquy* (rr. 23–27): 'Eala, leof hlaford, þearle ic deorfe. Ic ʒa ut on dæʒræd þypende oxon to felda, ꝉ iuʒie hiʒ to syl; nys hit spa stearc pinter þæt ic durre lutian æt ham for eʒe hlafordes mines, ac ʒeiukodan oxan, ꝉ ʒefæstnodon sceare ꝉ cultre mit þære syl, ælce dæʒ ic sceal erian fulne æcer oþþe mare. O, mi domine, nimim laboro. Exeo diluculo minando boues ad campum, et iungo eos ad aratrum; non est tam aspera hiems ut audeam latere domi pro timore domini

the riddle focuses on the pains suffered by the animal, represented in a situation of enslavement, to the point where the author renounces the genre's typical ambiguity. The poem uses an imaginary that links the animal to the human slave.[113] The ox is unmistakably placed under the yoke: it is 'bunden under beam' ('bound under a beam') and a chain, a 'beag' ('ring') (line 13a),[114] attached around its neck. Moreover, the emphasis on certain phonemes appears to link the lexicon of slavery to vocabulary indicating suffering and exile: the imperfect rhyme between 'bunden' and 'under', as well as the repetition of the sound 'ea' in 'sweartum' (line 11a), 'mearc-' (line 12a), 'beam' (line 13a), 'beag' (line 13b), 'wean' (line 14a), 'earfoða' (line 15a) and the sound 'æ' in 'træd' (line 12a), 'pæðde' (line 12b), 'hæfde' (line 14b), 'dæl' (line 15a) seem to highlight this peculiarity (Cavell, *Weaving Words*, 162–165; Irving, 208).

Indeed, #72/70 depicts an ox estranged from his original family and from its peers,[115] closely resembling other characters that similarly

---

      mei, sed iunctis bobus, et confrimato uomere et cultro aratro, omni die debeo arare integrum agrum aut plus' ('Alas, dear lord, I have to work very hard. I go out at daybreak to drive the oxen to the field and yoke them to the plough; not even in the stark winter would I dare to stay at home for fear of my lord, but, once yoked up the oxen and fastened plough and ploughshare to the plough, then I must plough a whole field or more for the whole day').

113 As noted by Irving (208), #72/70 portrays the ox as a 'slave-victim'. As seen in the preliminary chapter, the conceptual categories of slaves and domestic animals were easily associated in that they both were seen as property of their masters. Motifs developing the theme of servitude and slavery are addressed in several riddles, notably #12/10, which similarly seem to describe an ox and its use after death (see chapter 3), but also #52/50 and #28/26, both of which depict the items to be guessed with imagery of enslavement and suffering. For an in-dept study see Cavell, *Weaving Words*, 159–191.

114 According to Dale's interpretation (75), the riddle draws on the Christian idea expressed by Paul in the *Letter to the Romans* (8:22), whereby all creation suffers in unison the consequences of the original sin: 'Riddle 72 depicts a "groan of travail", drawing on the concept of the damaged relationship between humans and animals after the fall. Humans take the ox out of its pleasant, Eden-like environment constrain it and use it to work the land [...]. Humans, in their post-lapsarian state, do not have mere custody over the creature of this riddle but mastery, and this mastery is not benign.'

115 This choice contrasts with the iconographic evidence, which supports the hypothesis that teams of two oxen were employed for lighter work and teams of four or eight cattle for heavier work. See Banham and Faith, 51–52.

meditate about loneliness and grief. The riddle uses a diction and an imaginary akin to that of the so-called elegies, poems where the speaking subject's emotional state is placed at the centre of the narration. In these texts, the main character, often deprived of belongings and affections, usually complains about their exile in a painful confrontation with a happier past.[116] Similarly, in *#72/70*, the narrator laments the loss of childhood pleasures, which have been replaced by a present made of hardship and fatigue ('weorc þrowade' 'I suffered pain', line 14b); its continuous journey among the 'mearcpaþas',[117] 'paths across borders', which is also 'wean on lastas' ('a path of misery'), recalls all those *wræc lastas*, 'roads of exile', from *The Wanderer* (line 5a) and from *The Seafarer* (line 15b); and forces the ox to reflect on its share of hardships 'earfoða dæl'.[118] *#72/70* is one more riddle where a reversal of roles is enacted, because the plight of the ox – animal and therefore belonging to

---

116 It should be noted that the Old English elegies are neither poems composed in the elegiac couplet nor commemorative or funeral poetry, but rather a literary form that, often narrating a personal experience, dwells on the themes of absence, loss, and the transience of life (Klinck, 225). For instance, the main character in *The Wanderer* refers to himself as 'friendleasne' (line 27a) 'friendless' and reclaims sorrow as his only companion (lines 29b–31): 'Wat se þe cunnað, / hu sliþen bið sorg geferan, / þam þe him lyt hafað leofra geholena' ('Anyone who knew this understands what a cruel companion is sorrow for someone who has few good friends'). Several thematic threads run throughout the Old English elegiac corpus: in particular, the sensation of having lost a condition of grace, the direction that leads away from the homeland or from attachments, the continual movement and the necessity to endure a painful condition. On this, see, among others, Greenfield, 125–131.

117 On line 12 the manuscript read 'mearcpaþas walas træd'. Tupper (285) kept the reading, considering 'walas' as a not yet attested adjectival form of *Wealh*, thus, accepting Tupper's reading, in 1932 Mackie translates the verse as 'trod the paths on the Welsh march'; Krapp and Dobbie (*ASPR III*, 370) reject this reading and conjecture: 'it may be that *paþas* and *walas* represented two attempts by the scribe to reproduce a partly illegible word.' Similarly, Williamson (*The Old English Riddles*, 344): 'the original *mearcpaþas* was corrupted into something like *mearcwawas*, and [...] two scribal conjectures written in above the *-wawas* in the form of *paþas* and *walas* were then both incorporated into the text by a later scribe.' More recently Orchard (*A Commentary*, 456) argues that *walas* might have been an interpolated explanatory gloss, as Welsh people were identified as 'march-dwellers'.

118 See *Deor*, lines 28–30: 'Siteð sorgcearig sælum bidæled, / on sefan sweorceð, sylfum þinceð / þæt sy endeleas earfoða dæl' ('A grieved man sits, deprived of joys, grows dark inside, thinks for himself that his share of hardships is never-ending').

the natural realm – subjected to humans is shown as similar to the condition of humans – slaves but, above all, exiles – who are, in turn, exposed to the fickleness of natural forces.[119]

In this context, the animal's claim to have always been silent (line 16b, 'ic swigade') might signify a willingness to accept one's condition stoically.[120] However, in the opposition between *swigian* and *meldian*,[121] the riddle reminds the audience that the animal's speaking abilities are fictitious, that there is a distinction between the personal expression of non-human creatures in the 'real' world and the way in which these expressions take shape in the creative vehicle of poetry, and this difference is the reciprocal influence that is established in the *Exeter Book* riddles between literal and metaphorical forms of speech (Orchard, 'Performing Writing', 73–92). By emphasizing the ox's silence, the author of #72/70 recognises a distinction between those who truly possess a human voice and those on whom this voice is imposed from the outside.

Both interpretations on the silence of the animal, being not mutually exclusive, concur to emphasize the ox's position. The *Exeter Book* riddles, by depicting non-human creatures via a series of metaphors that evokes humanity, inevitably reduce the boundaries between things. Yet the animal's use of the human voice, while leading towards a major closeness among the species, never let this proximity become a complete symbiosis. Anthropomorphism, employed as 'a tool for exploring an intangible

---

119 Consider the struggles endured by the eponymous character in *The Seafarer* who is at the mercy of the terrible tumult of the waves (line 6a: 'atol yþa gewealc') in winter (see lines 8b–10b: 'calde geþrungen / wæron mine fet forste gebunden, / caldum clommum', 'my feet were crushed by chills, imprisoned in frost with frigid chains'); condition fairly identical to that met by *The Wanderer* as he sails among the dark waves (line 46b: 'fealwe wegas') in the midst of frost and snow mixed with hail (line 48: 'hrim ond snaw hagle gemenged'). On the elegiac elements in the Old English riddles, Borysławski (105) similarly notes how the authors are able to portray 'unusual powers of empathic insight into the nature of the portrayed beings, arising from the projection of the harsh conditions of human existence upon them'.
120 See Dale, 76 and Cavell, 'A poetics of Empathy'. According to Zweck (322), conversely, the choice to be silent is an act of resistance against the dominant culture.
121 *Swigian* generally means 'to be silent' but also, specifically, 'be silent about something, to refrain from the mention of something' (see *ASD*, s.v. 'swigian'); in contrast, *meldian* can mean 'to declare, announce, tell' or 'to inform against, accuse' (see *ASD*, s.v. 'meldian').

voice' (Dale, 68), preserves the living creature from total assimilation with the human being on the one hand, while on the other it transforms what is normally perceived as alien and distant into something close and familiar: the ox is still an external entity, but having access to its personal perspective allows us to better understand its existence. The tones of *#72/70* accentuate the animal's individuality while also highlight the truth that pain may be shared and understood even amongst different species.

3. Riddles and Metamorphosis

A riddle is a game that focuses on breaking down conventional categories in order to discover hidden similarities among things. As shown in riddles such as *#15/13* and *#72/70*, the human figure becomes an alter ego for the animal character thanks to anthropomorphic strategies. Man and animal alternate their respective positions in a perceptive movement that feel almost metamorphic to the audience.

Metamorphosis, as a rhetorical strategy, aims to illustrate the universe's fluidity and chaos: it recreates the circumstances under which an entity – with its own identity – changes into something else. Regardless of the metaphor's metamorphic illusion, many Old English riddles address the potential of an effective identity mutation in the creatures described. Instead of limiting the enigmatic proposition to the description of the main character, some *Exeter Book* riddles explore a narrative space, depicting a process of evolution – natural or forced by human intervention.[122]

As a case in point, in *#73/71*, rather than simply indicate its own physical features, the main character outlines the beginning of its 'life' in a first-person narration. The speaking subject can be identified as a bow (OE *boga*), it relates its earlier life a tree (OE *trēow*) residing peacefully in the woods:

	Ic on wonge aweox, wunode þær mec feddon
	hruse ond heofonwolcn, oþþæt me onhwyrfdon
3	gearum frodne, þa me grome wurdon,
	of þære gecynde þe ic ær cwic beheold,
	onwendan mine wisan, wegedon mec of earde,
6	gedydon þæt ic sceolde wiþ gesceape minum
	on bonan willan bugan hwilum.

---

122 According to Soper (841–865), for instance, the collection can be read as biographical (even autobiographical) texts; riddles are thus useful to narrate the experience of human beings and non-human beings.

[I grew up in a field, I lived where the earth and the clouds of the heaven fed me, until those who were cruel against me took me, old in the years, away from that condition I had when I was alive, they changed my ways, led me out of the earth, forged me so that I must bow under the will of murderer, against my nature.]

In a similar way, *#93/89*, a riddle companion for *#88/84*, depicts the intense metamorphosis from antlers into inkhorn (OE *blæchorn*). The poem is variously damaged at the beginning and at the end, the first scene (lines 1–14a) seems to describe the existence of a deer identified as 'frea' (lines 1a and 6a), the 'lord' to which the speaking subject owns its loyalty. But this joyful life is destined to end. In spring, the antlers get supplanted and thus end up in the hands of human beings who force a bloody and violent mutation on the speaking subject:

>   Ic on fusum rad
> 15   oþþæt him þone gleawstol   gingra broþor
>   min agnade   ond mec of earde adraf.
>   Siþþan mec isern   innanweardne
> 18   brun bennade;   blod ut ne com,
>   heolfor of hreþre,   þeah mec heard bite
>   stiðecg style.   No ic þa stunde bemearn,
> 21   ne for wunde weop,   ne wrecan meahte
>   on wigan feore   wonnsceaft mine,
>   ac ic aglæca   ealle þolige,
> 24   þæt [..]e bord biton.   Nu ic blace swelge
>   wuda ond wætre,   w[..]b[.] befæðme
>   þæt mec on fealleð   ufan þær ic stonde,
> 27   eorpes nathwæt;   hæbbe anne fot.
>   Nu min hord warað hiþende feond
>   se þe ær wide bær wulfes gehleþan;

[I rode on the swift lord until a younger brother of mine took possession of the seat of wisdom and drove me out of my dwelling. Later a shiny iron wounded me inside; no blood escaped, cruor from the heart, even though a strong, hard-bladed, steel bit me. I did not show distress for that moment, nor wept for the wound, nor could I avenge my misfortune on the warrior's life, but I suffer all the tortures that harm shields. Now I swallow dark wood and water, I enclose in my belly what falls from above where I am, something dark; I have only one foot. Now a raiding enemy guards my treasure, one who once carried away the wolf's comrades.]

The temporal break, signalled by the double recurrence of the adverb *nū* (line 24 and line 28) and by the present tense, shows that the transformation has already taken place; the moment is painful but the speaking subject endures this pain with the resignation of the defeated warrior. Like the ox-riddle *#72/70*, this poem uses a vocabulary that partly belongs to the heroic context, partly suggests a situation akin to the elegiac mood: the conflict between a miserable present and a joyful past. Just like the ox in *#72/70*, the speaking subject here choses to have a stance of stoic acceptance towards any adversities.

The metamorphic process finds a particularly articulated representation especially in *#12/10*, a poem depicting a creature that undergoes several transformations. *#12/10* can be considered as an additional *ox riddles*, like *#38/36* and *#72/70* it uses as sources the *aenigmata* by Symphosius and Aldhelm, but, here, the riddle-poet pays particular attention to the many iterations of the leather after the animal's death:

```
        Fotum ic fere,     foldan slite,
        grene wongas,      þenden ic gæst bere.
3       Gif me feorh losað,   fæste binde
        swearte Wealas,    hwilum sellan men.
        Hwilum ic deorum   drincan selle
6       beorne of bosme;   hwilum mec bryd triedeð
        felawlonc fotum,   hwilum feorran broht
        wonfeax Wale       wegeð ond þyð,
9       dol druncmennen    deorcum nihtum,
        wæteð in wætre,    wyrmeð hwilum
        fægre to fyre;     me on fæðme sticaþ
12      hygegalan hond,    hwyrfeð geneahhe,
        swifeð me geond sweartne.   Saga hwæt ic hatte,
        þe ic lifgende     lond reafige
15      ond æfter deaþe    dryhtum þeowige.
```

[I walk on my feet, tearing up the earth and the green fields, as long as I have life. If life leaves me, I bond tightly sometimes dark slaves, sometimes better men. Sometimes I give the brave men drinks from my inner parts; sometimes a bride tramples me proudly with her feet, sometimes a dark-haired slave takes me away, moves me and tramples me, the silly drunk maid, in the dark nights, moistens me in water and, sometimes, warms me pleasantly by the fire; a lustful hand places me on (their) lap, repeatedly rotates (me), makes me slip into the darkness. Say what my name is, I who, while living, turn the earth and, after death, serve men.]

The first two lines, which trace back to the Aldhelmian *Iuvencus*, briefly elucidate the ox's daily activities, picking up on the clue on turning the ground. The riddle's structure devotes a significant number of lines to recounting the many products that can be made from cowhide leather: laces used to bind prisoners and slaves, a bottle passed from hand to hand between drunken men, soles for a young bride's shoes, and a damp cloth dried on the fire. In this sense, *#12/10* fully exploits the life/death paradox by emphasizing the multiple services that animal-derived products may provide for humans, as evidenced by the closing verse: 'æfter deaþe dryhtum þeowige' ('after death, I serve men').[123]

The identification of the speaker lends itself to more than one answer because the living ox and the different things manufactured from its hide describe a single life experience. The speaking subject is clearly one, yet throughout its existence and after its death, it alters, it switches between numerous stages and multiple entities. Williamson (*Old English Riddles*, 166) and Murphy (59–60) propose a single solution because all the objects mentioned are incarnations of the bovine from which the hide is made; Niles (*Old English Enigmatic Poems*, 124–125), on the other hand, proposes a double alliterating solution that takes into account the *post mortem* uses, *oxa ond oxanhȳd*, 'ox and leather'. Klein (32) attempts to tackle the matter by introducing the concept of *allomorphs* in the interpretation of the Old English riddles; allomorph is a term loaned from chemistry and linguistics that can be used to define 'the alternative forms a riddle

---

[123] As seen, *#12/10* uses motifs linked to servitude and slavery, a thematic thread addressed in many other riddles (e.g. *#52/50* and *#28/26*, *#72/70*). Indeed, there seem to be a connection between the creature bound to serve (see *ASD*, s.v. 'þeōwian'), and the people destined for slavery as evidenced by the references to dark slaves ('swearte Wealas', line 4a) and the dark-haired slave ('wonfeax Wale', line 8a). On the social connotation for the adjective *sweart*, see section 2.3, n. 110. On the meaning of the noun *wealh*, it should be remembered that, although it appears to have been used to designate a 'foreigner', and more often a 'foreigner from Britain', it later acquired the meaning of 'slave of Celtic origin' or 'slave', presumably because many of the enslaved Britons in the south-west of the island had been put into slavery by the Anglo-Saxons (see *ASD*, s.v. 'wealh'). See Pelteret, and Cavell, *Weaving Words*, 159–172.

object may take in its various real and imaginative environments'. Even more than others, metamorphic riddles are inevitably characterized by unfixed solutions: in *#27/25*, the subject, mead (OE *medu*), illustrates its beginnings as honeydew (OE *mele-deāw*); in *#35/32*, the ore (OE *ōra*), discovered in the depths of the earth, develops into mail-coat (OE *byrne*); and *#83/79* depicts the entire lifecycle of a specific type of ore, which ends up producing objects and money (probably gold, OE *gold*).

It is true that ambiguity is a key component of the enigmatic genre, particularly in a collection like the *Exeter Book* one, which does not appear to be interested in maintaining any title or solution, but the shifting nature of the subjects described in these 'metamorphic' riddles favours a greater sense of ambivalence. Although it is understandable that the enigmatic genre would favour this kind of subject, it seems clear from the collection that the narration of mutability – which highlights the continuity between the different components of nature – is preferred. As a result, the metamorphic riddle is a valuable tool for reclaiming the areas where nature and culture converge. Thus, in *#26/24*, the narrative follows the speaking subject's metamorphosis from skinned animal to parchment, painting a comprehensive picture of the book-making process.

3.1 *#26/24*: From animal to book

```
        Mec feonda sum    feore besnyþede,
        woruldstrenga binom,   wætte siþþan,
3       dyfde on wætre,   dyde eft þonan,
        sette on sunnan,   þær ic swiþe beleas
        herum þam þe ic hæfde.   Heard mec siþþan
6       snað seaxses ecg,   sindrum begrunden;
        fingras feoldan,   ond mec fugles wyn
        geondsprengde speddropum    spyrede geneahhe,
9       ofer brunne brerd,   beamtelge swealg,
        streames dæle,   stop eft on mec,
        siþade sweartlast.   Mec siþþan wrah
12      hæleð hleobordum,   hyde beþenede,
        gierede mec mid golde;   forþon me glisedon
```

```
        wrætlic weorc smiþa,    wire bifongen.
15      Nu þa gereno    ond se reada telg
        ond þa wuldorgesteald    wide mære
        dryhtfolca helm –    nales dol wite.
18      Gif min bearn wera    brucan willað,
        hy beoð þy gesundran    ond þy sigefæstran,
        heortum þy hwætran    ond þy hygebliþran,
21      ferþe þy frodran;    habbaþ freonda þy ma,
        swæsra ond gesibbra,    soþra ond godra,
        tilra ond getreowra,    þa hyra tyr ond ead
24      estum ycað,    ond hy arstafum,
        lissum bilecgað,    ond hi lufan fæþmum
        fæste clyppað.    Frige hwæt ic hatte,
27      niþum to nytte;    nama min is mære,
        hæleþum gifre    ond halig sylf.
```

[A certain enemy snatched my life, deprived me of my life force, then wetted me, immersed me in water, then got me out again from there and placed me in the sun where I quickly lost the hair I had. Then the hard blade of the knife cut me, polished off impurities; fingers folded me, and the joy of the bird scattered useful drops on me, frequently left traces across the brown margin, swallowed the tree dye, stepped on me again with part of that stream, leaving a dark track. Then a brave man covered me with protective boards, wrapped me in hide, adorned me with gold; thus, the marvellous works of the smiths shine on me, wrapped in filigree. Now the ornaments and the red dye and the glorious decorations celebrate the protector of nations far and wide – the fool will find no mistake in it. If the children of men wish to make use of me, they will be the sounder and more victorious, the more valiant in heart and the happier in soul, the wiser in mind; they will have the more friends, the dearer and nearer, truer and better, finer and more faithful, then their glory and prosperity will gladly increase, and they will cover them with favours and services and will hold them tightly in embraces of love. Ask what I am called, I at the service of men; my name is famous, useful to men and sacred in itself.]

The response to the final query, 'Frige hwæt ic hatte' ('Ask what I am called') (line 26b), has generally been regarded as abundantly clear. The references to a 'protector of nations', ('dryhtfolca helm') (line17a), and the sacred name assumed by the speaking subject, 'halig sylf' (line 28b), establish a religious context; thus, it is reasonable to assume that *#26/24* depicts an illuminated book meant to help in the salvation of all who use it, a Bible (OE *biblio-þēce*) or a Gospel book (OE *godspell-bōc*).[124]

The riddle appears to be a poetic experiment aimed at delving into the space of the scriptorium's space, a widespread motif in the enigmatic tradition.[125] *#26/24* shows, in particular, numerous similarities with Tatwine's *De Membrano*, so much so that the Latin text might have been a direct source:

> Efferus exuuiis populator me spoliauit,
> uitalis pariter flatus spiramina dempsit;
> 3 in planum me iterum campum sed uerterat auctor.
> Frugiferos cultor sulcos mox irrigat undis;
> omnigenam nardi messem mea prata rependunt,
> 6 qua sanis uictum et lesis praestabo medelam.

---

124 Transmission of the complete text of the Vulgate was quite unusual; manuscripts containing the Gospels were more common. Niles speculates that this riddle could refer to a codex witnessing one or more Gospels. See Niles, *Old English Enigmatic Poems*, 118–119.

125 The scriptorium is a setting of particular interest for Symphosius and the Anglo-Latin riddle-poets: Symphosius begins his collection writing on stylus (*Graphium*) and calamus (*Harundo*); Aldhelm depicts wax tablets (*Pugillares*, enigma XXXII), pen (*Penna*, enigma LIX) and bookcase (*Arca Libraria*, enigma LXXXI); Eusebius's collection touches on inkwell (*De atramentorio*, enigma XXX), parchment (*De membrano*, enigma XXXII), a bag containing books (*De scetha*, enigma XXXIII) and the feather (*De penna*, enigma XXXV). Similarly, Tatwine writes on pen (*De penna*, enigma VI) and parchment (*De membrano*, enigma V). Further riddles on similar subjects are found in the *Lorsch* collection (*De penna*, enigma IX, and *De atramento*, enigma XII). Additionally, the *Bern Riddles* count a riddle on parchment (*De membrana*, enigma XXIV), one on papyrus (*De papiro*, enigma XXVII) and one on paper (*De charta*, enigma L). Within the *Exeter Book* collection, several riddles depict the writing and the book-making processes: *#88/84* and *#93/89*, as mentioned, deal with inkhorns; *#47/45* describe a book-moth and 'pen and fingers' have been identified as the solution for *#51/49*. Moreover, among the *Exeter Book* riddles of uncertain solution, *#28/26* has been interpreted, in analogy with *#26/24*, as a variation about the book-making process (Bitterli, *Say What I Am Called*, 178), while for *#49/47* different solutions were proposed, such as 'pen and paper', but also 'bookcase, book cabinet' (Dietrich, 'Die Räthsel des Exeterbuchs' [1865], 236). See Shook, 224–225.

[A cruel plunderer took away my covering and simultaneously deprived me of my breathing pores; a craftsman fashioned me into a flat field. The cultivator irrigates the fertile furrow; my meadows provide a diverse harvest of balsam, which is both food for the healthy and remedy for the sick.]

Both the Latin and Old English poems are *first-person riddles of personification*, thus the subject describes their experience through their own perspective. Moreover, both riddles depict the same specific locations: the scene moves from the abattoir, a site where animals are slaughtered, to the scriptorium, a place where the dead animal is brought back to life in a new form as an object of worship and beauty (Bitterli, *Say What I Am Called*, 173–174). The Old English text begins with a verse that vividly echoes the first two Tatwinian lines, referring to the loss of vital breath, 'Mec feonda sum feore besnyþede, woruldstrenga binom', where the 'populator', 'plunderer', mentioned by Tatwine is turned into 'sum feonda', 'a certain enemy'. Similarly, the many adjectives (lines 18–25) indicating the benefits intended for people who use the sacred book can be read as a deliberate expansion from the Old English poet's part on the final verse of the Latin text, 'sanis victum et lesis praestabo medelam'.

Notwithstanding these similarities, there are also several differences between the two poems. *De Membrano* develops a series of agricultural analogies. The Mercian bishop alludes to a theft committed against the speaking subject, and the pages derived from its skin are imaged as fields to be ploughed that will produce fruit; the literal clues related to the subject are almost completely absent, and the manufacture of the codex is only briefly mentioned in line 3, when Tatwine appoints an 'auctor', 'craftsman', who will model the fields-pages. Conversely, *#26/24* is primarily focused on the book-making process and shows an abundance of both literal and metaphorical clues; the riddle reflects the intent to recognize both the admirable – 'wrætlic', line 14a – work of the smiths as well as the sacrifice of the animal. The Old English riddle could be read as divided into two parts, structured on opposing pairs: it explores the animal, natural, and material aspects of the manufacture while also emphasizing the human, cultural, and spiritual aspects of the end product.

The account of the *wiht*'s initial experience centres on the corporeal and material aspects of the process. Rather than focusing on a static image, detailing shape and function of the creature to be guessed, *#26/24* looks into how a living thing that cannot be identified becomes a product intended for human consumption. The first part of the riddle describes step by step the process of making a manuscript. The animal is killed (lines 1–2a), its skin is tanned (lines 2a–5a), parchment is filed and individual sheets are folded (lines 5b–6b). Lines 7b–11a depicts the writing procedure and, on lines 11b–13a, the manuscript is finally bound.

Anyone involved in parchment-making process would consider cleaning and drying of the animal skin as a standard procedure, but this detailed description is characterized by a first-person narrator and, unlike other first-person poems in the *Exeter Book* collection, which often begin with an active voice,[126] here from the very first word the speaking subject is made the object of actions performed by others: the poem's opening line uses the accusative pronoun 'mec'. The only active character is an unnamed foe, whose first significant action is a crime, i.e. to rob the narrator of their life, 'feore', an act reiterated in variation the following line – 'woruldstrenga binom' ('deprived me of my vital force'). Moreover, in the next few lines the poet seems to adopt a lexical strategy developed in order to accentuate the speaking subject's passive stance, since the creature appears to be subjected to a sequence of deprivations.[127] The first experience the narrator goes through is expressed through the verb *besnyþþan*, meaning 'to deprive, to rob (someone of life)' (*DOE*, s.v. 'besnyþþan')[128]; only twice more in the Old English poetic corpus this

---

126 Several riddles in the collection use for the first line expression such as *Ic eom/Ic wæs*, e.g.: *#14/12*, 'Ic wæs wæpen wigan' ('I am an armed warrior'); *#17/15*, 'Ic eom mundbora minre heorde' ('I am the defender of my heard'); *#30/28*, 'Ic eom ligbsysig' ('I am occupied with flames'); *#60/58*, 'Ic wæs be sonde' ('I was on the shore'); *#62/60*, 'Ic eom heard ond scearp' ('I am hard and sharp'); *#72/70*, 'Ic wæs lytel' ('I was little'); *#74/72*, 'Ic wæs fæmne geong feaxhar cwene' ('I was a young maid, a grey-haired woman'); etc. This is also the case for all those riddles starting with the formulaic expression 'Ic eom wunderlicu wiht' (*#18/16, #20/18, #23/21, #24/22, #25/23, #27/25*).

127 The four verbs, in fact, are united by the prefix *be-*, which makes transitive an intransitive verb, and, in some cases, adds a sense of deprivation (see *OED*, s.v. *be-* and Deitz, 582–583).

128 *Besnyþþan*, derives from Proto-Germanic **sn(a)uþjanan* (see ON *sneyða* 'deprive'). However, it seems to be connected also with **sneuþanan* (from which both ON *snoðinn* 'bald, desert' and late MHG *be-schnotten* 'to cut' derive), might be linked to the Proto-Indo-European root **sneit-* and the Proto-Germanic **snīþanan* 'cut' (Goth. *sneiþan*, OE *snīðan*, OFr. *snītha*, OS *snīðan*, OHG *snīdan*; see Orel, s.v. '**sn(a)uþjanan*', '**sneuþanan*', '**snīþanan*').

verb does occur – in *Beowulf* and in *Andreas*.[129] In both instances, it is followed by an indirect object denoting vital breath or life (*feorh* or *ealdor*), suggesting an unnatural death. The following *beniman* (lines 2a), 'to take away, deprive', and *beleosan* (lines 4a), 'to lose, be deprived of (someone or something)', share a similar meaning, as does *begrindan* (lines 6b), which can indicate both 'to grind, scrape (something) free of', as well as 'to deprive, strip (oneself) of (something)'[130] (*DOE*, s.v., 'beniman', 'beleosan', 'begrindan').

The chosen images further emphasize the aggressiveness in the man's actions: a knife cuts forcefully on a powerless body (lines 5b–6a), the creature's hair is made to fall (lines 4b–5a), and unfamiliar fingers mould ('fingras feolda', line 7a) the subject's body without them being able to respond. The prolonged narrative assigned to this objectified voice, thus, seems to show a special interest for the most horrific aspects of the process. The description of apparently common activities, as reported from the alienating viewpoint of the creature subjected to them, conveys the sense that these same activities could be felt as torture.

Given that sacrifice and mortification of the body are central motifs in medieval Christian religious practice, some scholars (Bitterli, *Say What I Am Called*, 171–178; Marsden, 169–176) have seen in this

---

129 *Beowulf*, lines 2923a–2925: 'Ac wæs wide cuð / þætte Ongenðio ealdre besnyðede / Hæðcen Hreþling wið Hrefnawudu' ('But it was widely known that Ongentheow had snatched the life away from Hæthcyn Hrethli in the Ravenwood'). *Andreas*, lines 1324–1325: 'Þone Herodes ealdre besnyðede, / forcom æt campe cyning Iudea' ('Herod took his life away, the king of Judea defeated him on the field').

130 *DOE* records two meanings for *begrindan*, according to the two occurrences of the term. The privative sense of the verb is fundamental in the reading of the ambiguous locution 'sindrum begrunden'. For Williamson (*The Old English Riddles*, 213) and Bitterli (*Say What I Am Called*, 175) the expression applies to the edge of the knife, 'deprived of impurities', however, grammatically 'begrunden' can also be an accusative singular, thus the participle can be taken as apposition for 'mec'. Lester (*Sindrum begrunden*, 13–15) reads it as meaning 'ground away with pumice', reckoning that in the context of ninth-century parchment production, 'sindrum' might be an occurrence of a residual instrumental case. But pumice is not a very common translation for *sinder* and, as noted by Afros (*Sindrum begrunden*, 9), *begrindan* 'takes an accusative complement of person/object deprived of something and dative of the thing somebody / something is deprived of'. Thus, the meaning 'deprived of impurities' has to be preferred to 'ground away with pumice'.

passivity a body seemingly given up as a sign of sacrifice. For instance, *#26/24*'s speaking subject could be compared in their experience to the rood depicted in *The Dream of the Rood*. In the *Vercelli Book* vision-poem, the rood narrates its own experience: uprooted in the forest and then reduced to be an indecent display by the actions of cruel and strong men defined as 'strange feondas' (lines 28a–33a):

> þæt wæs geara iu,   (ic þæt gyta geman),
> þæt ic wæs aheawen   holtes on ende,
> 30   astyred of stefne minum.   Genaman me ðær strange feondas,
> geworhton him þær to wæfersyne,   heton me heora wergas hebban.
> Bæron me ðær beornas on eaxlum,   oððæt hie me on beorg asetton,
> 33   gefæstnodon me þær feondas genoge

> [It was long time ago (I still remember it), that I was cut down at the edge of the forest, removed from my root. There strong enemies took me, made me into a spectacle for themselves, ordered me to raise their criminals. Warriors carried me on their backs, until they placed me on a hill, where very hostile people stared at me to the ground.]

Men are here portrayed as hostile because they designed and built the torture mechanism that ultimately kills Christ.[131] Nonetheless, after being transformed into a cross, the wood becomes eventually a companion for Christ, so much so that the wounds inflicted on the rood mirrors Christ's sorrows.

The sufferings of the rood could be read as a useful comparison with the violence inflicted on the animal skin in *#26/24*: the speaking subject of the *Exeter Book* riddle could similarly metaphorically refer to a Christian martyr – or even to Christ himself, because they silently suffer and endure the humiliation of death and bodily torment in preparation for a future resurrection. In *#26/24*, the immersion in water and the removal of impurities may be both allegorical allusions to the baptism ceremony. In this light, even the initial references to the mortification of the body would be part of the process that leads to heavenly glory: just as the

---

131   The poem suggests that the blame for this atrocious act does not fall exclusively on the soldier or on the Roman officials or on the Jewish people; the whole humanity is at fault here. Therefore, the whole humanity is *feōnd*. See Swanton, 66–74.

Christian is rewarded for their tortures with eternal life in the eyes of God, the sacrificed animal would resurrect in the form of a magnificently decorated manuscript (Marsden, 146).

As a matter of fact, the riddle opens focusing on the animal's sacrifice and gradually progresses towards a more anthropocentric perspective, finally depicting a piece of human craftsmanship. When the riddle illustrates the process of writing, two additional components are incorporated into the narrative, two kennings emphasize the organic origin of the manuscript: the feather is defined as 'fulges wyn' (line 7b), 'the bird's joy', while the ink is literally 'beamtelge' (line 9b), 'tree dye'.[132] The gush arising from the pen's stroke wets the parchment, forming a symbiotic relationship among the manuscript's constituent parts: the feather absorbs (or swallows, 'swealg', line 9b) the ink, which in turn seeps the page in a black trace ('siþade sweartlast', line 11a). Already explored in Aldhelm's *Penna*[133] and in the *Exeter Book* collection in *#51/49*,[134] this image compares the act of writing to the route made by footprints left by walking on unpaved roads. The metaphor describes writing but it also implies a major aspect of the reading process, which is to say,

---

132 Black ink was made from carbon or a compound of iron and gall. On the production of the gall see https://www.nottingham.ac.uk/manuscriptsandspecialcollections/researchguidance/medievalbooks/materials.aspx.

133 Aldhelm, LIX: 'Me dudum genuit candens onocrotalus albam, / Gutture qui patulo sorbet de gurgite limphas. / Pergo per albentes directo tramite campos / Candentique uiae uestigia careula linquo, / Lucida nigratis fuscans anfractibus arua. / Nec satis est unum per campos pandere callem, / Semita quin potius milleno tramite tendit, / Quae non errantes ad caeli culmina uexit' ('The dazzling pelican, which absorbs seawater in its wide throat, once begot me (as white as I was). I proceed in a straight line through the whitened fields, leaving dark-coloured traces on the gleaming route, darkening the shining fields with my blackened meanderings. It is not enough to open a single path through these fields, rather, the trail branches out in a thousand directions, leading those who do not err to the heavenly summits').

134 *#51/49*: 'Ic seah wrætlice wuhte feower / samed siþian; swearte wæran lastas, / swaþu swiþe blacu. Swift wæs on fore / fuglum framra; fleag on lyfte, / deaf under yþe. Dreag unstille / winnende wiga se him wegas tæcneþ / ofer fæted gold feower eallum' ('I saw four wonderful beings traveling together; black were the footsteps, and very black the traces. Swift it was on the trajectory, faster than birds; it flew through the air, plunged into the wave. Tirelessly he worked, the fighting warrior who showed it – all four of them – the pathways on ornate gold').

the ability to interpret, to understand. Just like footprints on the ground have no meaning for people who do not know how to distinguish in them the passage of a specific animal, the reader must be able to carefully study and analyse the sign they see in order to continue on their progress towards knowledge, or, as stated by Aldhelm, to be led towards heaven, 'ad coeli culmina' (line 8).

This particular metaphor associated to the verb *swelgan* does not seem an accidental choice. *Swelgan*, first and foremost, denotes the process of consuming food or drink but, in a figurative sense, it might also mean 'to understand'.[135] It occurs multiple times in the *Exeter Book* collection, especially in riddles related to the scriptorium's space,[136] but its use is particularly noteworthy in *#47/45*:

> Moððe word fræt —   me þæt þuhte
> wrætlicu wyrd   þa ic þæt wundor gefrægn,
> 3   þæt se wyrm forswealg   wera gied sumes,
> þeof in þystro,   þrymfæstne cwide
> ond þæs strangan staþol.   Stælgiest ne wæs
> 6   wihte þy gleawra,   þe he þam wordum swealg.

[A moth ate words. It seemed a curious fate to me when I heard that marvel, that a worm, a thief in the dark, devoured a man's songs, his glorious speech, and his strong foundation. Even though he gorged on words, the thievish guest didn't get any wiser.]

#47/45 focuses on the paradox of the book-moth, a creature that continuously ingest speeches and words and yet has no awareness of what they

---

135 See *ASD* s.v. 'swelgan': 'to swallow; to take in, drink, absorb [...] to take in to the mind'.

136 In *#93/89*, the antler turned into an inkhorn says it is forced to swallow black wood and water ('Nu ic blace swelge woda ond wætre', lines 24b–25a). Similarly, in *#49/47*, the speaking subject reveals that a servant's hand made them swallow useful gifts ('se oft dæges swilgeð þurh gopes hond gifrum lacum', lines 2b–3) and others precious things more expensive than gold ('golde dyrran', line 6b). These priceless items could be read as fine manuscripts, assuming 'book cabinet' or 'bookcase' as solutions; otherwise, they could simply be a reference to the incalculable value of the written word, if we assume the riddle describes, instead, 'pen and inkwell'. See Shook, 224–225.

could mean.[137] This paradoxical intent is emphasized, indeed, by the reiterated use of *(for)swelgan*: the moth consumes word in a physical sense, but is unable to comprehend them; a moth cannot interpret the footprints of those who came before it. The book-moth is one of those people, *errantes* in the words of Aldhem, who are barred from understanding the signs left on any page. Conversely, in *#26/24*, the quill absorbs and the parchment page stores the message, for the benefit of people who will know how to understand the meaning of the black traces (line 18); in this manner, the page can somehow give back the knowledge and wisdom stored ('ferþe þy frodran', line 21a).

The negative tone of the preceding lines has been flipped at the end of the poem. At this stage, the speaking subject's torment is finished; the mortification of the body has reached the point of sublimation since material demands have been replaced by spiritual blessings. Thus, the human being, introduced as a *feōnd* in the first line, has morphed into someone worthy of respect, a hero ('hæleð') in line 12, and the parchment is no longer merely skin, but an artefact deserving reverence because it can lead towards redemption in a Christian sense. Having absorbed the knowledge derived from God's word – a tool for obtaining safety, victory, glory, and prosperity (as remarked in lines 19–23) –, the speaking subject may now claim its own famous name – 'Nama min is mære' (line 27b) – and its own holiness 'halig sylf' (line 28b). Moreover, the subject can finally claim their own voice: the accusative 'mec' can ultimately become a nominative 'ic' (line 26b), the object becomes subject. The final part of the riddle seems to emphasize the spiritual and cultural advantages of the Gospel book. It may be argued that this is an attempt to justify the initial act of violence, as if it were essential to recast the animal sacrifice in a Christian and anthropocentric perspective, thus the emphasis on comfort, knowledge, and other benefits that the book promises for humans.

---

137 The riddle, with its parodic intent, can be read as a short meditation on the perishable nature of knowledge. The beginning of the poem, 'word fræt' (line 1a) and the following 'forswealg wera gied sumes' (line 3), both imply a physical (or material) act of consuming the page, while the last two lines are built on a contradiction between 'ne wæs wihte þy gleawra' (lines 5b–6a) and 'wordum swealg' (line 6b), a paradox created by a semantic juxtaposition: the acquired knowledge is going to be wasted. See Marino, 259 and Borysławski, 115.

Yet, the poem does not convey the sense of a completely positive outcome: all of that amazing insight is achieved at the expense of the animal whose life was taken, through the joy denied to the bird and the sap stolen from the tree. *#26/24*'s *wiht* has gone through an irreversible process of change, and yet, even after being irrevocably altered by the craftsmen's expert hands, the parchment preserves traces of its original state. As anybody who has worked on parchment can tell, and as many scholars have noticed, indications of organic origin never entirely vanish: parts of the spine, veins, and arteries – hallmarks of animal life – may occasionally be seen and felt on the page.[138] As a result, notwithstanding the sense of comfort obtained from the final use of the book, *#26/24* can largely be read as the portrayal of a tormented and hybrid body: as observed by Mittman (*Maps and Monsters*, 109–110), the poem is primarily focused on the life of the constituent parts of the manuscripts. Poetry, in a sense, gives back their vital breath to each component required to make the book. Part of the animal soul returns into the skin for it to convey its story, and similarly the feather needs its lost spirit as a 'bird's joy' to glide over the page and absorb wisdom. The item depicted in *#26/24* reveals itself to be what it initially was: the skin of a living creature, ripped from its body, and inscribed with the help of a bird's feather. Then, this biological origin is physically covered with an extra layer of skin, while metaphorically invested by a series of positive ideals, mostly comfort and knowledge represented by the Bible in a religion that places the Book at its core. The riddle's concluding sentences place the process's end as an obvious accomplishment for humanity, because, as noted by Neville (114), the capacity to control a natural creature is seen as a happy result.[139] However, the emphasis on the animal genesis and on the efforts required to make

---

[138] On how the materiality of a manuscript can influence the reading process, see Treharne, 465–478, and Kay, in both 'Legible Skin: Animal and the Ethics of Medieval Reading' and *Animal Skin and the Reading of the Self in Medieval Latin and French Bestiaries*.

[139] Jennifer Neville (114) investigates how Old English poetry often puts humans at a disadvantage in nature, allowing external forces to rule humanity. The *Exeter Book* collection, instead, depicts all of the natural components that humans are able to manage and dominate. 'These objects become valuable when they have been

the manuscript appear to indicate a wish to depict those early acts in a different light. The focus on the animal's voice in the opening fourteen lines is an explicit acknowledgement of the animal sacrifice and the human effort: they both are essential requirements for the book to exist. *#26/24* appears to endorse the animal origin of the book-object, recognizing an ethical issue.

The poem is built on the juxtaposition of conflicting factors. On one hand, the attention paid to corporeal imagery in the initial section of the text indicates an interest for the earliest steps in the production of a book; the depiction of the dead animal, from its own perspective, goes on contrasting a vision of natural resources as solely instrumental (Dale, 99). The second half, on the other hand, with its special emphasis on the spiritual and cultural benefits of the book-object, appears to be an attempt to justify the act of violence that opens the text, as if there was a desire to re-frame the animal sacrifice in a Christian and anthropocentric perspective. Hence the poem's emphasis on wisdom, comfort and all the other benefits of the manuscript. The poem appears to be attempting to justify the sacrifice of the animal for what it is deemed to be a greater good – the manuscript's cultural and spiritual significance.

The strategies used throughout the whole collection to depict nature stimulate some reflection on the Anglo-Saxons' possible regard for non-human creatures. The space granted to the point of view of a slaughtered animal in *#26/24* opens up to different perspectives, similar to the voraciousness of the human character in *#77/74* and the stoic resignation to pain of the ox in *#72/70*: the *Exeter Book* collection appears to recognize in animals a vital force analogous to that of men. Furthermore, the riddles exhibit a clear understanding of the suffering imposed on them.

As suggested by Holsinger (616–623), *#26/24* acknowledges somehow the complexities of the ethical question of book production: for a long time, parchment manuscripts were the best way to preserve the greatest examples of human civilization but could exist solely because a great number of animals were killed. Probably, the ethical problem would not be felt in the same way in Early Medieval England, but if it is true that the *Exeter Book* riddles open a different perspective on any transformed

---

forcibly "denatured", that is, when their natural state, characteristics and power have been removed and replaced by traits conferred by human art and skill.'

creatures for the use and consumption of men, *#26/24* points out the violence suffered by the animals, making the book-making process's contradictions painfully clear for anyone who reads the text, considering it in its original context.

4. *Wonders of the East*: Men, Animals and In-Between

The sense of interconnection among the various entities expressed in the *Exeter Book* collection can be also found in *Wonders of the East*, albeit through different paradigms: if the creatures populating the riddles have the ability to move from one identity to another through the riddlic game of revealing-obscuring clues, the beings described in *Wonders of the East* could be interpreted as the material expression of a combination amongst several identities. The monstrous people protagonists of the text muddle any clear categorizations because they display both animal and human features.

Wonders of the East represents the Anglo-Saxon interpretation of a textual tradition resulting from a context fascinated by the idea of the monstrous coming from an indistinct East. This tradition first developed during the second century CE, in the eastern part of the Roman empire, drawn by the legends on Alexander the Great and his travels; then in Late Antiquity and in the Early Middle Ages these stories spread also in Western Europe.

The almost-human beings described in the text must have piqued the interest of Anglo-Saxon readers for a long time: the text has been preserved in three manuscripts produced on the island between the end of the tenth century and the mid-twelfth century, they contain two versions of the Latin text and two versions in Old English. Evidence of a peculiar interest for these kinds of works can be found in other similar texts preserved and produced in the Old English area. Another book of monsters in Latin, most likely composed in the Anglo-Saxon context, is the *Liber monstrorum de diversis generibus*; it is a work halfway between the fields of teratology and zoology, written between the eighth and ninth centuries, and shares much of the subject matter and the encyclopaedic intent with *Wonders of the East*.

4.1 Origin and circulation of the texts: From the *Letter of Pharasmanes* to *Wonders of the East*

Wonders of the East[140] thus constitutes the Anglo-Saxon contribution to the textual tradition of the so-called *Letter of Pharasmanes*, a fictitious, lost epistle addressed to a Roman Emperor, Hadrian or Trajan. The original core of the *Letter*, which was most likely written in Greek around the second century CE[141] and later translated into Latin between the fourth and the early seventh centuries,[142] can be variably reconstructed by comparing the preserved versions. Based on the distortion of the name of the alleged writer, Φαρεσμάνης, a king of Iberia[143] during the reigns of Trajan and Hadrian (ca. 100 CE), the known versions have been split into two main groups, typically denoted by the letters F and P. The *Letter* reveals itself to be the account of a journey through known and unknown

---

140 The Latin and Old English texts have been jointly published for the first time by Cockayne, in *Narratiuncula anglice conscriptae:* 33–39 and 62–66. Among the numerous following publications, the main critical editions are: Rypins, *Three Old English Prose Text in MS Cotton Vitellius A. XV*, E.E.T.S. o.s. 161; Gibb, *Wonders of the East: A Critical Edition and Commentary*; Knock, *Wonders of the East: A Synoptic Edition of the Letter of Pharasmenes and the Old English and Old Picard Translations*; Orchard, *Pride and Prodigies*, 173–203; Fulk, *The* Beowulf *Manuscript*, 15–31; Mittman and Kim, *Inconceivable Beasts: The Wonders of the East in the Beowulf Manuscript*, 39–71.

141 Proof of the Greek origin of Pharasmanes's *Letter* is not only the name of the alleged author, whose corruption in F and P implies a derivation from /ph/ as a transliteration of the Greek /φ/; we must also consider the Greek measurements in *stadia* kept in most versions of the text, as well as the names given to the monstrous races, which are frequently of Greek origin. See Knock, 25–26.

142 More specifically, two rivers, Brixo and Gargarus – otherwise known only through the *Letter* – are identified in the grammatical treatise *Catholica*, which is thought to have been written around the fourth century and attributed to M. Valerius Probus; this would be the oldest evidence of the Latin text's existence. In any case, the *terminus ad quem* is identifiable in the elements of the *Letter* that Isidore includes in his *Etymologies* (XII, iv, 18 and XVII, viii, 8) in regard to the Corsias serpents and the pepper they kept, § 6 in *Wonders of the East* (see Faral, 358–359 and 366). For a more detailed discussion on the dates of composition see Knock, 31–34, and Lendinara, 'Di meraviglia in meraviglia', 186.

143 A region in the Caucasus area, precisely the South-East of modern Georgia.

regions, a chain of descriptions about places and creatures positioned on the edges of the known universe, a marvellous East whose geographic coordinates are not exactly defined.

Interpolations, transpositions, and omissions characterize the relations between the two branches of the tradition.[144] The two texts known by the conventional titles of *Letter of Fermes to Hadrian*[145] and *Feramen Rex ad Adrianum imperatorem*[146] are part of the F group. A version of the text placed in book III (chapters lxxii–lxxxi) of Gervase of Tilbury's *Otia Imperialia* is also attributable to this branch of the tradition (ca. 1211). On the other hand, the P group is characterized by a significant reduction in the initial chapters; the *Epistola Premonis Regis ad Trajanum imperatorem*,[147] the *Epistola Parmoenis ad Trajanum imperatorem*,[148] the translation in Old French known as *Lepistle le roy Perimenis a lempereur*[149] and *Wonders of the East* are all part of the P group.

Among the versions produced in England, the codex London, British Library, Cotton Vitellius AXV[150] (ca. 990–1020), also known as the *Beowulf* manuscript, contains the oldest known copy in Old English, preserving thirty-two chapters and thirty-one illustrations (ff. 98v–106v). The manuscript London, British Library Cotton Tiberius BV/1[151]

---

144 For an in-depth analysis on the relations between the two branches of the tradition see the fundamental works by Gibb and Knock.
145 This is the longest and most detailed version of the text, it is kept in Paris, Bibliothèque Nationale, nouv. acq. lat. 1065, ff. 92v–95v (ninth century). Citations from Faral, 199–215.
146 Copied in four manuscripts: Montecassino, Archivio dell'Abbazia, 391, ff. 82v.84v (eleventh century); Cava dei Tirreni, Archivio dell'Abbazia, 3, ff. 393r–394v (eleventh–twelfth century); Madrid, Biblioteca Nacional, 19 ff. 198v–199r (thirteenth century); Paris, Bibliothèque Nationale, anc. fond. lat. 7418, ff. 268–270v (fourteenth century). All citations are from Knock, 933–940.
147 Once kept in Strasbourg, C IV 15. The manuscript has gone missing in a fire of 1870; in 1827, however, Graff had published a diplomatic edition of the text. Citations from Faral, 199–215.
148 It was transmitted in a manuscript belonging to Isaac Vossius in Leiden, the codex is no longer identifiable. The text was partially transcribed in 1884 by Pitra, 648–649. Citations from Pitra.
149 Copied in Bruxelles, Bibliothèque Royale, 14562, ff. 5vb–6vb (thirteenth century), it was firstly published by Hilka in 1923, 92–103. Citations from Knock, 907–914.
150 Henceforth, V.
151 Henceforth, T.

(mid-eleventh century, ff. 78v–87v) includes thirty-seven chapters of Old English text followed by a Latin version with the corresponding images. A third manuscript (Oxford, Bodleian Library 614,[152] twelfth century, ff. 36r–48r) preserves the Latin text and images, including also twelve new chapters.[153]

The texts copied alongside *Wonders of the East* in V and T belong to genres significantly different from one another. T is a miscellaneous codex made up by didactic works on time measurement, astronomy, and geography, such as a copy of Ælfric's *De Temporibus Anni* (ff. 24r–28v) and Priscian's *Periegesis* (ff. 57r–73r); additionally, the manuscript also includes a calendar (ff. 2r–19r), lists of popes and bishops (ff. 19r–22r), and genealogies of kings and emperors (ff. 22r–23v).[154] A structure of this kind implies that the manuscript was assembled as a work intended for consultation. On the other hand, the Nowel Codex,[155] folia from 94 to 209 in V, is composed by several literary texts in verse and prose: in addition to the two poems, *Beowulf* (ff. 132r–201v) and *Judith* (ff. 202r–209v), *Wonders of the East* is accompanied by two prose works, a hagiography about Saint Christopher (ff. 94r–98r) and the sole copy in Old

---

152 Henceforth, B.
153 Henceforth, the Old English versions will be mentioned by the conventional title of *Wonders of the East*, while the corresponding Latin texts produced in Anglo-Saxon England will be identified by the Latin title, *Mirabilia*, in place of *De rebus in oriente mirabilibus*. Unless otherwise specified, quotations from *Wonders of the East* and the *Mirabilia* are taken from the editions by Orchard, who uses the T-text for both the Old English and the Latin text, published in the appendix in *Pride and Prodigies*, 173–203.
154 For a more detailed description of the manuscript see McGurk et al., 4–108.
155 London, British Library, Cotton Vitellius B XV, as is well known, is made up of at least two manuscripts that were bound together in the seventeenth century, most likely by Sir Robert Cotton. The Nowell Codex is named for the volume's most likely owner in the sixteenth century (see Malone). The first section of the manuscript, ff. 4–93, belongs to another codex, denominated Southwick, which dates from the second half of the twelfth century and contains four prose works, including the Old English versions of Augustine's *Soliloquia* (ff. 4–59v), the Gospel of Nicodemus (ff. 60–86v), a prose on Solomon and Saturn (ff. 86v–93v), and part of a homily on Saint Quentin (f. 93v) (Cross and Hill, 14; Ker, 279–281).

English of the *Letter of Alexander to Aristotle* (ff. 107r–131v).[156] The criteria underpinning the Nowell Codex's compilation appear to be tied to the presence of physical or metaphorical monstrosities in the narrative structure of the texts. Sisam (96) probably did not go too far from truth when he anticipated how the work may have been catalogued:

> [I]f a cataloguer of those days had to describe it briefly, he might well have called it 'Liber de diversis monstris, anglice'.

The two manuscripts' distinct contexts consent to read *Wonders of the East* from different angles. Included among the pseudoscientific-didactic texts in T, the work appears as a treatise on teratology, a catalogue of places, animals, and peoples with exceptional characteristics; in the context of V, instead, the text could be seen as travel literature, as the tale of a journey through distant regions occupied by extraordinary figures and peoples.[157]

In comparison to the continental versions of the *Letter*, the epistolary frame, already reduced in group P, is completely absent within the manuscripts produced in the Anglo-Saxon area, and the text sequence has undergone significant changes in the central part due to the inversion of two sections.[158]

Another distinguishing feature of *Wonders of the East* is the inclusion of an iconographic set depicting the scenes or the beings described in the treatise, a kind of visual support for a text probably meant for silent reading or, in any case, for individual study (Mittman and Kim, 7). The miniatures that adorn the three manuscripts are images of a textual type, that is, they aspire to visually represent what the text describes; furthermore, the relationship that binds text and images is not only thematic: the

---

156 The fictitious epistle covers the Macedonian leader's journey to conquer the regions of the East, as well as his meetings with remarkable animals and peoples. As a result, themes and episodes makes it a very close work to *Wonders of the East*, and the Alexandrian matter has entered the transmission of the treatise. In *Wonders*, the figure of Alexander occurs twice: in § 2 he is referenced in relation to some imposing buildings; in § 27, he fights against a race of hybrid women, see section, 5.2. The *Letter*'s most recent editions are available in: Orchard, *Pride and Prodigies*, 224–252 and Fulk, *The Beowulf Manuscript*, 34–83. Citations from Orchard.
157 For detailed studies on the two codices, see Howe, 155–156, and Ford.
158 See section 4.2.

105

layout of the pages reveals how the reduction of spaces and the interaction between the modes of representation can bring the text's characters closer to the reader; most of the portrayed figures seem to be on the verge of overstepping beyond the limits imposed by the frames. In other words, because leaving the delimited space is comparable to entering the observer's world, the iconography in *Wonders of the East* questions the boundaries that separate text and image, reader and written page, depicted creature and observer, East and West. Some of the monsters that occupy the manuscript in V wander beyond their limits, frequently invading the space intended for the text, and the images are not always contained inside a frame. The illustrations in T, and its derivative B, seem to be more rigorous, but, in some cases, hands and feet expand up to exceed the boundary of the frame: an example of the outward-facing attitude that characterizes most of the depicted figures is the headless man (f. 82r) – Blemmye, for most of the teratological literature – who, looking directly over the page towards the reader, grasps the borders of the painting containing him as if he were in the process to jump out (Friedman, 'The Marvels-of-the-East Tradition', pp. 319–341).

The versions written in Anglo-Saxon territory are based on a single Latin exemplar that arrived on the island towards the end of the eighth century.[159] The Old English texts, on the other hand, retain variants that, while absent in the Latin version of T and B,[160] occur in other texts of the P group; thus, the Latin text used for the Anglo-Saxon translation would not be identifiable among those extant and should correspond to a slightly earlier version than that of the *Mirabilia*.[161]

---

159 Among the corruptions shared by all the insular versions, see § 11 on the two-faced giants: *Mirabilia* refers to the creature's black hair, 'capillis nigris' (f. 81r in T, f. 40r in B), corresponding to the Old English to 'sweart feax' (f. 101v in V, f. 81r in T), where elsewhere it refers to the creature's shoulders or shoulder blades; both the *Epistola Premonis* (XVII, 2) and the *Epistola Parmoenis* (V) read 'scapulas nigras', while the Old French version reads 'noires espaules' (XIV). See Knock, 76 and 675–684; see also Lendinara, 'Di meraviglia in meraviglia', 179–180.
160 Gibb (5–13) proved the derivation of B from T, while Knock (81–91) established that the copy was indirect.
161 In their depiction of the two lakes ruled by the Sun and the Moon (§ 18), the *Mirabilia* use the incorrect 'loci' instead of the more accurate *laci* (T, f. 82v: 'Sunt et alibi loci duo'; B, f. 42r: 'Sunt et alibi loca duo'); in *Wonders of the East*, these locations are referred to as 'seaðas' (T, f. 82v: 'Ðær syndan ii seaðas'; V,

The Old English translation is, in general, equivalent to the Latin text. Small additions to clarify statements not easily understood by Anglo-Saxons appear in some paragraphs (Fulk, xi–xii). Indeed, among the translation strategies implemented by the antigraph's copyist a few interventions seem to be added for explanatory purposes: for example, the regular insertion of the Latin league alongside the measurement in Greek *stadia*; there are also some explanatory glosses for words considered unfamiliar, such as *balsamum* explained as 'se deorweorðesta ele' (§ 19) 'the most precious oils', and *cinnamomum* 'ðam deorweorðestan wyrtgemangum þe man cinnamomum hateð' ('with the most precious spices which are called cinnamon') (§ 35); similarly, some of the Latin ethnonyms are kept in the Old English text and immediately glossed, as is the case for 'Homodubii [...]þæt bioð twylice' ('Homodubi [...] that is doubtful') (§ 8); finally the narrative material appears sometimes adapted to the new audience, for example, references to the Gorgons are replaced by those to the Valkyries (§ 9).

The Old English versions have common ancestry but are not dependent to one another (Lendinara, 'Di Meraviglia in Meraviglia', 181). Despite multiple corruptions,[162] the V-text includes, in several cases, readings from an earlier tradition than the T-text. One of the most notable examples is the section about the two-headed giants (§ 11) and, in particular, the form of travel they use to get to India to procreate.[163] V reads

---

f. 103r: 'Ond þar syndon twegen seaþas'). In Old English, *seāþ* usually means 'a pit, hole, well, reservoir, lake' (see *ASD*, s.v. 'seāþ') and, in the tale of Jamnes and Mambres (§ 37), an added chapter in T (f. 87r), it appears as a translation of 'lacus'. See Knock, 92–93.

162 There are significant omissions in the V-text, including one chapter missing at the beginning of the text (§ 5), two chapters missing at the end of the treatise, and nine words that have been completely obliterated. For the first omission, Knock (103–110) speculates that the text was copied from a bilingual manuscript with an arrangement similar to T; in that scenario, the copyist in V may have overlooked an Old English passage between two paragraphs in Latin. The omission of the final chapters corresponds with the last section of the displacement in chapters § 17– § 24 and could have been caused by it; the missing word, on the other hand, could be due to a partial compromission – possibly caused by a stain – of the text arranged on four columns in the manuscript from which the V-text is copied.

163 The white two-faced giants are expressly defined as men who can morph into storks in the F group. There are no classical sources on this, although the oral legend has

107

'on scipum' (f. 101v), corresponding to the *Epistola Premonis*'s Latin 'in navibus' (XVII, 2) and to the Old Picard 'en nes' in the French translation (XIV). This reading is an intermediate stage between the older variant 'in avibus', found in the *Letter of Fermes* (XVII, 3), and the reading of *Mirabilia*, 'suis manibus'. The periphrasis is completely absent in the Old English text in T (f. 81r). Another case where V keeps an older reading is the toponym Ciconia (§ 12), which has been renamed *Liconia* in both *Mirabilia* and Old English T (f. 81r).

Overall, there are eight instances when the Old English translation is in line with texts from group P but disagrees with *Mirabilia*. Five of these are found exclusively in V and were most likely removed from the copy when the Old English text in T was adapted to conform with the evolution of the *Mirabilia*.[164]

4.2 Structure and organization of *Wonders of the East*

Whether read as travel literature in a fantastic world, or as an encyclopaedic treatise with pseudo-naturalistic and allegorical purposes in the vein of the *Physiologus, Wonders of the East* depicts a series of heterogeneous creatures and places, associated with each other merely by being out of the ordinary.

Places, beasts and people are all portrayed in a neutral tone and an extremely simple style: every chapter normally indicates a vague location, then the marvel presented is introduced with a name and a physical description; occasionally the text includes a reference to some unusual customs.[165] When compared to classical travel literature, *Wonders of the*

---

been preserved in a variety of traditions. Thompson records several variations in *Motif-Index of Folk-Literature* (Vol. 2, D624.1 and D155). See Knock, 675–679.

164   For a more in-depth examination of all the variants, see Knock, 92–102.

165   Aside from this system, which can be considered as an essentially objective account of the wonders, the text does not leave much room for any subjective observations, except in two unusual chapters. In § 18, the treatise introduces a barbarian (*ellreord*) people who, despite having no physical defects, are described as 'ða wyrstan men ⁊ þa ellreordingestan' ('the worst men and the most barbarous'). This judgement appears to be based on their wrongdoing: they subdued a large number of

East has a tendency to exaggerate the size of both beings and regions mentioned. The narrative rarely pauses to detail habits and rituals; it is a continuous sequence of small illustrative pictures,[166] barely stating whether or not the creatures are dangerous or hostile.[167]

In this setting, the semi-human monster races play a significant role.[168] Monstrous people dwell in the most remote corners of the globe, have a humanoid shape, but differ from humans in various physical ways, such as having an excessively big or an excessively small size, having extra limbs or missing one, or showing bestial features in their body.

The narrative begins with a description of Antimolina's territory (§ 1), an island inhabited by sheep, whose largest city, Archemedon, is populated by merchants and rams the size of oxen, figures fairly distant from everyday life, yet still somehow plausible. The chapters that follow introduce places and beings that are increasingly more unlikely and detached from reality: the land of Hascellentia (§ 5), where only good things are born, is home to double-headed snakes with lantern-like eyes. Animals with unusual characteristics alternate with monstrous peoples: the gigantic gold-digging ants (§ 9) and the Lertices (§ 14), which

---

monarchs. The second instance is on § 27, when the narrative depicts a people of hybrid women being slain by Alexander the Great because their bodies are deemed unworthy and shameful ('for ðam hi syndon æwisce on lichoman Ᵹ unweorðe'). See section 5.2.

166 As noted by M. Campbell (71): 'When there are no travelers to stimulate them into movement it would seem that they simply eat, sleep and reproduce.'

167 They either avoid contact with the outside world – for example, the animals with two heads and fiery eyes (§ 4), the lion-headed giants (§ 12), the onocentaurs (§ 17), the men with big ears (§ 21) – or they attack any visitors, either for self-defence – red hens (§ 3) and Corsias serpents (§ 6) – or because they see the men as prey – Hostes (§ 13) and Donestres (§ 20).

168 Already present in travel narratives since Ctesias' (fifth–fourth century BCE) and Megasthenes' (fourth century BCE) accounts on India, monstrous peoples are also mentioned in the Plinian encyclopaedia (in particular the books: V on the geography of Africa, the Middle East, and Turkey, VI on the geography of Asia, and VII on human physiology) and find diffusion throughout the Middle Ages through the Solinian compendium of the *Naturalis Historia*. The fragments of the two Hellenistic historians are contained in Jacoby's inventory *Die Fragmente der griechiscen Historiker*, Ctesias: nr. 688, 416–517; Megasthenes: nr. 715, 603–639. For a more in-depth examination on the diffusion of fantastic travel literature in medieval Europe, see Wittkower, 159–197.

have donkey ears, sheep's wool, and bird's feet, are described among the Cynocephali (§ 7)– humanoid beings with a dog's head– a population of fish-eating men called Homodubii (§ 8), the white two-faced giants (§ 11), the lion-headed people (§ 12), the Hostes– another species of giants (§ 13)–, the headless people – called Blemmyes in the teratological tradition – and a race of onocentaurs, also called Homodubii (§ 17).[169] In the final section, the extraordinary nature of the peoples encountered shifts from physical deformities to purely cultural differences: in § 25, on the largest mountain between Media and Armenia, there are men who are said to have power and dominion over the Red Sea and are characterized by their kindness, whereas § 29 introduces a population of men whose peculiarity is being hospitable, despite having subdued many tyrants. The V-text continues the journey with a brief chapter on the black people, named *sigelwaras*[170] (§ 32). The T-texts adds four more chapters,

---

169 In most cases, the human and humanoid populations portrayed have no denominations; even populations mentioned in prior teratological literature, such as Blemmyes – headless men (§ 15) – or Panotti – men with large ears (§ 21) – do not get distinct names. In both branches of the *Letter of Pharasmanes*, the dark-skinned peoples of § 32 are classified as Ethiopians, the ethnonym was widely employed in antiquity to indicate different dark-skinned populations south of Egypt. Hostes, for the anthropophagous giants (§ 13), Conopoenas, for the Cynocephali (§ 7) and Homodubii, for ichthyophagi (§ 8) and for onocentaurs (§ 17), are readings unique to the P group, acquired by the tradition during their diffusion in Latin-speaking Europe. The name Donestre, which refers to a polyglot and cannibal race of monsters (§ 20), appears only in the insular manuscripts and has an unknown etymology.
170 The T-text reads *silhearwan*. It is a compound word made up by *sigel* 'sun' and *wara* 'inhabitant'; the noun *wara* is primarily used in the plural or as second part of compounds in the formation of nouns such as *burhwaran* 'inhabitants of a city' and *eorþwaru* 'inhabitants or populations of the earth', or with toponyms such as *Cantware* 'Kentian, inhabitant of Kent' or *Lundenwaru* 'Londoners, people from London' (see *ASD*, s.v. '-waru'). Thus, the *sigelwaras* would literally be referred to as 'sun dwellers' or 'inhabitants of the sun'. In Old English documentation, this compound word is frequently used to denote the Ethiopians; see, for example, *Exodus*, vv. 68–71a: 'Nearwe genyddon on norðwegas, / wiston him be suðan Sigelwara land, / forbærned burhhleoðu, brune leode, / hatum heofoncolum' ('The difficulties pushed them on the road to the north, they knew that to the south there were the high fortresses burned by the hot coal of the sky, the land of the Ethiopians, brown people').

regarding wonderful locations (a country of vineyards, a fiery mountain) and mythological creatures (the griffin and the phoenix).[171]

Wonders of the East differs from any other version of the *Letter* because an entire section of the text had been displaced. The portion § 17–§ 24 (*V*: ff. 102v–104v; *T*: ff. 82v–84r) corresponds to chapters XXVI.2–XXVII[172] in the *Letter of Fermes* and XXIV.2–XXVII in the *Epistola Premonis*, and the section from § 24 to § 32 corresponds to the sequences XVIII-XXII in the *Letter of Fermes* and XVIII–XXIV.1 in the *Epistola Premonis*.[173] The displacement may have been caused by an antigraph codex being dismembered and thus to a subsequent accidental movement of a single folio (James, 25), or it could have been caused by the erroneous folding of a bifolio if the antigraph had been an illustrated codex.[174] It is also possible that the alteration is not due to a technical error, but rather to a purposeful choice made by the compiler of the island versions' antigraph. In fact, the adjustment moves further down the text a group of chapters centred on positive images (§ 25: decent people and precious gems; § 28: men who live on honey; § 29: hospitable kings; § 30: generous men), anticipating another group of chapters dedicated to monstrous races and purely negative figures, depicting, among others, the onocentaurs (§ 17), the 'most barbarous' people (§ 18), and the Donestre people (§ 20). Thus, in comparison to the continental versions of the *Letter*, the structure of the subject matter in *Wonders of the East* appears to follow a specific trend: the first chapters contain the greatest concentration of animal descriptions, the central part of the text is primarily dedicated to the monstrous races, while the people described in the final part lack particularly monstrous features and appear closer to the Western norm of humanity.[175]

---

171 The chapter on Jamnes and Mambres (§ 37), despite being copied in B, is regarded as spurious due to significant inconsistencies with the remainder of the tradition. See, for example, Fulk's (15–31) decision not to include the chapter in his edition of the text.
172 Following the numbering of the sections proposed by Faral, 199–215.
173 Using Orchard's proposed groupings for the chapters in *Wonders of the East*, the sequencing order would have been: § 1–§ 16, § 25–§ 32, § 17–§ 24, § 33–§ 36. See Orchard, *Pride and Prodigies*, 24–25, for an analytic confrontation.
174 See Sisam (77): 'Wrong folding of a conjugate pair of leaves is likely.'
175 On this, see the observations made by Austin (28): 'The anonymous compiler rearranged the order of the text and images so that the marvels begin with animals,

Nevertheless, even if the rearrangement of the chapters in the insular versions was the result of a deliberate editorial choice, it is not possible to recognize an effective classification in the structure of the work, in the manner, for example, of the *Liber Monstrorum*, which is organized in three distinct books, with relative prologues and epilogues, where the semi-human monsters (*De monstris*) are separated from the animal monsters (*De belvis*) and from the snakes (*De serpentibus*) (Porsia, 4–69). Rather, it appears that *Wonders of the East* portrays animals, hybrid creatures, and fully human individuals as part of a continuum with no clear divisions. As in the colour spectrum, where the brighter tones of red and violet can be distinguished but the transition where one becomes the other cannot be seen, creating the illusion that the colours blend, the creatures found in the marvellous east are put in continuity with each other. Thus, in our text, the first monstrous races, Cynocephali (§ 7) and Homodubii ichthyophagi (§ 8) are included in a section dominated by animals, such as huge donkeys with bovine horns (§ 6) and giant gold-digging ants (§ 9). Lertices (§ 14) and dragons (§ 16), both monstrous but wholly animal entities, emerge in a section devoted entirely to the Plinian races. In the final section, bearded ladies (§ 26) and hybrid women (§ 27), two populations labelled as dreadful, are placed among the races depicted as being 'more human'.

According to Austin (26–29), the seeming inconsistency could be ascribed to a compiler who arranged the sequence of the exceptional inhabitants of the East using a soteriological criterion. In fact, the text appears to depict creature after creature with a scientific curiosity, maybe aiming at defining their place in the natural world. As a result, all the living creatures in the text would be introduced into a progressive disposition based on the potential for salvation. The text would begin by depicting a greater number of animals on the lower rungs of this hypothetical salvation ladder, then move on to hybrid creatures in an intermediate position between grace and damnation, and finally to entirely human beings.

Gibb (62–66), on the other hand, proposes an allegorical reading: the thematic structure of *Wonders of the East* could be a binary opposition

---

progress to humans, with bestial characteristics, and end with humans who enjoy cooked food, clothing, and political organization.'

between figures of Good and figures of Evil, in which, in an alternation of positive and negative meanings, each argument would connect to the next, through the identification of a defining feature. Thus, § 3 and § 4 describe animals whose touch is incendiary, § 4 is linked to § 5 since they both depict two-headed entities with glowing eyes, and the snakes with flaming eyes of § 5 are connected to the Corsias serpents in § 6.[176] A macrostructure would also correlate to this microstructure: a first section occupied by creatures that allude to Evil, such as monsters and individuals who commit heinous acts, would be countered by a final section populated by emblems of Good, such as the decent and hospitable peoples. Just like the *Physiologous*, each species or place described in *Wonders of the East* would be a representation of something else; hence, the treatise would be structured on the basis of the typological interpretations commonly given to the treated subject. Corsias serpents (§ 6), which have a lethal touch for humans, could easily be associated with the devil, as could the dragons (§ 16) and the Donestre people (§ 20). In contrast, in the final chapters, the symbology becomes more positive: the focus shifts to images such as the Lakes of Sun and Moon (§ 18), the laurel and olive tree (§ 19), the precious gems (§ 25), and the golden vineyard (§ 24); in this light, the insertion in T of other figures that can be interpreted positively, such as the phoenix (§ 35), could also be explained. Thus, Gibb (73) sees in the text a moralizing drive and a Christian authorship that would have redesigned the structure of the continental version in a direction that goes 'from the temporal to the eternal, from the moral to the eschatological, from man to God'.

Furthermore, it must be noted that monstrous figures indicated a relationship with the divine and its manifestations already in classical Latin: the noun *monstrum* was frequently used in conjunction with supernatural phenomena used by the gods to warn humans. The meaning that the classical world ascribed to the signifier *monstrum* emphasizes, on the one hand, the premonitory role that was ascribed to it, and, on the other, the belonging of monstrous animals to a sphere that is not solely physical. The idea of the monster as a communication link with the divine appears to be declined also in the medieval universe as explained by Isidore in the *Etymologies* (XI, iii, 1–3):

---

176 For further investigations see also Ramazzina, 309–329.

> Portenta esse Varro ait quae contra naturam nata videntur: sed non sunt contra naturam, quia divina voluntate fiunt, cum voluntas Creatoris cuiusque conditae rei natura sit. Unde et ipsi gentiles Deum modo Naturam, modo Deum appellant. Portentum ergo fit non contra naturam, sed contra quam est nota natura. Portenta autem et ostenta, monstra atque prodigia ideo nuncupantur, quod portendere atque ostendere, monstrare ac praedicare aliqua futura videntur. Nam portenta dicta perhibent a portendendo, id est praeostendendo. Ostenta autem, quod ostendere quidquam fururum videantur. Prodigia, quod porro dicant, id est futura praedicant. Monstra vero a monitu dicta, quod aliquid significando demonstrent, sive quod statim monstrent quid appareat; et hoc proprietatis est, abusione tamen scriptorum plerumque corrumpitur.
>
> [Varro defines portents as beings that seem to have been born contrary to nature – but they are not contrary to nature, because they are created by divine will, since the nature of everything is the will of the Creator. Whence even the pagans address God sometimes as 'Nature' (*Natura*), sometimes as 'God.' A portent is therefore not created contrary to nature, but contrary to what is known nature. Portents are also called signs, omens, and prodigies, because they are seen to portend and display, indicate and predict future events. The term 'portent' (*portentum*) is said to be derived from foreshadowing (*portendere*), that is, from 'showing beforehand' (*praeostendere*). 'Signs' (*ostentum*), because they seem to show (*ostendere*) a future event. Prodigies (*prodigium*) are so called, because they 'speak hereafter' (*porro dicere*), that is, they predict the future. But omens (*monstrum*) derive their name from admonition (*monitus*), because in giving a sign they indicate (*demonstrare*) something, or else because they instantly show (*monstrare*) what may appear; and this is its proper meaning, even though it has frequently been corrupted by the improper use of writers.][177]

In contrast to Varro's belief that monsters and portents existed in opposition to the natural order of things, Isidore views every prodigy to be the result of divine will, and monstrous creatures are regarded as a natural part of the world. It's no surprise that teratology treatises were transcribed alongside reconstructions of the celestial vault, calculating works, and computations of dates based on terrestrial movements, as in T: monster catalogues were regarded as representations of reality (Mittman and Kim, 12–13). Nonetheless, the monster, like any other member of the so-called *liber naturae*, serves as a conduit for other meanings. If portents and wonders announce and forecast the future, the monster is a warning,

---

177 Translation by Barney et al. 2006.

in that it has the power to suggest a meaning that is not immediately apparent.

Moreover, if monstrous races are a part of the natural world, the second question they raise concerns their place in the order of creation. In *De Civitate Dei* (XVI, viii–ix), Augustine does not appear to be particularly convinced by the possibility of monstrous peoples existing in the East, but in recognizing the birth of children with obvious deformities, he finds himself admitting the possibility that God might have included in his creation project the various Cynocephali, Blemmyes, and all the other Plinian races:

> Verum quisquis uspiam nascitur homo, id est animal rationale mortale, quamlibet nostri inusitatam sensibus gerat corporis formam seu colorem siue motum siue sonum siue qualibet ui, qualibet parte, qualibet qualitate naturam: ex illo uno protoplasto originem ducere nullus fidelium dubitauerit. Apparet tame quid in pluribus natura obtinuerit et quid sit ipsa raritate mirabile.
>
> Qualis autem ratio redditur de monstrosis apud nos hominum partubus, talis de monstrosis quibusdam gentibus redid potest. Deus enim creator est omnium, qui ubi et quando creari quid oporteat uel oportuerit, ipse nouit, sciens uniuersitatis pulchritudinem quarum partium uel similitudine tamquam deformitate partis offenditur, quoniam cui congruat et quo referatur ignorant.
>
> [Even in the hypothesis that in some place a man is born, that is a rational mortal animal, although he presents to our senses an unusual somatic typology of shape, colour, movement, voice or characteristics in terms of strength, organs and properties: the faithful man must not doubt that he comes from the first man. However, what nature has achieved in several subjects and what is extraordinary because of rarity is manifested.
>
> The justification that we give to deformed examples of men is the same that can be given for the deformity of some peoples. In fact, God is the creator of all and He knows the place and the time in which it is opportune or it was opportune to make a being exist because He knows the equality and inequality of the parts with which to accord the harmony of the cosmos. But whoever cannot grasp the whole is shocked by the apparent deformity of a part, because he does not know who he conforms to and what it leads back to.]

Monstrous peoples are descended from the first man and, as such, are identical to any other man, that is, a mortal rational animal. Even in the Augustinian vision, however, monsters and wonders are part of a divine plan, serving a moral teaching function in regard to sin and virtue. The malformations of these beings are difficult to accept and understand due to a lack of information about the divine plan as a whole. The Christian model, as articulated by Augustine, must sympathetically recognize all monstrous peoples' participation in humanity, but in reality, as a sign, the Plinian races help men understand themselves and their place in the world; more than being human, they thus assume the role of symbolic guide for men.

The language of *Wonders of the East* conforms to the perspectives emphasized in Augustine and Isidore's thought: monstrous peoples are part of creation and are frequently regarded as human, even if their humanity is constantly questioned. The work gives the required information to differentiate the unusual creatures belonging to the animal kingdom from creatures that, despite their deformity, are considered human. In contrast to the animal hybrids usually introduced as *wildeōr*, as in the case of the Lertices (§ 14), 'Ðonne syndon on Brixonte wildeor' ('there are wild animals on the Brixonte'), or *Catinos* (§ 28) 'be þæm garsecge wildeora cyn' ('on the ocean there is a species of wild animals'), monstrous peoples are directly introduced by expressions such as 'þær beoð men acende' ('there are generated men'). Thus, similarly to the *Sigelwaras*, also known as Ethiopians (§ 32) and to the hospitable kings (§ 29), who are not characterized by any physical anomaly, the text classifies as humans a series of hybrid races: the white two-faced giants (§ 11), the lion-headed men (§ 12), the Hostes (§ 13), the headless men[178] (§ 15), the Donestre people (§ 20), the men with big ears (§ 21), the men with fiery eyes (§ 22), the bearded women (§ 26) and the hybrid women (§ 27).

This cataloguing notation, however, fails to neutralize the paradoxes inherent in monstrous figures, particularly in human-animal hybrids, whose bodies are the union of disparate elements that are difficult to reconcile.[179] In both textual and iconographic depictions, congenital

---

178 In this case, the two manuscripts have different readings: V omits 'menn akende'. V (f. 102v): 'on þon beoð buton heafdum þa habbað on hyra breostum heora eagan ⁊ muð' ('on which there are headless (creatures) who have ears and mouth on their breasts'); T (f. 82r): 'on þam beð menn akende butan heaftum, þa habbaþ on breostum heora eagan ⁊ muð' ('on which there are born men without heads, that have ears and mouth on their breasts').

179 See how J. Cohen (*Hibridity*, 2) defines the hybrid: 'a conjoining of differences that cannot simply harmonize'.

ambiguities in Plinian races are frequently stressed. For example, the description of the Cynocephali, denominated Conopoenas in the text (§ 7) – the only population that is not explicitly classified as human or animal – demonstrates a clear contrast between the text, which highlights their animalistic aspect, and the illustrations, which depict the figure as humanoid. Even the humanity of the ichthyophagi (§ 8) and the onocentaurs (§ 17) is openly questioned: based on the name given to them, Homodubii, these creatures are identified as beings of doubtful nature. Identification of the lion-headed men (§ 12) and of the Donestres (§ 20), creatures with a hybrid appearance and ambiguous behaviour that generate more than a few questions about their nature, is also difficult. The traditions that gave rise to these two chapters were built on animal figures, which were anthropomorphized during the textual transmission. In this context, moreover, the position of hybrid women (§ 27) stands out: explicitly condemned in text, they seem to be directly dehumanized.

Man, monster, and animal are not put in completely antithetical positions; rather, the distinctions are regarded as varieties within the same classification system. There are no polar oppositions in this setting, and the distinctions between the Self and the Other are obliterated (Tally Lionarons, 170–172).

The Plinian races are liminal creatures because they are placed at the boundaries of the known world and because they bring together and confuse aspects of different categories and, thus, are all 'abject' as defined by Kristeva (12–13): neither subject nor object, the monstrous being is an entity that upsets order and identity, because it does not respect borders, rules, and positions and forces us to confront the fragile states in which man enters the territories of the animal. Since the monster is ambiguous by nature, like everything liminal and belonging to two distinct groups, it ends up being regarded as taboo (Leach, 39–40). Human-animal hybrids, in particular, highlight the frailty of the human identity to which they relate. By questioning the borderline between man and other animals, these figures of almost-men become *loci* of horror (Davidson, 36): the representation of hybrid forms puts any kind of identity in jeopardy. As a result, the monstrous races of *Wonders of the East* can be viewed as transitional figures, serving as a bridge between animals and the more distinctively human populations of the final section.

5. Uncertain Humanity Denied Humanity

Hybrid beings have an important role in the treatise's overall organization: they could be viewed as the point of convergence between what is deemed animal and what is considered human. The ambiguity about their nature raises concerns about the basic concept of humanity, about what it is to be human. As a result, there are hybrids in the treatise who cannot be considered, directly or indirectly, to be part of any human race. They are not part of any *manncynn*. This fairly unclear category contains the dog-like people (§ 7) and both Homodubii communities (§ 8; § 17). The representation of the Cynocephalus reveals a tension between the written text, which emphasizes the most animalistic elements of the creature, and the pictures, which, instead, depict the figure as humanoid. The two people identified as Homodubii are perceived as 'doubtful men' for very different reasons: the former (§ 8) are seen as strangers because of their peculiar eating habits, thus, they are 'wonderful' from a social perspective, they do not conform to Western society expectations; the latter (§ 17) are human-donkey hybrids, a perfect example of a man-animal monster, that, because of their inherent ambiguity, is subjected to an ongoing process of revision by all artists and copyists succeeding one another in the textual transmission.

Even more complicated in respect to the perceived humanity of a specific race described is the situation of the hybrid women (§ 27), who are openly condemned in the text. As a result of a total rejection of their inherent humanity, these monstrous women are the sole race to face moral censorship and to be slain in the text.

5.1 Doubtful men: Cynocephali, ichthyophagi and onocentaurs

The catalogue of monstrous peoples begins in § 7 introducing a race of giants with a dog-like head and a humanoid body. These dog-men have been known to Western society since Ctesias (*Fragment* 45, 37); mentioned by Augustine (*De Civitate Dei*, XVI, viii) and by Isidore (*Etymologies*, XII, iii, 15), they appear in several *mappae mundi*[180] and Alexander's legends (*Letter of Alexander to Aristotle*, § 29). Moreover, in the apocryphal hagiographic tradition, transmitted also in the Nowell Codex, Saint Christopher is depicted as a cynocephalus giant.[181]

Tradition assigns various characteristics to the Cynocephali: usually associated with giants, they hunt with bows or javelins and cover themselves in animal skins, live on raw meat,[182] sometimes even human, and are unable to communicate other than by barking. Many of these traits are not covered in *Wonders of the East*. The text introduces the image of a fiery breath and emphasizes on physical characteristics that can only be explained through animal images: boar tusks and a horse mane are added to the canine head.

> Similiter ibi nascuntur Cenocephali, quos nos Conopoenas appellamus, habentes jubas equorum, aprorum dentes, canina capita, ignem et flammam flantes.

---

180 Cynocephali are depicted both in the Hereford Map (thirteenth century, Hereford Cathedral) and the Ebstorf Map (the original is lost, but a facsimile is available for consultation at the British Library); even the T-O map copied in T (f. 56v) records the presence of Cynocephali on the external coast of Africa.

181 *The Passion of Saint Christopher*, copied in the Nowell Codex, is an acephalous text, where, thus, the standard initial description of the main character is omitted (Fulk, 2–13). Nevertheless, the *Old English Martirology* (73) allows us to learn about the Anglo-Saxons' perspective on the figure of Christopher. The book provides a physical description of the saint on his feast day (28 April): 'he hæfde hundes heafod, ond his loccas wæron ofer gemet side, ond his eagan scinon swa leohte swa morgensteorra, ond his teþ wæron swa scearpe swa eofores tuxas' ('He had the head of a dog, his locks were excessive, his eyes shone as bright as the morning star, and his teeth were as sharp as the tusks of a boar').

182 See section 4.1.

> Eac swylce þær beoð cende Healfhundingas ða syndon hatene Conopoenas. Hi habbað horses manan ⁊ eoferes tucxas ⁊ hunda heafda, ⁊ heora oruð byð swylce fyres lig.
>
> [Similarly, there are born half-dogs that are called Conopoena. They have horses' manes, boars' tusks and dogs' heads and their breath is like a fiery flame.]

The Cynocephali exemplify the liminality of the monstrous races. The monster depicted is partially herbivorous, partly carnivorous, partly omnivorous; partly domesticated beast of burden, partly hunter and at the same time game, partly companion animal; it is placed on the boundary between numerous categories. This mingling of physical characteristics from many species, however, affects solely the monster's head. In fact, any semi-human feature of the beast can only be gleaned through the iconographic apparatus or the fame of this race of monsters. In addition to the more general reference to the dog-like head, the text specifies their having a mane (*manu*), tusks (*tucxas*), and fiery breath (*oroþ*); the observer's sight does not fall beyond the monster's lips. As in the rest of the tradition, therefore, even in *Wonders of the East*, the hybridity of the cynocephalus finds its *locus* in the creature's head, and the representation does not seem to be interested in other parts of the body.

Human-animal hybridity is always symbolic of transcending and refuting the categories prescribed by science and logic; yet, when the combination affects the head, monstrosity points to problems about the boundaries between rationality and irrationality. Placing a human head on an animal body is a physical distortion that preserves the creature's seat of reasoning and hence its human nature; nevertheless, placing an animal head on a human body favours the bestial side (Williams, 137–140). This particular issue has always piqued the interest of medieval intellectuals. In his Latin commentary on Aristotle's *Problemata* (1310), Peter of Abano argued that the shape of a creature's skull might be used to determine if it belonged to the human race:

> Et scias quod maxime decernitur in figuracione capitis: si aliquid animal debet dici nostrum genitum: si enim caput habuerit plene vt generans figuratum: etiam si in multis aliis partibus sit monstruosus potuit dici nostrum: quid et doctores legis nostre considerantes percipiunt baptizari tanquam recipiendum sit in specie nostra.[183]

---

[183] *Problemata Aristotelis cum Commento*, Paris, 1520, IV, 13 (f. 57v). In the absence of critical editions, the text is cited from Friedman, *The Monstrous Races*, 252–253.

> [You should know that this is determined mostly by the form of the head: if any animal must be said it is generated from us: if indeed the head had completely the shape of the generating one, even if in many other parts it is monstrous, it can be said to be ours; that is what, carefully considering, the doctors of our law understand: that being baptized is like being accepted in our species.]

If, apart from any other monstrous features, a completely developed human head is a sign of humanity, then an animal head is a sign of animality.

As a point of fact, this monstrous breed is the only one among the hybrid populations that is not introduced as belonging to the human race, and the text demonstrates difficulties in its classification. Already in the *Epistola Premonis* (XIV), these beings are described in words that indicate a degree of ambiguity about their nature:

> Nascunturque canis cenonulli, homines vel bestiae quaedam vel verius homine mixti cum capitibus canum, habentes jubas equorum, quorum capita canina sunt ignium flammas flantes.
>
> [And there are born Cenonulli dogs, men or some animals or actual men blended with the head of a dog, they have horses' manes; their dog's heads are breathing flames of fires.]

The epistle labels these people as 'cenonulli' and includes a brief explanation for their classification: 'cenonulli' could be human beings, animals, or human hybrids with the head of a dog. In the Old French rendition (X), these monsters are referred to as 'cenophale', variant of *cynocephale* found only in this text:[184]

> Et la naissent cenophale qui ont testes de kien et ont alainnes de flamme.
>
> [And there are born the Cenophale who have dog's heads and breaths of flame.]

The reading in the *Epistola Parmoenis* (X) is very similar to *Wonders of the East*, these half-dog men are denominated both *cynocephali* and *Conopenras*:

---

184 According to Knock (612), it may be derived from a Latin form that had already lost the -*ce*- element, analogous to the changes between the names 'lertices' and 'celestices' in § 14.

> Nascuntur ibi cynocephali, quos Conopenras appellatis: comas equorum, dente aprorum, capita canica, ignem et flammam flantes.
>
> [There are born Cynocephali, who are called Conpenras: (they have) horses' hair, boars' teeth, the head of a dog, fire and flames breathing.]

Similarly, the term 'cenocephali', translated in Old English with the compound noun 'healfhundingas',[185] is reinforced by the alternative name 'conopoenas' in the *Mirabilia* and *Wonders of the East*. This supplementary designation appears exclusively in these copies of the text and may be related to one of the other names reserved for the Cynocephali, *cynopenae*, a form of dubious etymology first documented in Tertullian's works (*Apologeticus* 8, 5; *Ad Nationes*, I, 8, 1).[186]

The addition of a second denomination for a single population could be interpreted as an attempt to return the monstrous being to the realm of what is understandable; it is a strategy to domesticate the Other and to practise a form of hegemony. It could be compared to *Genesis* 2:19, where Adam is appointed dominion over creation because he is required to provide names for every creature (Barajas, 249; Mittman, 84).

The images that accompany the text portrayal broaden the view of the cynocephalus, who is depicted in full-length as a humanoid figure. The visuals assist in identifying them as members of a monstrous community that is also human, and thus contribute to demonstrating the liminal state of this particular species.

In B and T (f. 80r), the cynocephalus is pictured naked, and because nudity represents both a proximity to barbarism and the animal side of the depicted subject, the creature appears to be placed in a position distant from humanity. Nonetheless, in contrast to what the textual description highlights, the artwork softens the more animalistic traits: the boar tusks are scarcely noticeable, the horse's mane barely brushes the creature's shoulders, and the remainder of the body is completely hairless. The monster is shown in the act of eating a leaf from a plant growing on a black rock, which takes up a large portion of the image. Its right

---

185 This compound noun is made up by *healf* 'half' and *hund* 'hound, dog' (see *DOE*, s.v. 'healf' and 'hund') with the suffix *-ing*, used to form masculine nouns denoting affiliation, lineage or derivation from. See Torre Alonso, 44.

186 An older hypothesis linked the name to the adjective κυνώπης, denoting someone with dog-like eyes, see Schneider, 191–192.

hand, with two fingers pointing to the plant, may be an invitation to the observer to join in the feast (Barajas, 249).

The miniaturist in V made a different choice (f. 100r): with its dog-like head and boar tusks, the monster is dressed in regal clothing, its garment is made up of three separate layers denoted by three different colours; the figure also bears the symbols of royalty, a globe and a sceptre. The attention paid to its attire and adornment would appear to inform the observer that a pure alterity is never attainable (Mittman-Kim, 9–11).

While T's gesture of welcome may be interpreted as a hint to minimize the barrier between monster and viewer, V's picture appears to symbolize a kind of monstrous civilization: the cynocephalus's garments evoke a familiar image, but his elongated muzzle disrupts this familiarity. The ambiguous and liminal quality of the hybrid creature is clearly represented in both images, which may be seen as both welcoming and disturbing.

The text assigns the name Homodubii to two distinct peoples, thus conveying uncertainty about their humanity and the duality of their nature through their own names. Chapter § 8 depicts a race of fish-eating men:

> In aliqua regione nascuntur homines statura pedum .vi. barbas habentes usque ad genua, comas usque ad talos, qui Homodubii appellantur et pisces crudos manducant.

> On sumon lande beoð menn akende ða beoþ on lenge six fotmæla lange. Hi habbað beardas oþ cneow side ⁊ feax oð helan. Homodubii hi sindon hatene, þæt bioð twy-lice, ⁊ be hreawan fisceon hi libbað ⁊ þa etað.

> [In a certain land there are born men who are six feet long. They have beards to their knees and hair to their heels. They are called Homodubii, that is 'doubtful ones', and they eat raw fish and live on it.]

Originally, the term 'ichthyophagi' was used to describe dietary patterns of coastal communities living between the Arab Peninsula and Asia; their distinctive feature was, in fact, that they followed a fish-based diet.[187]

---

187 Beyond the mere mention of the name, the first descriptions of this people date back to the Hellenistic period. Nearcus of Crete's travelogue and Agatharchides of Cnidus' geographical treatise were later reused by various Greek and Latin writers, including Arrian of Nicomedia and Pliny the Elder. For an in-depth historical examination see Nalesini, 9–18. Even Isidore, in the *Etymologies* (IX, ii, 131), describes them among the African populations: 'Ichthyophagi quod venando in mari valeant,

To name this population, the group F of the *Letter of Pharasmanes* retains the historically more appropriate name, using variants of *ichthiophagi*,[188] but this ancient ethnonym vanishes in the P group's adaptations. Two new names for the population are proposed in the *Epistola Premonis* (XVI, 1). The first is 'cenodubii', which appears to be formed by the first element of *cenonulli* (as seen, the only name given by the *Epistola Premonis* for the Cynocephali) and the second element of *homodubii*; the second designation, proposed as a gloss, is 'homunculi', a reference to the population's small stature:

> Ibi nascuntur homines statura pedum binorum in longitudine barbas usque ad genus habentes, qui cenodubii appellantur, id est homunculi.
>
> [There are born men, a couple of feet in height; they have long beards up to the knees, who are called Cenodubii, that is little men.]

Similarly, the Old French text (*Lepistle*, XI) identifies this people simply as 'hommeles':

> En lequele naissent homme qui nont que II pies de lonc, et leur pendant leur barbes lusques as genous. On les apele hommeles. Et menguent les poisons tous crus, lesquels il prendent en le riviere de Cabes.
>
> [In which men are born who are only two feet in height and they let their beards fall up to their knees. They are called little men. And they eat completely raw the fish that they catch in the river Cabe.]

Conversely, in the *Epistola Parmoenis* (II, iv), they are referred to as 'Homines Durci'; a scribe paying attention to the plural form of the verbal voice would appear to have corrected *homo* with *homines*. The

---

et piscibus tantum alantur. Hi post Indos montanas regiones tenent, quos sub actos Alexander Magnus piscibus vesci prohibuit' ('Ichthyophagi, because they are capable of hunting in the sea, and are fed only by fish. They occupy the mountainous regions, after the Indians, which under Alexander the Great prevented them from eating fish').

188 See for instance the *Letter of Fermes* (XVI, 1): 'A dextra parte ducent [*corr.* ducens] ad Ægyptum; hinc ad insulam in quo nascuntur homines longi [*corr.* longa] habentes barbas usque ad genua, qui appellantur idtofagi, pisces enim crudos vescuntur' ('From the right part leading to Egypt; from there to an island where are born men who have beards long up to the knees, that are called Ichthyophagi, they indeed feed on raw fish').

reading 'Durci', while difficult to interpret, is undeniably closer to the *Mirabilia* version.

> Dexteriores partes (*cod.* dexteriore parte) ducent in Aegyptum, in qua nascuntur ... (trogloditae?) pedum binum, barbas habentes usque ad genua. Homines Durci appellantur. Hi pisces crudo manducant.
>
> [The right parts lead to Egypt, where are born (troglodytes?) two feet tall, having beards up to the knees. They are called Durci Men. They eat raw fish.]

The ichthyophagi in the *Mirabilia* are six feet tall and thus can no longer be classified as 'homunculi'; the text therefore calls them Homodubii. The Latin appellative is recorded in Old English, both in V and T, but an equivalent Old English word is inserted soon after to clarify its meaning. T glosses with 'twylice' an adjective attested in various contexts that has a semantic significance comparable to the Latin *dŭbĭus*,[189] indicating something doubtful, uncertain or ambiguous. However, in the same paragraph, V (f. 100v) reads 'twimen'. The compound word does not occur anywhere else and is configured as a direct calque from the Latin *homodubius* in accordance with the Germanic *Wortbildung*. Just as the Latin *dŭbĭus*, even *twi-* (or *tweō-*) is connected to the root indicating the number two and alludes to a duplicity that provokes a sense of doubt, uncertainty, or ambiguity.[190] The V-text reading is especially useful for reinstating the compound's double meaning: both *homodubius* and *tweōman* can simultaneously mean 'double man' or 'doubtful man'.[191]

Contemporary English translations focus on the ambiguity conveyed by the term: according to Gibb (144), *twylic* and *twimen* have roughly the

---

[189] See some occurrences in Ælfric. *Grammatica, De generibus*, VI: 'Sume synd gecwedene dubii generis, þæt is, twŷlîces cynnes' ('Some are said dubii generis, that is of uncertain kind'); 'Sermo in Aepiphania Domini': 'forðan ðe hit bið twylic, hwæðer hit on life a olige oðþæt hit þam lareowe mid geleafan andwyrdan mage' ('because it is uncertain, weather to keep on living until it can answer to the master with faith'); 'Depositio Sancti Cuthberrhti Episcopi': 'Þa andwyrde hire se halga mid twylicere spraece' ('then the holy man answered with an ambiguous speech').

[190] See, for example, the nouns *tweō* 'doubt, uncertainty, hesitation', *tweōn* and *tweōgung* 'doubt'; the adjective *tweōgend-līc*, used to designate something 'doubtful' or 'uncertain' and the verb *tweōgan/tweōñ* 'to inspire doubt into a person (with acc.)' and 'to feel doubt, to doubt, to hesitate'. See *ASD*, s.v. 'tweō'.

[191] See *ASD*, s.v. 'tweōman'; see Mittman and Kim, 74.

same meaning 'double-ones', whilst Knock (1021) glosses *twiman* as 'a creature not indubitably man', and *twylic* as 'dubious'. Using the T-text as his primary source for his critical edition, Orchard (*Pride and Prodigies*, 189) translates *twylic* as 'doubtful ones'. In contrast, both Fulk (23) and Mittman-Kim (66), editing only the Nowell Codex's version, propose for *twimen* 'maybe-people' and 'doubtful people', respectively.

The ambiguity of this people is reinforced by both designations, *homodubii* and *twimen*; this population practises customs felt as too distinctive to be regarded as truly human. The doubt surrounding their nature does not appear to stem from their external appearance, which is marked by a height slightly above average and a very long beard; rather, it appears to emerge from their eating habits: they only eat raw fish. In truth, in Old English literary documentation, particularly in poetic literature, there is a notable lack of positive references to food. For instance, as seen, in riddle *#77/74* the human being is described while eating merely to emphasize their greed and lack of moderation; similarly, in other poems, human beings are rarely represented while consuming food; eating is an action for animals, inhuman or nearly human creatures;[192] in convivial scenes, the symbolic representation of mutual loyalty characterizing the warrior society is always entrusted to the sharing of drinking, almost never involving food. The act of sharing a meal can also have symbolic and social significance. In the introduction to his translation of *Genesis* (22–23), Ælfric stigmatizes anyone who refuses to obey the New Testament, judging them unworthy of sharing a meal.

> Gyf hwa wyle nu swa lybban æfter Cristes tocyme, swa swa men leofodon ær Moises æ oþþe under Moises æ, ne byð se man na cristen, ne he furþon wyrðe ne byð þæt him ænig Christen man mid ete.
>
> [If, now, after the arrival of Christ, someone wishes to live as men did before or under Moses' law, he is not a Christian at all, nor he is deserving that any Christian man should dine with him.]

---

192 For example, eight of the twelve lines in *Beowulf* that mention food are about Grendel, while one is about his mother: lines 120b–125; 276–277a; 442–450a; 559–564; 731–736a; 739–745a; 1331b–1333a; 1580–1582; 2078b–2080. Three other passages refer, instead, to the bodies of the deceased consumed by animals: lines 2445b–2449; 2939–2941a; 3024b–3027.

More often than not, however, the act of eating food appears to cause discomfort because it serves a biological purpose shared by men, animals, and monsters.[193]

The eating customs of peoples depicted in *Wonders of the East* are only described when they are seen as exceptional: the giants Hostes (§ 13) and the Donestres (§ 20) are cannibals, while the men in § 28 are unique because they consume honey and raw meat, as do these fish-eating Homodubii. Eating raw food was specifically considered an eccentric practice, alien to shared social customs, and thus was regarded as a sign denoting the inability to assume a conduct in keeping with a codified social context, an important trait to determine if a certain people could be considered human (Friedman, *The Monstrous Races*, 27–32; Neville, 33–35). Anthropologically, regulations on eating practices, that is to say the ways of consuming food, have been discriminating components to determine admissions or exclusions from the community (Adamson, 181–183), and the contrast between raw and cooked has a central place from this perspective.[194]

A further feature questioning the humanity of this Homodubii is provided by the iconographic apparatus: in V, chapter 8 is not accompanied by any picture, but in T the figure meant to represent the entire people is portrayed in the act of biting a fish while being completely naked[195] (f. 100r).

---

193 See Magennis (51–84), who conducted an extensive investigation on the symbolic significance of food-related activities discovered in the Old English literary record. See, also Frantzen's *Food, Eating and Identity in Early Medieval England* (42), which focuses on the appraisal of historical-archaeological evidence and the material component, noticing how: 'The textual network proves too preoccupied with isolating various meanings of the feast and ensuring that its enormously important spiritual significance was not compromised by the material aspects of either food and drinks.'

194 It will be remembered that, according to Lévi-Strauss (43–71), the raw is the natural state of the food, which can evolve in a natural way into the putrid, or in its cultural transformation, the cooked; thus, cooking food becomes a peculiar feature of the human being; the opposition between raw and cooked is an opposition between nature and culture, which is, predictably, elaborated in the many myths in which a founding hero lights a fire to cook meat.

195 The text in *Wonders of the East* does not give any indication, but the *Letter from Alexander to Aristotle* clearly suggests that the same people used to be naked.

The willingness to show a naked body, a violation of modesty, is another element that could be seen as denoting whether a person, or a Plinian race, possesses any reasoning ability, and thus could be seen as human. Firstly, in the formation of human consciousness, the development phase of self-awareness – defined as the ability to reflect on and worry about what others think of us (Miller, 1) – and the increase in signals of embarrassment are predictable stages in child development but not in other living beings. Covering one's nakedness with clothing would thus be a sign of self-awareness, separating man from animal (Friedman, *The Monstrous Races*, 189; Wilcox, 'Naked', 275–309). Furthermore, nudity has a significant moral aspect in the medieval Christian worldview, which *Wonders of the East* participate in, because the naked body symbolically becomes the primary sign of sin. The necessity for mankind to manufacture garments to cover oneself would thus be a result of Adam and Eve's actions, who became conscious of their own nakedness after eating the forbidden fruit. As may also be seen in Ælfric's Old English translation of *Genesis* (III, 7–11):

> And heora begra eagan wurdon geopenode. Hi oncneowon þa þæt hi nacode wæron and siwodon ficleaf and worhton him wædbrec. Eft þa þa God com and hi gehirdon hys stemne, þær he eode on neorxenawange ofer middæg, ða behidde Adam hyne, and his wif eac swa dide, fram Godes gesihþe, onmiddan þam treowe neorxenawanges. God clipode þa Adam and cwæþ: 'Adam, hwær eart þu?' He cwæð: 'Þine stemne ic gehirde, leof, on neorxnawange and ic ondred me, for þam þe ic eom nacod, and ic behidde me'. God cwæð: 'Hwa sæde þe þæt ðu nacod wære, gyf þu ne æte of þam treowe, þe ic þe bebead þæt þu ne æte?'

> [And both their eyes were opened. They realised they were naked, wove fig leaves and made belts for themselves. Then God came and they heard his voice, He was walking in the garden at midday, then Adam hid himself, and his wife did the same, from the sight of God, among the trees of the garden. God called Adam and said: 'Adam, where are you?'. He replied: 'I heard Your voice in the garden, Lord, and I was afraid, because I am naked, and I hid myself'. God said: 'Who told you you were naked if you didn't eat from the tree from which I forbade you to eat?']

Adam justifies his reaction citing a sense of shame, but God's response instantly returns to the subject of the violation of the prescribed restriction: nudity is intrinsically linked to sin. This correlation is made apparent also in *Genesis B* (lines 777b–784a), along with references to the need for prayers and repentance:[196]

        Hwilum to gebede feollon
        sinhiwan somed,   and sigedrihten
        godne gretton   and god nemdon,
780   heofones waldend,   and hine bædon
        þæt hie his hearmsceare   habban mosten,
        georne fulgangan,   þa hie godes hæfdon
783   bodscipe abrocen.   Bare hie gesawon
        heora lichaman.

[Several times the spouses together prostrated themselves in prayer, and turned to the good Lord of victory whom they call God, king of heaven, and implored Him so that they could receive his punishment, which they would have gladly fulfilled, since they had disobeyed the order of God. Naked they saw their bodies.]

T's pictorial cycle depicts all of the monstrous races as unclothed,[197] even in those cases for which the text does not supply clothing details. Conversely, the peoples represented in the last chapters wear brilliantly coloured stoles and dresses.[198] Depicting the monstrous creatures as naked is a conventional choice because it facilitates the display of their anatomical peculiarities, but it works also as a symbol for bestiality, denoting a particular closeness to wilderness and to that animal nature, unable to discern sin, which was believed to characterize those who lived beyond the borders of the Christian world in the medieval Western universe (Friedman, *The Monstrous Races*, 31–32).

---

196 See Ericksen (258): 'The Junius 11 *Genesis* narrative [...] uses literal nakedness to emphasize the need for figurative clothing and defines part of that clothing as confession and penance.'

197 See f. 80r, Cynocephali and Homodubii ichthyophagi; f. 81r, two-faced men; f. 81v, lion-headed men and Hostes; f. 82r, headless men; f. 82v, Homodubii onocentaurs; f. 83v, Donestres and men with big ears; f. 85r, monstrous women.

198 See f. 84r, the priest in the Heliopolis' temple; f. 84v, decent men; f. 85v, men eating raw meat and honey and hospitable men; f. 86v, generous kings and Ethiopians.

Eating raw food and not wearing clothes appear to be presented in *Wonders of the East* as activities incompatible with the idea of humanity proposed in the text; practices alien to a civilized world, and thus closer to wilderness and to an animal realm.

The second monstrous race identified with the denomination Homodubii (§ 17) in the treatise, on the other hand, shares more than merely antisocial behaviours with the animal world:

> Ubi nascuntur Homodubii qui usque ad umbilicum hominis speciem habent, reliquo corpore onagro similes, longis cruribus ut aues, lena uoce: sed hominem cum uiderint longe fugiunt.
>
> Þær beoð kende Homodubii þæt byð twylice. Hi beoþ oð ðene nafelan on menniscum gescape ⁊ syððan on eoseles gescape; hi habbað long sceancan swa fugelas ⁊ liðelice stefne. Gyf hi hwylcne mon on ðam landum ongitað oððe geseoð, þonne feorriað hi ⁊ fleoð.
>
> [From there are born Homodubii, that is 'doubtful men'. They are of a human shape to the navel and then they look like donkeys; they have long bird-like legs and a soft voice. If they see or perceive somebody on their land, they run and fly away.]

The hybrid character of this race is obvious from the outset and is the source of their moniker of 'doubtful men': they have human traits in the upper half of their bodies, but donkey features from the navel down. These creatures can be considered to be members of a broader family of figures halfway between man and horse or man and donkey, they are commonly referred to as onocentaurs in teratological literature. However, in contrast to the customary appearance of onocentaurs, these creatures in *Wonders of the East* have peculiar characteristics: long legs similar to those of a bird and a delicate voice.[199] The text in this chapter contradicts the pictures because the drawings, both in T (f. 82v) and in V (f. 102v),

---

[199] The presence of a gentle voice, as a distinguishing feature, points to another race with a dual nature, half human and half equine, the hippocentaurs, implying a higher level of species mingling. For example, the *Liber Monstrorum* chapter dedicated to them (*De Hippocentauris*, I, vii) depicts their voices and lips as unsuited for human speech: 'Hippocentauri equorum et hominum habent commixtam naturam habent et more ferarum sunt capite setoso, sed ex parte aliqua humanae normae simillimo, quo possunt incipere loqui: sed insueta labia humanae locutioni nullam in verba distinguunt' ('Hippocentaurs have a mixed nature of horse and man and their hairy heads are like beasts, but they are partly similar to the human shape, with

depict the animal with donkey's studded hooves. The illustrative sequence was apparently inserted before the *Mirabilia* underwent the alterations leading to the current text; these changes were not as significant as the discrepancy between the visuals and the words may suggest. The trail of corruption may be reconstructed by comparing this passage to the same chapter in *Lepistle*, which has the numeral 'xii' to indicate the length of the creature's feet. The digit has most likely been lost, and the punctuation in *Mirabilia* has changed. As a point of fact, moving the punctuation and adding the number xii would be enough to make the *Mirabilia* version in T entirely consistent with both the Old French text and the figures depicted in the illustrative sequence (Knock, 184). Compare:

> qui usque ad umbilicum hominis speciem habent. reliquo corpore onagro similes longis pedibus [xii] ut aues lena uoce. (*Mirabilia*, §17)[200]
>
> qui ont fourme domme isques a le boutine et apres fourme dasne sauuage. Il ont .xii. pies de lonc. et souef vois comme oisel (*Lepistle*, XIV)

Unlike the previous episode about the fish-eating people, both the *Epistola Premonis* and the Old French version here concur with the *Mirabilia* in assigning the name Homodubii to the onocentaurs described in this chapter.[201]

As in § 8, the Old English version in the T-text retains the Latin name and adds the gloss intended to clarify its meaning ('þæt byð twylice'); V, on the other hand, has an omission:

> þær beoð cende homo dubii, þ beoð.[202]

Because the missing word is the Old English name for the creatures discussed in the chapter, the ellipsis could be caused by a space left blank for rubrication in the antigraph (Knock, 783). Fulk's (22) edition compensates for the omission by repeating the gloss from § 8: 'þæt byð twi-men'. Mittman and Kim (49), on the other hand, propose focusing on what the

---

which they can start talking: however, their lips, ill-suited for human speech, cannot organize sounds in words').
200 Citation from the T-text diplomatic edition by Knock, 890.
201 The chapter appears solely in group P. The Latin denomination implies that the addition came after the Greek translation. See Knock, 781.
202 Citation from the V-text diplomatic edition by Mittman and Kim, 49.

omission might imply about how people perceived onocentaurs. Beyond the accidental nature of the error, the elision triggers a reading pause, forcing the reader to look at the text a second time; as expressed in V, the sentence – 'þær beoð cende homo dubii þæt beoð' ('there were men born who are') – needs to be reassessed. It appears that such a proposition simply contributes to emphasize the existence of the monstrous creature described: a donkey-man hybrid that may or may not be a human being.

> We can translate 'homo dubii' into twimen, and from there into as many other languages as we might wish, but the pair of double men they describe will never merge from their doubtful status. For this reason, the lipography of the *Wonders* is, perhaps, more meaningful than the 'correct' version in Tiberius. While Tiberius tells us that the double men / men of doubt are, in fact, double men/men of doubt, instead the *Wonders* tells us simply that they are [...] they exist. Their existence confirms an utter absence of certainty about human identity (Mittman and Kim, 49).

The existence of hybrid species, such as Cynocephali and Homodubii, demonstrates a lack of certainty about what may be classified as unequivocally human. Just like any hybrid body, the onocentaur's body is, at the very least, a double body. Half man, half donkey: while inextricably linked, the two components remain in contradiction with each other and offer no chance of classification. More than in its textual description, the onocentaur in V's illustration (f. 102v) appears to emphasize this lack of distinctions. The frontal angle through which the creature is depicted makes it difficult to recognize the second pair of legs, a crucial aspect for distinguishing between human and donkey. Therefore, due to both the readily apparent abnormalities and the difficulty in identifying the less obvious ones, the depictions of these onocentaurs pose a threat to and compromise the integrity of the human body, which is constantly compared to the hybrid body (Mittman and Kim, 79–84).

Ichthyophagi and onocentaurs, as described in *Wonders of the East*, share no traits other than the Homodubii designation. The term, which describes the onocentaurs in all versions of the P group, may have originated as a simple attribute in relation to the human-donkey hybrid and, later, a scribe of an antigraph version of the *Mirabilia* may have extended the designation to the people depicted in § 8 through dittography or in an attempt to rationalize an incomprehensible reading.

Homodubii becomes an appropriate denomination to characterize two such disparate people merely because whoever composed the manuscript expresses hesitation in assigning human characteristics to both groups. According to this logic, the appellation would be adequate to define every and each monster population depicted in the treatise.

5.2 The dehumanization of the hybrid women

Among these *almost*-human peoples, there is a breed of hybrids counting only women; § 27 describes a race of females with boar tusks and a bovine tail. Just like other hybrid peoples, their monstrous character is determined by the violation of several boundaries: these monstrous women not only allude to the overlapping of the human and animal categories, but they also let emerge an anxiety for the gender distinctions between male and female. They seem to express in a monstrous form the generalized association between the feminine and the natural sphere.[203]

Female creatures represent a small portion of the monstrosities described within the text, which, otherwise, implies that monstrous peoples are mostly masculine.[204] Besides the creatures portrayed in § 27, there is only another female race; the preceding chapter, § 26, illustrates

---

203 On this, see the aforementioned work by Plumwood, *Feminism and the Master of Nature*, especially the first two chapters: 'Feminism and Ecofeminism' and 'Dualism: The Logic of Colonisation'; see also the previous and fundamental essay by Ortner, 68–87.

204 The first sentence of each paragraph frequently refers to conception and birth of each people represented, implying the existence of both sexes for each species; however, while the text generally alludes to the entire population, each creature is depicted in isolation (with the sole exception of the Ethiopians, represented in § 32); without any reference to sex or age distinctions, it is therefore impossible to imagine these people in a social structure. Nonetheless, T's illustrations often display the male primary sexual features (f. 82v, f. 80r, f. 83v); implying that the monster was typically perceived as masculine. See Oswald, 'Unnatural Women', 1–33 and Lendinara, 'Mostruosità femminili', 209–210.

a people of bearded women who wear horse-skin clothes and hunt wild animals with the help of other fierce beasts:[205]

> Circa hunc locum nascuntur mulieres barbas habentes usque ad mamillas, pelliculas equorum ad uestimentum habentes, et hae uenatrices maxime sunt: pro canibus tigres et leopardos nutriunt, et omnia genera bestiarum quae in eodem monte nascuntur cum illis uenantur.
>
> Ymb þa stowe beoð wif akenned, ða habbað beardas swa side oð heora breost, ⁊ horses hyda hi habbað him to hrægle gedon. Þa syndan huntigystran swiðe genemde, ⁊ fore hundum tigras ⁊ leopardos þæt hi fedað þæt syndan þa kenestan deor. ⁊ ealra ðæra wildeora kynn, þæra þe on ðære dune akenede beoð, þæt hi gehuntigaþ.
>
> [Women are born around these places, with long beards reaching up to their breasts, dressed in horse hide clothing. They are known as hunters all over the world, and instead of dogs, they rear the most fearsome creatures, tigers and leopards. They hunt all manner of wild beasts that are born in the highlands.]

Androgynous both in appearance, as evidenced by the long beard – a strong indicator of virility – and in behaviour – hunting is an activity associated with the male gender[206], these wild women manifest their monstrosity by dissolving the differences between male and female, as well as altering society customs by being accompanied by tigers and leopards instead of dogs, and by using horses to produce raw hides.[207]

---

205 Tigers, lions and lynxes in V: 'tigras ⁊ leon ⁊ loxas' (ff. 105r–105v); tigers and leopards in T: 'tigras ⁊ leopardos' (f. 84r).

206 *Hundicge* (V) and *huntigystre* (T) are both feminine forms found only in these texts; the rarity of these occurrences may prompt us to consider the distinctiveness of the costume: unlike the monstrous women of the East, Western women do not go on hunting trips. Furthermore, in the translation of 'cum illis uenantur', V's interpretation differs slightly from T's faithful rendition 'þæt hi gehuntigaþ'. V reads 'mid heora scin*** þæt hy tohuntiaþ' ('which they hunt with their magic'). The stem *scin-* could be from *scīnlac* (Sisam, 81) and it should mean magic or sorcery. It could be an inaccurate translation of *cum illusio* mixed up with *cum illis* as read in the Latin text. On this see Knock, 743. For more on the androgynous ambiguity of these female-hunters see Oswald, *Monsters*, 53–58, and Lendinara ('Mostruosità femminili', 216–217) who draws a link with the Amazons of classical mythology.

207 Banham and Faith argue that in Anglo-Saxon England horse skin could have been used for clothing based on the particular marks of wounds discovered on the equine bones; yet, as is well known, the manufacture of textile fibres was predominantly provided by sheep's wool. The horse, on the other hand, was primarily used as a form of transportation in a personal, domestic, or even commercial capacity. The

Conversely, the monstrous ladies described in § 27, just like the Cynocephali and the onocentaurs, are monstrous because they are defined by the aggregation of body parts derived from several animal species; they have boar tusks, camel feet, and an ox tail:

> Et alie sunt mulieres ibi, dentes aprorum habentes, capillos usque ad talos, in lumbis caudas boum, quae sunt altae pedum .xiii., specioso corpore quasi marmore candido, pedes habentes cameli, dentes asininos, quarum multae ex ipsis ceciderunt pro sua obscenitate a magno nostro Macedone Alexandro quia illas uiuas adprehendere non potuit, occidit, ideo quia sunt publicato corpore et inhonesto.

> Ðonne sindon oðre wif þa habbað eoferes tucxas. ⁊ feax oð helan side. ⁊ on lendenum oxan tægl. þa wif syndon ðreottyne fota lange ⁊ heora lic bið on marmorstanes hwitnysse. ⁊ hi habbað olfenda fet ⁊ eoferes teð. for heora mycelnysse hie gefelde wurdon fram ðam mycclan macedoniscan alexander þa he hi lifiende gefon ne mihte, þa acwealde he hi for ðam hi syndon æwisce on lichoman ⁊ unweorþe.[208]

> [There are other women who have boar tusks and hair down to their toes and an oxtail on their loins. These women are thirteen feet tall and their bodies are of marble whiteness. And they have camel's feet and boar's teeth. For their massiveness they were killed by Alexander the Great of Macedonia. He killed them because he couldn't capture them alive, because they have unworthy and shameful bodies.]

The creature's animal features increase and evolve during textual transmission. In a variant of the P group, recorded in the *Epistola Premonis*, the women acquire donkey's teeth ('dentes asinorum') instead of boar's teeth ('aprorum dentes', 'dentes aprinos') described elsewhere. Both readings are preserved in V's Old English version, thus giving to these women both boar tusks, 'eoferes tuxas', and donkey's teeth, 'eoseles teð'. The repercussion of this duplication in information may be seen in the Old French version – which retains the reference to the donkey but replaces the teeth with another characteristic, the ears – and in both *Mirabilia* and Old English text in T, which describe teeth and tusks as

---

horse's relevant position in the symbolic hierarchy of animals was primarily tied to its affiliation with the nobility for pursuits such as hunting, horse racing, and, most importantly, the arts of war. See Banham and Faith, 79–82 and 118–121.

208 In this specific occasion, it was decided to refer to the diplomatic edition edited by Knock (883), which retains the manuscript reading 'mycelnysse' rather than Orchard's emendation 'unclænesse', proposed for analogy with the Latin *obscenitas*.

being comparable to those of a boar ('eofere tuxcas' and 'eoferes teð'; 'dentes aprinos' and 'aprinos').[209]

The main textual difference between the insular texts and the corresponding chapters in the continental tradition is the mention of Alexander the Great.[210] The writings in the F Group and the *Epistola Parmoenis* include no reference to the Macedonian leader, and the massacre of the women is imputed to ordinary soldiers:

> In eodem monte silve sunt, in quibus nascuntur et alie mulieres, aprorum dentes habentes, capillos usque ad talos et in lumbis caudam quasi bos, alte pedes vii, reliquum corpus pilosum quasi structio et camelus. Propter vero desiderium cupivi ut aliquas caperem, atque vivas Romanniae adducerem. Tres autem comiti armati ut unam occiderent quippe ut evadere potuissent diu multoque pugnaverunt (*Letter of Fermes*, XXII).

> [In the same mountain, there are woods, on which are born other women, having wild boars' teeth, hair up to the ankles, and at the loins a tail like an ox; (they are) seven feet high, (and have) the rest of the body hairy like ostrich and camel. On account of my desire, however, I wanted to catch some, and to bring them alive back in Romania. But (it took) three armed comrades to kill one, because they fought for a long time in order to escape.]

> Is eisdam montibus silve sunt, in quibus nascuntur et alie mulieres, aprorum dentes habentes, capillos usque ad talos et in lumbis causa bobis, alte pedes xii, reliquum autem corpus pilosum, quasi strutio et camelus. (*Feramen Rex*, XXII).

---

209 B omits the second 'aprinos'. See Knock, 757.
210 Alexander has always been portrayed as an insatiable conqueror in classical and medieval legends. In *The Letter from Alexander to Aristotle*, the Macedonian warrior appears inclined to observe with curiosity the spectacle offered by the marvellous peoples; see § 3 of the *Letter*: 'Seo eorðe is to wundrienne hwæt heo ærest oþþe godra þinga cenne, oððe eft þara yfelra, þe heo þæm sceawigendum is æteowed. Hio is cennende þa fulcuþan wildeora ⁊ wæstma ⁊ wecga oran, ⁊ wunderlice wyhta, þa þing eall þæm monnum þe hit geseoð ⁊ sceawigað wæron uneþe to gewitanne for þæere missenlicnisse þara hiowa' ('The earth arouses wonder first and foremost for the good things it produces, then for the bad ones, through which it reveals itself to observers. It is the producer of well-known wild beasts, stones, metals, and wondrous creatures, many of which are difficult to comprehend for people who see and observe them due to the variety of their shapes'). For a more in-depth analysis of the characterization differences between the Alexander of the *Letter* and *Wonders of the East*, see Joy, 209–229.

[In the same mountains, there are woods, on which are born other women, having wild boar's teeth, hair up to the ankles and on the loins a ox's tail; (they are) twelve feet high, (and have) the rest of the body hairy like ostrich and camel.]

Sunt et aliae ibidem mulieres, dentes aprinos habentes, capillos usque talos in lumbis et caudas habentes boum. Altae sunt, speciosae corpore, quasi marmore candido, pedes habentes camelinos: propter quarum inspectionem tres ex his occiderunt socii nostri, quoniam vivas prendere non potuerunt. (*Epistola Parmoenis*, XXII).

[There are other women, having donkey's teeth, hair up to the ankles and having a tail of an ox on the loins. They are tall and have a beautiful body, like pure white marble, and feet like camels; because of this inspection, our comrades killed three of them who could not be caught alive.]

Thus, the presence of Alexander appears to be an innovation introduced in some texts in the P group:

Sunt enim et aliae mulieres Rubro mari proximae, capillos usque ad talos habentes et in lumbis caudas boum, statura pedum tredecim, cum specioso corpore vel ut marmor, quae pedes camelorum et dentes asinorum habent; et ex his decem occidit Alexander magnus, quia vivas eas capere non poterat. (*Epistola Premonis*, XXII).

[There are also other women, close to the Red Sea, having hair up to the ankles and an ox's tail on the loins, thirteen feet of height, with a beautiful or marble-like body; they have camels' feet and donkeys' teeth; and Alexander the Great killed ten of them, because he couldn't catch them alive.]

Et la sont autres femmes qui ont dens de saingler. et les kaulas lonz iusques au talon. et ont keues de buef et .xiiii. de lonc. et sont ossi blankes que marbres. et ont blaus cors. et pies de kamel. et oreilles dasne. Nos gens en tuerent .ii. et li grans alexandres ne les peut prendre vives. mais il les ochist. (*Lepistle*, XXII)

[And there are other women that have boar's teeth and hair up to the ankles, and they have an ox's tail and are fourteen feet in length and they are as white as marble and have pale bodies and camel's feet and donkey's ears. Our people killed two of them and Alexander the Great could not catch them alive, but he killed them.]

The Macedonian leader was already mentioned at the beginning of *Wonders* in association to the building of some enormous monuments (§ 2), but in this chapter he assumes the role of the Western explorer, thus representing the point of view of the reader who does not seem to recognize any form of humanity in the monstrous women; their animalized body appears to be perceived as a danger that can only be overcome through complete annihilation.

In the context of *Wonders*, it is possible to speculate that every monstrous people could be seen as the result of an observation point that supports an animalizing perception of anything that appears unusual. As seen, even though Christianity claimed that all persons, no matter their physical or cultural differences, were equally human, as explained by Augustine (*De Civitate Dei*, XVI, viii–ix), some categories were perceived as less human than others. The notion of *bestial men* was born in the Greek world as a result of a conceptual shift between the idea of slave, considered as a figure next to animality, and the concept of barbarian. This semantic contiguity permitted the developing of ideas concerning the bestiality of the foreigners (Volpato, ch. 1; Salisbury, 133). The use of animal analogies and metaphors in regard to otherwise human creatures can be viewed as a mental strategy employed to deny the other's humanity; in other words, it could be considered a form of dehumanization.[211] As observed, the text considers each monstrous people as part of a *manncynn*; yet, affiliation with animalistic elements results in a partial loss of the status of 'human'. Dehumanized people are generally seen as vulgar and amoral, as well as unable to function in society (Haslam, 252–264).[212] The hybridity that defines these women and all the other

---

211 Dehumanization refers to both a psychological process and a social issue. As defined by Volpato: 'Deumanizzare significa negare l'umanità dell'altro – individuo o gruppo – introducendo un'asimmetria tra chi gode delle qualità prototipiche dell'umano e chi ne è considerato privo o carente' ('Dehumanizing is rejecting the humanity of the other – individual or group – by introducing an asymmetry between those who possess paradigmatic human qualities and those who are judged lacking or completely missing them'). Volpato, ch. 1.

212 Consider how, relating the origins of the English nation from two opposing perspectives, the works of Bede and Gildas refuse to acknowledge the existence of a median space between Britons and Germanic peoples and highlight, in their narratives, the opposing population's bestial and monstrous characters. Gildas depicts the Saxon 'invaders' as wolves in a pen, eager to devour any sheep that crosses their path. A few lines later, the analogy to wolves is followed by a reference to other predators, reinforcing their ferinity and linguistic extraneity. The Saxons are the perilous children of a barbarous lioness who leaps from her den (see Gildas, *De Excidio Britanniae*, XXIII, 1). In his *Historia Ecclesiastica*, Bede, on the other hand, attributes bestial cruelty to the British king Cadwallon and his people, accusing them of having waged war against King Edwin of Northumbria, causing his death, without sparing either women or innocent children (Bede, *Historia Ecclesiastica Gentis Anglorum*, II, 20, 2).

hybrid races depicted in the treatise could be the inevitable outcome of this viewpoint, of medieval European ethnocentrism that sees any other population as inferior.

Significantly, however, in an otherwise detached and descriptive narrative, the hybrid women of § 27 are the only monstrous people to face an explicit moral censorship. Even the Hostes (§ 13) and the Donestres (§ 20), two anthropophagous races, a danger for any traveller, receive a more tolerant treatment. As a result, we can infer the presence of a discriminant factor separating these hybrid women from other monstrous peoples. The text appears to support the notion that Alexander's outburst of violence was caused by the presence of a sexual threat. Compared with the chapter in the *Epistola Premonis* and the Old French version, the *Mirabilia* provide a justification for the Macedonian king's actions. The text mentions that these women must be killed because of the obscenity ('pro sua obscenitate') of their bodies labelled as 'publicato', 'public' or 'that is devoted to prostitution',[213] and 'inhonesto', 'dishonest',[214] deficient in honesty and contemptible.

If it were not for a single variant that could modify the reading of the section, the two Old English versions would appear to be basically equivalent to the Latin text. The adjectives *ǣwisc* and *unweorþ*, which, respectively, translate the Latin *pūblicātŭs* and *ĭnhŏnestus*, convey the same idea of indecency associated with the monstrous women's bodies. According to the *DOE*, *ǣwisc* implies a lack of modesty in its various meanings of 'shameless, indecent, foul'; for example, it is used as an element for compound words in reference to the figure of the tempting woman; in the poetic version of *Genesis A* (line 896), after persuading Adam to eat the forbidden fruit, Eve is designated as 'ides æwiscmod'

---

213 Among other meanings, *publicare* could refer to 'expose oneself to the public use' thus 'prostitute oneself'; see Plautus, *Bacchides* (4, 8, 22): 'corpus publicat'. See *Forcellini Lex*, s.v. 'pūblĭco'.

214 Forcellini's *Lexicon* defines *ĭnhŏnestus*: '1. Stricto sensu est turpis, inhonorus, foedus, *vergognoso, disonorato, disonesto* [...] 2. Latiori sensu ponitur pro sordido, *deformi, brutto, sporco*'. Thus, it means 'shameful, dishonest' but also 'deformed, ugly, sordid'. See Terentius, *Eunuchus* (II, iii, 65): 'Illum ne, obsecro, inhonestum hominem, quem mercatus est heri, senem, mulierem?'. See *Forcellini Lex*, s.v. 'ĭnhŏnestus'.

('an indecent woman' or 'a woman with a shameless soul').[215] *Unweorþ* can refer to something that is 'worthless' or 'of little value', as well as something that is 'unworthy' or 'undeserving'. It is frequently employed in translation for both *vilis* and *indignus*.[216] The two Old English texts, however, diverge from the *Mirabilia* because, in lieu of the Latin 'pro sua obscenitate', the Old English texts read 'for heora mycelnysse' ('because of their massiveness'). According to both Gibb and Knock, the different reading is due to confusion between the vertical strokes of the first letters of *micelness* 'greatness, exaggerated size' and *unclænness* 'uncleanness, impurity, obscenity',[217] most likely an original reading with a closer meaning to the Latin *obscēnĭtas*.[218]

Regardless of any further conjecture, the presence of this discrepancy between the Old English *micelness* and the Latin *obscēnĭtas* prompts us to consider a possible interpretative inconsistency of the passage, revealed in the iconographic apparatus. The depictions in V and T highlight the physical qualities of this monstrous race through different

---

215 On the difference in meaning between *ǣwisc* and *ǣwisc-mōd*, Powell (160) notes: 'Admittedly, *ǣwisc* and *ǣwiscmod* seem to encompass somewhat different semantic fields: while *ǣwisc* seems to describe an innate and exteriorly observable characteristic of things, *ǣwiscmod* suggest the interior condition of a person who has been perverted by *ǣwisc* things. This distinction aside, women often seem to be associated with shame in some way and, whether or not forms of the word *ǣwisc* are used of them, they are more often represented as causing shame through their temptations than as being ashamed.' As a noun, finally, *ǣwisc* occurs in the Old English glosses of Aldhelm's *De Virginitate* as a gloss for *obscēnĭtas* (Napier, 113, 161 and 167).
216 See *ASD*, s.v. 'unweorþ': 'of no value; of no dignity, little esteemed; unworthy, not of sufficient merit; worthless, bad, contemptible, despicable, ignoble; ignominious, dishonouring'. See, for instance, the Old English translation of the Benedictine Rule (VII, 7): 'Gif munuc hine sylfne yttran and unweorðran talaþ ðonne ænigne oþerne' ('If a monk recognise himself as inferior and unworthy of anybody else'); see also Ælfric's translation of the *Cura Pastoralis*: 'Sua Sua Saul s[e] cyning, æresð he fleah ðæt rice, & tealde hine selfne his suiðe unwierðne' ('Just as king Saul, he firstly fled the kingdom and saw himself as very unworthy').
217 See *ASD*, s.v. 'unclǣnness': '1. in a physical sense, uncleanness, impurity, foulness, squalor [...] 2. in a moral sense, uncleanness, impurity, obscenity'.
218 See Gibb, 171 and Knock, 757. Both Orchard (see section, 5.2, n. 208), and Fulk (28) emend with 'unclennesse'.

modalities, and appear to reflect two separate assessments of what is seen as shameful and terrifying in these women.

V – which, as previously seen, includes only the Old English version – depicts a woman with her gigantic breasts almost completely exposed; her portrayal makes clearly discernible the boar's tusks, the camel's hooves and a huge tail projecting from her right side (f. 105v). Through the representation of powerful arms and legs, the drawing conveys the idea of a size out of the ordinary; moreover, the woman wields a stick or a club in her right hand: her entire appearance is frightening. The danger in this image is associated with the risk that these monsters will physically overrun and hurt the traveller (Powell, 150–151).

However, the artwork in T – which includes the Latin text with the reading 'obscenitate', as well as the Old English text – seems to suppress any major bestial feature while accentuating the femininity of these creatures. The woman depicted is a thin, unclothed figure discreetly covered by her flowing hair; overall, her tusks and hooves look to be extremely minimized. Her bovine tail appears in a prominent position, but is dramatically relocated on the back of the figure, in contrast to the text's information, which put it ambiguously on the loins; a correction that reveals a certain anxiety on the artist's part with this phallic protrusion on an otherwise female creature (f. 85r).[219]

---

219 The Latin noun *lumbus*, usually used in the plural, denotes the muscular regions on the sides of the spine, although it can also refer to hips and kidneys. However, already in classical Latin, *lumbi* is used in relation to the sexual sphere; it frequently appears to describe the necessary movements to copulate. Consider Catullus' *Carme XVI*, v. 11: 'duros nequeunt mouere lumbos' ('who can't move their loins'); see also in Martial's *Epigrams* (V, lxxviii, vv. 28–29) 'nec de Gadibus inprobis puellae / vibrabunt sine fine prurientes / lascivos docili tremore lumbos' ('neither dissolute girls from Cadiz, with their infinite lust, will shake in sweet rhythm their lascivious loins'). The lumbar region was thus regarded to be the part of the body in which sexual desire was born, as evidenced also by Isidore (*Etymologies*, XI, i, 98): 'Lumbi ob libidinis lasciviam dicti, quia in viris causa corporeae volupatatis in ipsis est, sicut in umilico feminis' ('The loins are thus called from the lasciviousness of lust, because in males the cause of bodily pleasure is located there, just as in women it is in the navel'). On the definition of *lumbus*, see *Forcellini Lex*, s.v. 'lumbus' and Adams, 48. Old English *lendenu* (pl.) is often used to indicate the kidneys, but, in some occasions, it is also employed to denote the seat of desire in forms akin to Latin *lumbi*. In a homily for the 'Commons of Virgins', (*Catholic Homilies II*), Ælfric prompts the correct reading of a verse from the *Gospel of Luke* (12:35),

The hybrid woman depicted in § 27 could thus be viewed as a perverse figure who, by returning the subject to the distinction between male and female, as well as the distinction between human and animal, would embody the abject according to Kristeva's definition, that is, would push towards confrontation with the limits of the self and pose a threat to its integrity.[220] Alexander and his followers react so brutally to their presence because they recognize the frailty of these boundaries; this awareness necessitates a cleansing by highly violent means.

As Joy (220) explained:

> The readers of the Old English *Wonders* may very well have been drawn to the image of these women as both frightening and attractive, leading to feelings of both sexual desire (or sexual astonishment), followed by feelings of violent revulsion, the relief of which [...] might have been provided by Alexander's decisive act of execution.

---

urging his audience to stay chaste: 'On þam ymbgyrdum lendenum is se mægðhad and on þam byrnendum leohtfatum sind þa godan weorc to understandenne' ('The belt on the loins is the maidenhood, and the lit lights are to be understood as [symbol of] good work'). Similarly, in an exegesis of *Exodus* (12:11) for an Easter homily (*Catholic Homilies II*), the abbot of Eynsham explains: 'On lendenum is seo galnys þæs lichaman' ('The lust of the body is on the loins'); the link is also made clear in a pastoral letter to Wulfstan (II, 28): 'On þam lendenum is, swaswa we leornigað on bocum, seo fule galnys and we sceolan fæstlice þa gewriðan and gewealdan us to clænnysse' ('As we learn from the books, the vile lust is on the loins and we must bind them tightly and govern ourselves towards purity'). As Oswald pointed out, the oxtail placed on the seat of sexual desire could have caused discomfort in the artist tasked with depicting the image of these monstrous women. Even though there is no open censure in this case, the caudal protuberance is significantly repositioned in a more usual, and hence less ambiguous, location. The hermaphroditic traits of hybrid women are thoroughly analysed by Oswald in 'Unnatural Women', 18–22 and in *Monsters*, 59–63.

220 'Abject. It is something rejected from which one does not part, from which one does not protect oneself as from an object. Imaginary uncanniness and real threat, it beckons to us and ends up engulfing us. It is thus not lack cleanliness or health that causes abjection but what disturbs identity, system, order, what does not respect borders, positions, rules. The in-between, the ambiguous, the composite' (Kristeva, 5).

If the hybrid races described in *Wonders of the East* can be regarded as a threat to the preservation of the boundaries delimiting the human identity of those who observe them, the danger of this provoked threat is perceived as greater in the case of monstrous women, because they also question the distinctions between masculine and feminine.

6. Alien and Familiar

The treatise on the *Wonders of the East* is, as seen, the extant product of a long textual transmission. Most peoples and creatures depicted originated in the travel literature of Hellenistic origin, however, the text describes as well some 'wonders' that changed significantly because of textual corruptions, mistakes, revisions, and different evaluations about the copied text made by the several scribes alternating in the process. In particular, the portrayal of the lion-headed giants (§ 12) and the Donestres (§ 20) underwent what could be called an anthropomorphizing evolution. The earliest sources on these two chapters described creatures that were considered simply animals: in one case hippopotamuses, and in the other hyenas and crocodiles. These original animal forms were partially lost in the textual tradition, giving rise to these new human-animal hybrids. As if they were a crystallization of the inevitable textual alteration, these hybrids, by being both familiar and destructive, exemplify what can be defined an 'anxiety for change', because the hybrid body continuously challenges borders of the Self, by holding it together with the Other.

6.1 Anthropomorphizing the animal: Lion-headed giants and Donestres

Among the various human-animal hybrids described in *Wonders*, § 12 portrays a race of lion-headed giants. Their look, typified by the accumulation of mismatched human and animal parts, appears to be the consequence of the overlaying of interpolations, errors, and corrections in the textual transmission.

> Item Ciconia in Gallia nascuntur homines tripertito colore, quorum capita capita leonum, longi pedibus .xx., ore amplissimo sicut uannum; hominem cum

cognouerint, aut si qui persequatur, longe fugiunt et sanguinem sudant: hi putantur homines fuisse.

Ciconia in Gallia hatte þæt land þær beoð men acenned þreosellices hiwes þara heafda beoð gemona swa leona heafdo, ꞇ hi beoð twentiges fota lange ꞇ hi habbað micelne muð swa fann. Gif hi hwylcne man on ðam landum ongitað oððe geseoþ oððe him hwylc folligende bið, þonne feorriað hi ꞇ fleoð, ꞇ blode þæt hi swætað. Þas beoð menn gewenede.

[There is a land in Gallia that is called Ciconia where men are born with a triple form, their head have manes like lionheads, and they are tall twenty feet long and they have mouths as big as fan. If they see or recognize someone in those lands, or if someone is following them, then they withdraw and flee away and they sweat blood. It is thought they are men.]

As can be observed from the extant chapters in the P group, these creatures were associated to hippos:[221]

et quadrupedia colorem equorum, pedes leonum, ore amplissimo sicut vannum, habentia regunt: verum hos si aliquis sequitur, longe fugiunt et sanguinem sudant. Hos potamos appellant. (*Epistola Parmoenis*, XV)

[and four-footed animals, with the complexion of horses, feet of lions and a mouth as big as a fan, govern those possessions: but if somebody follows them, they flee for a long time and sweat blood. They are called *potamos*.]

Nascuntur etiam ibi animalia triplici coloris, quorum capita sunt leonum, longa pedum decem et octo, ore amplissimo; homines cum viderint, si eos aliquis insequatur, longe fugiunt, ita ut sanguine sudent: hyppotami appellantur. (*Epistola Premonis*, XVII, 4)

[There are also born animals of a threefold complexion, whose heads are lion-like, (they are) eighteen feet tall, with a very large mouth; when they see men, if somebody follows them, they flee for a long time, until they sweat blood: they are called hippopotamuses.]

Apres en vne region qui a non galle en le quele naiscent tripaire. qui ont testes de lion. et .xiiii. pies de lonc. Et ont si grant guele quil i porroit bien vn van. Sil voient homme qui les sieuent il fuient bien loins. Et suent sanc. on les apele ypotames. (*Lepistle*, XV)

---

221 The F group's reading, which labels these monsters as ἱπποφάγοι, 'hippophages', or 'horse meat eaters' (see Liddell–Scott–Jones' *Greek-English Lexicon* (*LSJ*), s.v. 'ἱπποφάγοι'), is a later one, resulting from the displacement of the term assigned to the headless men in the next chapter in the P group. See *Letter of Fermes*, XVII, 4, and *Feramen Rex*, XV. See Knock, 700.

[After this, in a region where there isn't any gall, there are born tripartite (creatures) who have lion's heads and are fourteen feet long. And they have such big mouth that they could be a fan. If they see a man who follows them, they flee very far. And they sweat blood. They are called *ypotames*.]

The description of the physical traits to be assigned to the animal differs across the two branches of the tradition. The creature in the *Letter of Fermes* has the skin of a horse[222] and the feet of a lion, as does the being depicted in the *Epistola Parmoenis*, which stands out from the rest of the writings in the P group. In fact, in this branch of the tradition, it is the creature's head, rather than its feet, to possess leonine features. Furthermore, any allusion to horses is removed. Finally, the mantle colour of the animal is described as 'triplice', in the *Epistola Premonis* and 'tripertito'[223] in the *Mirabilia*.

In relation to this tripartite nature of the animal, it is possible that the Latin *Letter from Alexander to Aristotle* (§ 27), might have influenced the textual transmission:

> Belua noui generis prosiliuit serrato tergo, duo capita habens, alterum leoni simile, hippotamo pectore, corcodrilli gerens alterum simillimum duris munitum dentibus.
>
> [A beast of a new kind appeared with a dented back, having two heads, one looking like a lion, the breast of a hippopotamus and the other of the genre of the crocodiles, armed with hard teeth.]

In this case, too, the new beast that Alexander encounters on his journey is depicted through a comparison among three different animals: one of its two heads resembles a lion, the second a crocodile, and its chest a hippopotamus.[224]

---

222 The overlap of hippopotamus and horse can be explained by traditions formed around the figure of the hippopotamus, which are linked to the literal meaning of the Greek term, ἱπποπόταμος, from ἵππος 'horse' and πόταμος 'river' (see *LSJ*, s.v. 'ἵππος' and 'πόταμος').
223 T's image (f. 81v) appears to depict a humanoid figure with a golden-brown mane, a grey-pink upper half of the torso, and a lighter lower part. This is the description provided by Knock (694), who conducted the analysis on the manuscript; nevertheless, the quality of the image provided by the British Library does not allow to notice clearly this distinction in tone.
224 Knock (692–693) accurately observes that the juxtaposition of a hippopotamus and a lion's head is too bold to suggest a parallel and separate genesis.

What plainly differentiates the lion-headed giants in *Wonders* from the rest of the tradition just examined is their human affiliation. The introductory formulas in T and V – 'nascuntur homines', 'þær beoð men acennned' – declare their humanity from the start, whereas the corresponding chapter in the *Letter of Fermes* begins introducing some beasts, 'bestiae', the *Epistola Premonis* refers to animals, 'animalia', and the other versions of the P group do not specify anything in this section of the text. The *Mirabilia*'s antigraph might have been forced to replace 'bestiae' and 'animalia' with 'homines' as a necessary provision to reconstruct the meaning of the chapter's final sentence, which from an original 'hyppotami appellantur', as we read in the *Epistola Premonis*, becomes 'hi putantur homines fuisse' in the version attested in the *Mirabilia*. The textual corruption appears to have occurred in stages: the first syllable of 'hyppotami' may have separated from the remainder of the word and then been classified as a pronoun. The *Epistola Parmoenis*' version 'hos potamos' represents an intermediate stage. The entire expression is replaced by a verb in *Mirabilia*, 'putantur' with the addition of the predicate 'homine fuisse'. The Old English translation, 'þas beoð menn gewenede',[225] effectively ties up a complete reinterpretation of the passage.[226]

It seems thus clear that a gradual anthropomorphizing process was completed in the insular manuscripts in order to resolve the interpretative quandary that developed as a result of the chapter closure error. The hippopotamuses into lion-headed men in § 12 are not the only beings depicted in *Wonders of the East* to experience anthropomorphization. The beings in § 11, for example, could have gone through a similar process. The related versions of group F narrate a legend about storks, who were formerly men with the ability to change their shape, but the animals

---

225 Instead of T's 'gewenede', here V reads 'gewende'. According to Mittman and Kim (79–80), this variant should not be interpreted as preterite tense of *gewēnan*, 'to hope, expect, suppose, think, esteem' (see *ASD*, s.v. 'gewēnan'), rather as preterite of *gewendan*, 'to turn, change, translate, incline, bring about' or 'to turn [one's self], change, go, return' (see *ASD*, s.v. 'gewendan'). Thus, 'þas beoð men gewende' could be rendered as 'these are changed men', rather than 'it is thought they are men'. *Gewendan*'s past participle conveys an idea of movement and transformation, which could be seen as a warning: metamorphosis from one species to the other, or degeneration, is indeed possible.
226 For an accurate reconstruction see Knock, 687–702.

depicted in group P have lost all the features relating to the migratory birds, they are classified as two-faced white giants:

> Nascuntur et ibi homines habentes staturam pedum .XV., corpus habentes candidum, duas in uno habentes capite facies, rubra genua, naso longo, capillis nigris; cum tempus gignendi fuerit, sui nauibus transferuntur in Indiam et ibi prolem reddunt.
>
> Ðær beoð akende men, ða beoð fiftyne fota lange ⁊ hi habbað hwit lic ⁊ tu neb on anum heafde, fet ⁊ cneowu swiðe read, ⁊ lange nosu ⁊ sweart feax. Þonne hi kennan willað, þonne farað hi on scipum to Indeum, ⁊ þær hyra gecynd on weorold bringað.
>
> [There are born men, who are fifteen feet tall and they have white body and two necks on one head, feet and knees very red, a long nose and dark hair. When they want to give birth, then they travel on ship towards India and there they bring their offspring to the world.]

These textual changes, from animals to monstrous human beings with bestial traits, are unmistakably the result of copying errors in the textual transmission; however, it can be assumed that in conjecturing the lost meanings, the copyists, compiling the different versions, might have found more likely and comprehensible the existence of these peoples than that of the animals originally described. Returning to § 12, for example, the hippopotamuses described in the alleged *Letter of Pharasmanes* must have been viewed as remote and impossible to imagine. Despite being transported to Rome for the first time by Marcus Aemilius Scaurus[227] and thus known in medieval Europe for a long time, hippopotamuses remained a distant and rare vision.

As it has been shown for the Old English riddles, techniques of personification and anthropomorphization are often unavoidable in works of fiction with animals as central characters: the human approach of seeing and exploring the world is, after all, anthropocentric by nature.[228] Because the animal experience is forbidden to man, the only way to comprehend it is to transfer human voice and human emotions to animals. The anthropomorphization of some creatures throughout the textual tradition of

---

227 According to Pliny's account. See *Naturalis Historiae*, VIII, 26.
228 Fudge (89) justifies the centrality of anthropomorphic narratives in human perception of animals as the realization of an essential desire for knowledge: if these narratives did not exist, humans would not have the possibility of coming into contact with, and thus attempting to understand, the surrounding world. On this, see also Budiansky, 16–23.

Wonders of the East might be explained by similar logics: it could be the result of a lack of imagination combined with a desire for knowledge. If we consider the human perspective to be the natural position from which man observes the world, one might imagine that, in a context where monstrous races are an integral part of culture, a scribe forced to conjecture to what or to whom the meaning of a descriptive detail refers, might believe that the interpretation is somehow linked to elements belonging to the known dimension of the human.

Any creature formed as a result of this progressive anthropomorphization, precisely because it retains animal vestiges, combines categories of familiarity and strangeness. In this regard, the case of the Donestres is interesting (§ 20); these monsters combine the original features of the crocodile, the hyena and its hybrid offspring, the crocotta (Lendinara, 'I donestri', 259–273).

The term Donestre occurs for the first time in the *Mirabilia* and *Wonders of the East* to describe a monstrous race that lives on an island in the Red Sea and lures every unfortunate visitor to eat them by exploiting an extraordinary ability to speak all the languages of the world. Only the visitor's head is spared from this act of violent consumption, for which the creature sheds tears of repentance at the end of the meal.

> Itaque insula est in rubro mari. In qua hominum genus est quod apud nos appellatur donestre. quasi divine. a capite usque ad umbilicum quasi homines. reliquo corpore similitudine humana nationum linguis loquentes. Cum alieni generis hominem viderint ipsius lingua appelabunt eum & parentum eius & cognatorum nomina blandientes sermone ut decipiant comedunt. et postea comprehendunt caput ipsius hominis quem comederunt et super ipsum plorant.[229]

> Ðonne is sum ealand in ðære Readan Sæ, þær is moncynn þæt is mid us Donestre genemned, þa syndon geweaxene swa frihteras fram ðan heafde oð ðone nafelan, ⁊ se oðer dæl byð mannes lice gelic. ⁊ hi cunnon eall mennisc gereord. Þonne hi fremdes kynnes mann geseoð, ðonne næmnað hi hine ⁊ his magas cuðra manna naman, ⁊ mid leaslicum wordum hine beswicað, ⁊ him onfoð, ⁊ þænne æfter þan hi hine fretað ealne butan his heafde ⁊ þonne sittað ⁊ wepað ofer ðam heafde.

---

229 Orchard's edition alters T's punctuation in an attempt to match the Latin and Old English versions, dramatically affecting the meaning. As a result, it was decided in this situation to quote the text from Knock's diplomatic edition of T, which retains the original punctuation. See Knock, 891.

[Then there is an island on the Red Sea where is a race of men that among us is named Donestre, they are born like soothsayers from the head to the navel, and the other part is human like. And they know all human languages. When they see someone of a foreign kind, they call them and their kinsmen by known names, and with false words they entice them, and capture them and after they eat them all except the head, they seat and weep over their head.]

Within the *Letter of Pharasmanes'* tradition, the chapter is an interpolation found exclusively in some versions of the P group.[230] This type of monster is mentioned in the *Epistola Premonis* but without a name:

> Est quoque insula in Mari rubro in qua est genus hominum qui a capite usque ad umbilicum sunt homines, reliquum vero corpus dissimile humano, omnium nationum linguis loquentes, et, si alienigenam viderint, ipsius lingua appellant et parentum cognatorumque dicunt nomina, blandientes sermone ut decipiant et comprehendant; et, cum comprehenderint, perdunt illos et comedunt. (*Epistola Premonis*, XXVI, 3)

> [There is also an island in the Red Sea where is a breed of men that are men from the head up to the navel, the rest of the body is actually dissimilar from human, speaking the languages of every nation; if they see somebody from a foreign race, they call them in their language and they say the name of their parents and their relatives, attracting with their speeches in order to deceive and seize; and, when they seize, they destroy and eat those people.]

In this case, the name is omitted, as is the final description depicting the creature during its fleeting moment of regret following the meal. The corresponding Old French section includes the final reaction, but the denomination is still missing:

> Et la en le rouge mer est vne isle. en le quele sont gens qui parolent de tous langages. et saluent tous chlaus qui la vont. chascun en sen propre langage. Et leur nomment leur cousins et leur lignage. et par beles paroles les decholvent et les prendent et menguent et quant il les ont mengie si se metent en orisons sur les testes. (*Lepistle*, XXIX)

---

230 There is a good probability that the F Group chapter on the Soraci (or Tritonides), animals with divination abilities, is related to this Donestres chapter. There is a line in the *Letter of Fermes* (XXV) that sounds quite close to *Mirabilia*'s reading here: 'In illo loco nascuntur soraci, qui apud vos tritongides appellantur, quasi divini'. See Knock, 797.

[There is an island in the Red Sea, in which there are people who speak every language and they greet everyone they see, each with their own language. They name their cousins and their relatives and through nice words they deceive them and seize them and eat them and when they have eaten, they pray on their heads.]

The name Donestre is thus an addition of the insular manuscripts. The text, however, does not elucidate the meaning given to the term, as opposed to what transpires in both episodes on the Homodubii races. According to the three manuscripts, the monster is given the name Donestre, 'mid us', 'apud nos' ('among us'), a clarification that may specifically refer to the Anglo-Saxon context, thus implying that the denomination may have been easy to understand for the insular audience. The names given to the monstrous races in the treatise are usually self-explanatory; that is to say, their meaning is often deducible based on the appearance or behaviour of the creatures: the cannibalistic giants in chapter 13 are named Hostes, Latin for 'enemies' because they attack anyone they meet, and the chapter on the Cynocephali (§ 8) contains a reference to dog-like features in any name assigned to them (*healfhundingas*, *cenocephale* or *conopoenas*). Thus, even in regard to § 20, the meaning of the name Donestre might be deduced by the behaviour of the monster.

One of the plausible arguments links the name's etymology to the root of the Old English word *dōn*, which means 'to do, act, or cause'.[231] In this light, the term, which would mean 'maker/causer', would imply the monster's active role in its interactions with the visitors. The suffix -*estre*, which is generally employed to make feminine agent nouns, would point towards an androgynous interpretation of the creature. Despite having a masculine physical aspect, with its misleading words, the creature seems to act according to vices stereotypically assigned to women, namely deception and dishonesty, in opposition to Anglo-Saxon strictly male warrior society's codes of respect and honour (Lehr, 183–184; Saunders, 26–27). According to other interpretations, however, the ethnonym could also refer to the monster's prophetic abilities: given the likely interference of the Old English suffix -*estre*, Donestre could be a corruption of the late Latin form *dīvīnātores* (Friedman, *The Monstrous Races*, 15; Lendinara, 'I donestri', 270–271).

---

[231] See *DOE*, s.v. 'dōn'. Among the many connotations, the primary meaning is referred as 'to do, perform, act, achieve, make'.

The creature's divinatory powers are actually one of the key factors that contribute to its monstrous nature, since they provide a supernatural explanation for its ability to guess the language of each visitor. In the Latin text, the Donestre's prophetic abilities are expressed as an apposition for the monster's name, 'quasi divine'; in the Old English version, however, they become one of its physical characteristics: the creature's body is depicted as divided into an upper part, similar to that of soothsayers (T: 'swa frihteras', V: 'swa frifteras'), and a lower part human in form, 'mannes lice gelic'. This odd difference is the product of interpretative decisions that were clearly influenced by a corrupted textual tradition. The Latin text provided to the translator in this passage was most likely unclear.

The *Mirabilia* text in T agrees with the *Epistola Premonis* in depicting the upper portion of the creature as human, but the rest of the description shows an error:

> Itaque insula est in rubro mari. in qua hominum genus est quod apud nos appellatur donestre. quasi divine. a capite usque ad umbilicum quasi homines. reliquo corpore similitudine humana nationum linguis loquentes.[232]

Syntactically, 'quasi homines' and 'similitudine humana' are placed in contradiction, but there is no semantic opposition because both the upper part, 'a capite usque ad umbilicum', and the lower part, 'reliquo corpore', are described as human in form. If the Old English version's translator worked from a Latin text with a reading similar to T's *Mirabilia*, it can be assumed that he attempted to overcome this illogicality by modifying the sentence structure; 'quasi diuine'[233] is read as a physical detail to which the verb 'syndon geweaxene' is added, and the double repetition ends up being removed:[234]

---

232 T's translitteration, f. 83v: 'Itaq: insuḷa est in rubro mari. in qua hominũ | genus est qd̄ apud nos appellatᵣ donestre. | q̊si diuine. a capite usq: adumbilicum quasi | homines reliq̊ corprore similitudine humana | nationũ linguis loquentes'.
233 It should be noted that T's 'quasi diuine' would seem to confuse the adjective *dīvīnus, -a, -um* 'divine, of the gods; extraordinary, wonderful; prophetic, inspired by the gods' with the noun *dīvīnus, -i*, 'soothsayer' (see *ALD*, s.v. 'dīvīnus, -a, -um' and 'dīvīnus, -i'). As a result, Orchard emends to 'quasi diuini'. See Orchard, *Pride and Prodigies*, 179.
234 B, following probably both the Latin and the Old English versions, replaces both 'quasi homine' and 'similitudine humana'. The sentence is thus formed: 'quasi

153

þær is moncynn þæt is mid us Donestre genemned, þa syndon geweaxene swa frihteras fram ðan heafde oð ðone nafelan, ⁊ se oðer dæl byð mannes lice gelic.

In its sole occurrence in the Old English corpus, the noun *frihtere* appears to be a vernacular translation of the Latin *dīvīnus*, 'diviner, soothsayer'. It would be an agent-noun from the verb *frihtan* or *frihtian* 'to divine, to practice divination',[235] sharing the root with the abstract noun *friht*, which indicates a request for prediction, 'divination, augury', but also 'omen, auspice'; it also appears to be linked to prohibited heathen rituals.[236] The reading in V 'frifteras', on the other hand, may point towards a different etymology. Considering the Donestres' anthropophagy, *frifteras* might be an unknown or corrupt form linked to the verb *fretan* 'to devour, to eat with voracity' or the adjective *frettol* 'voracious'.[237]

Whatever the meaning of *frihtere/frifteras* was, it is apparent that the creature's exterior appearance should have been defined by a distinction between a human-like part and a visibly separate part. Indeed, all of the illustrations in the manuscripts depict the figure as a human-animal hybrid. V portrays the monster as having a humanoid torso and an animal head with a protruding snout (f. 103v); in its left hand, it wields a severed limb, waving it at the terrified female figure with whom it shares the frame. In T's picture (f. 83v), the lower section of the monster's body is plainly human, while the upper half bears animal-like features: the figure is coloured as if it had fur, and the head has a lion mane. T depicts

---

divinum. a capite usque ad umbilicum deformatum ab hominum spetie. reliquo corpore similitudine existens humana' (Knock, 891); B's translitteration, f. 42v: 'quasi di | vinū. a capite usq: ad umbilicū deformatū | ab hominū spetie. reliq̇ corpore similitudine | existens humana'. For a more detailed discussion, see Knock, 797–799.

235 Weak verb, I or II class, equivalent to the Latin *facere auguria*, see gloss n° 55, in Meritt, *Old English Glosses*.

236 See *DOE*, s.v. 'friht': 'that which forecasts or anticipates the future; a. divination, augury (ref. to heathen practices)'. Thus, it would imply a request for foresight. The noun *auspicium* is translated as 'auspice, omen' in a prayer rubricated as *Ora' ad barbas tondendas* (Thompson and Lindelöf, 97). However, in the other two occurrences, *friht* appears in legal codes, on lists of prohibited practices, and is associated with the practice of blood sacrifices. See *Cnut*, II, 5, 1 and *Norðhymbra preosta lagu*, 48.

237 See *DOE*, s.v. 'frettol': 'glossing *edax*, "voracious, gluttonous"'. See Mittman and Kim, 19.

a meeting between a Donestre and a traveller, developing it in three scenes: in the first, the two are engaged in a peaceful conversation; in the second, at the bottom right, the Donestre assaults the traveller, forcing him to the ground to devour him; and in the third, the monster regrets its actions and sheds tears on the visitor's severed head. B's image (f. 42r) is largely based on T.[238]

The animalistic aspect emphasized in both illustrative cycles appears to indicate the illustrators' strategy to visually represent the sense of hybridity expressed in indefinite terms in the textual description; at the same time, it may still reflect the legacy of this race's animal origin. The Donestres go through the same anthropomorphizing process that occurred during the transmission of the chapters on the lion-headed men (§ 12) and the stork-men (§ 11). Unlike these previous examples, which occur also in the F group, the direct sources of § 20 are not immediately traceable within the extended tradition of the *Letter of Pharasmanes*; nonetheless, the attributes of the Donestres correspond to an older intermingling among the hyena, crocotta, and crocodile legends.

Since Late Antiquity, the hyena had been seen as an animal to be despised, because of its purported hermaphrodite nature. It was a widespread belief that the hyena could change sex every year and it had also some magical powers, including the ability to enchant humans, causing them to lose their minds.

> Hyaenam Magi ex omnibus animalibus in maxima admiratione posuerunt, utpote cui et ipsi magicas artes dederint vim que, qua alliciat ad se homines mentes alienans. (*Naturalis Historia*, XXVIII, xxvii, 92)
>
> [Among all animals, the hyena has been held in the highest admiration by magicians, who have gone so far as to attribute to it some magical arts, and the power of alluring human beings and depriving them of their senses.]

Pliny provides some information about this animal that he himself deemed unusual: it seemed that hyenas used to station outside shepherds'

---

[238] The main distinction between B and T is the visibility of the monster's genitals, which are highlighted in red ink in T but completely suppressed in B. In V, the reproductive organs are also quite visible, albeit partially obscured by a triangle of tissue.

huts, and, imitating human speech, learned their names to call them out and, eventually, destroy them:

> Multa praeterea mira traduntur, sed maxime sermonem humanum inter pastorum stabula adsimulare nomen que alicuius addiscere, quem evocatum foris laceret, item vomitionem hominis imitari ad sollicitandos canes quos invadat. Ab uno animali sepulcra erui inquisitione corporum. (*Naturalis Historia*, VIII, xliv, 106)
>
> [Many more fantastic things are told about this animal, but the wildest of which is that it imitates the human voice among the shepherds' stalls, and while there, it learns the name of one of them, and then calls him away and devours him. It is also reported that it can simulate a man vomiting, and that by doing so, it draws dogs and subsequently falls on them. It is the only animal that digs up cemeteries to get the bodies of the deceased.]

A similar behaviour was assigned also to the crocotta, the spotted hyena, which in Antiquity was identified as a hybrid born out of the union of a male striped hyena and a lioness. Because of their violent and deceptive nature, Claudius Aelianus (*De natura animalium*, VII, 19) defines both animals as evil, κακόηθες.

There is a clear parallel between the behaviour of the Donestres and the actions attributed to hyenas and crocottas. The main core of the chapter may have evolved from the portrayal of the crocotta, with the final detail emerging instead from traditions concerning the crocodile. The image of the crying crocodile on the bodies of its victims is based on observations of the reptile's behaviour in the wild, where tear secretions are triggered by the animal's need for hydration when forced to feed away from water (Shaner and Vliet, 615–617).[239] In the Greek *Physiologus* tradition, the traits previously assigned to the crocodile are merged with descriptions of the dragon and the snake.[240] Only from the tenth century

---

239 This peculiarity on the crocodile is, according to Knock (178–179), an element that was associated to the description of the crocotta in the Latin area in Late Antiquity. Lendinara ('I Donestri', 267–268), on the other hand, suggests the hypothesis that the interpolation is of Greek origin, because the motif of the crocodile grieving after a meal is attested for a long time only in Greek works; as a point in fact, crocodile's tears are mentioned for the first time by Asterius of Amasea (380–410 ca.).

240 See the *Physiologus*' chapters § 10 and § 11, on viper and snake, in addition to all the chapters reserved to the dragon's enemies (§ 16 on the panther, § 30 on the stag, § 43, on the elephant).

onward, in the B version of the Latin *Physiologus*, is the crocodile recognized as a separate animal. *De bestiis et aliis rebus* (II, viii) – a work attributed to Hugh of Saint Victor that consists of several chapters from the *Physiologus* with interpolations from Solinus and Isidore – contains the summary of knowledge about the crocodile available during the late eleventh century:

> Crocodilus a colore croceo dicitur, et nascitur in Nilo flumine, quadrupes animal, terra et aqua vivens, longitudine plerumque viginti cubitorum, dentium et unguium immanitate armatum, cuius cutis tantae duritiae dicitur, ut quamvis percutiatur in tergo lapidum ictibus, nihil laedatur. Nocte in aquis, die in humo quiescit; qui si aliquando inveniat hominem comedit eum, si vincere potest, et postea eum semper plorat.
>
> [The crocodile is named after the colour of saffron, and is born within the river Nile; a four-footed animal living in land and on water, for the most part it is twenty cubits in length, armed with teeth and claws for great savagery; it is said that its skin is so hard that, if anyone were to throw stones on its back, it wouldn't be hurt at all. It rests in water by night and in earth by day; if it ever meets a man, eats him, if it can win, and afterwards always weeps for him.]

The manuscripts of group P in the *Letter of Pharasmanes'* tradition make no reference to crocotta or crocodile. The blending of the two traditions was most likely caused by the similarity of the names: along the textual transmission, a scribe may have had access to a bestiary or a comparable encyclopaedic work arranged alphabetically (Knock, 70–71). The Latin adjective *crŏcĕus* was used to describe the yellowish colour of saffron, derived from the Greek κρόκος, meaning 'saffron', and gave a false etymology to the name of the crocodile both for Isidore and Hugh of Saint Victor; it had long been thought to be at the origin of the name crocotta, due to the animal's yellowish-reddish fur.[241] This initial uncertainty could have been exacerbated by the iconographic depictions; the scales of the reptile and the mane of the mammal were commonly portrayed with the same crested back in bestiary illustrations. In the New York manuscript

---

241 The *Dictionnaire ètymologique de la langue latine*, edited by Ernout and Meillet, notes *crocŭta*, among the derivatives of *crocus*, *-ī*, citing this etymology. In actuality, the word was never used with this meaning in Greco-Roman sources. *Crocŭta* actually derives from Greek κροκόττας 'spotted hyena', probably from Sanskrit *koṭṭhâraka*, originally referring to the golden jackal. See Funk, 154–155.

bestiary, Pierpont Morgan Library M. 81 (twelfth century; Lincoln or York), for instance, both the hyena (f. 14v) and the crocodile (f. 70r) are depicted with a coral-coloured body – which could be described as croceus – long legs, and a crested back, while their enormous jaws are busy devouring a human being.[242]

The anthropomorphizing process of crocotta and crocodile is not completely traceable, but has deep roots. Even beyond a few factual and naturalistic observations, already in Pliny and Aelianus, the hyena is clearly endowed with anthropomorphic traits: attributing one's own will to the animal is a first step towards an anthropomorphization, an attempt to transfer a human mindset to the animal. The impersonation of human voices, on the one hand, and the tears produced after eating, on the other, are further humanizing features.

According to Harpham (9), the animal element lost in textual transmission has been restored in the illustrations, which depict the monster as a hybrid, thus leading towards an interpretation of its behaviour as infused with 'primitivism or bestiality'. Nonetheless, this position does not appear totally convincing: it does not seem that the text and visuals accentuate exclusively the bestial side of the Donestres; there is more to this monstrous race's conduct than just animal instinct. Rather, their main characteristic appears to be a powerful ability to manipulate. The Donestre seems to emerge from the spectrum between humanity and animality, presenting a disconcerting combination of savage brutality and superior rationality. The creature overcomes visitors' hesitations not with an aggressive attitude, but with the seductive use of words; this is the reason the monster can overwhelm its victim with minimal physical effort. If, as J. Cohen claims, in T's illustration, the lion's mane and the elongated muzzle become more prominent when the monster attacks (J. Cohen, *Of Giants*, 2), it is also true, and perhaps more surprising, that the first scene depicts a completely peaceful conversation: the Donestre faces his guest, and the two's gesticulating arms suggest an engaging dialogue.

---

242 The image of the leucrota, another hybrid lion-hyena that is frequently confused with the crocotta, appears to be very similar, both in colour and in the depiction of its long legs (f. 47v). See Lendinara, 'I Donestri', 269.

The Donestres, unlike any other monstrous race, can communicate through human speech, and, in the tendency to exaggerate typical in the treatise, they know all human languages 'eall mennisc gereord', and can guess the language of any traveller. As a result, while this creature transcends the boundaries of misunderstanding put on the people of the world, its ability to use human language pushes it beyond the barrier between humans and animals (Williams, 141). In this respect, the Donestre might be viewed as a response to the human fantasy of hearing an animal talk, a fantasy that, in the end, can only generate a hybrid and unsettling creature, because, as pointed out by Fudge (89), an essential aspect of the anthropomorphized animal is the ability to 'upset all kinds of assumptions by saying something we don't want to hear'.

The Donestre, more than any other monstrous creature, is defined by its appearance as both familiar and destructive (Kim, 'The Donestre', 162–180); in fact, it could be said that the monster is fundamentally destructive *because* it is familiar: by appearing familiar and welcoming, it transforms what seems safe into something alien and frightening, creating a threat in familiarity.[243]

Deceptive and aggressive, the Donestres could be read as one of the most dangerous populations met on the journey among the *Wonders of the East*. As polyglot and anthropophagous, this monstrous race oversteps the confines of the mouth, a fundamental threshold in the body, because the mouth is the organ around which all its deceptive activity revolves and, moreover, it circumscribes the boundaries of the Self (Williams, 141–149). The Donestres, therefore, simultaneously embody a monstrosity linked to the body and a monstrosity linked to language, thus compromising both the distinctive characteristics that Isidore of Seville attributed to humans as opposed to animals. Indeed, we read in the *Etymologies* (XII, i, 5): 'Pecus dicimus omne quod humana lingua et

---

[243] In this context, Roby's (176) latest observations are also noteworthy; the scholar stresses the emotional complexity shown by the Donestre while emphasizing the human attributes assigned to the monster. In short, the creature surprises, seduces, assaults, and then cries. Its implicit psychology helps to investigate undesired components within the cultural context. 'They compel us to analyse how medieval English readers might have considered the monsters' behaviours of crime and sorrow as emanating from within their own cultural context; they do not reveal the other, but the self.'

effigie caret' ('We call "cattle" any creature who lacks human language and form'). Man identifies as man through language and through his appearance, and thus through his body.

The Donestre claims its connection to the more human side of the human-animal continuity spectrum by physically appearing, at least in part, like a man, 'mannes lice gelic', and employing a familiar language for the visitor. The familiarity of the dialogue initially persuades the traveller, since the monster's ability to speak reawakens memories of home and family. The creature entices the visitor to the point of gaining his trust before devouring him. As a result, language becomes the cause of body destruction: because man's identity is expressed through language, the Donestre's choice of words, namely the traveller's name and the name of his family, ensure that he recognizes himself in them, but it is impossible for the man who comes into contact with the monster to maintain both human appearance and human language. Thus, the distinction between signifier and signified becomes the sense of alienation found in the Self, a form of dissociation between the Self represented through language and the Self experienced as a body (Kim, 'Man-Eating Monsters', 42).

The ensuing cannibalistic episode can be interpreted as an exploration of the fear of losing the boundaries that define human identity. The human body is materially assimilated within the monstrous body during the anthropophagic act, and the traveller becomes a constituent part of a new hybrid entity, in a complete fusion between victim and murderer, subject and object, human and monster. As previously examined, the Donestre, as a polyglot and a hybrid creature, represents the Other from both a cultural and a linguistic perspective and, by being able to appear familiar and by changing what is safe into something alien and scary, produces a rupture inside the subject. In T's pictures (f. 83v), after devouring the traveller, the monster observes his severed head with fascination and compassion; J. Cohen (*Of Giants*, 1–4) sees in this illustration the alienating result of anthropophagy: the traveller has been absorbed by the monster, becoming one with it, but he is also a victim of his own inherent differences. He weeps over what is left of a body that no longer belongs to him, observes and examines what he once was from the outside, and realizes that he has always been a stranger to himself. The encounter with the monster then reveals the subject's 'intimate alterity', an unavoidable alienation from the Self, 'the restless presence at its centre of everything it abjects in order to materialize and maintain its borders' (J. Cohen, *Of Giants*, 4). To be fully human, one must reject the space that the inhuman, the monstrous, occupies within any subject capable of expressing itself via language; the Donestre is the figure of a cultural body that must constantly devour itself in order to survive. In this sense, the hybrid reveals what one does not want to know about human nature; when the creature cries over the severed head is a crucial moment that might be viewed as the recognition of a betrayed human identity.

6.2 Monstrosity: A necessary Otherness

The Plinian races sprang from the psychological desire to construct contrasting figures to delimit the boundaries of humanity. As seen, they arise from the very attempt to draw boundaries and represent those peripherical elements of society returning to trouble the individual consciousness. Moreover, the interest in hybridity that emerges from the text of *Wonders of the East* reflects an attempt to impose a classification on the world's heterogeneity. The characters inhabiting the treatise, while evoking dread and awe because of the boundaries they overstep, symbolize an attempt to understand a fluid and unsystematic universe (Bynum, 31).

Resulting from the fantasy of ejection for impure elements of society (Stallybrass-White, 193), these creatures, as hybrids of the human and the animal, end up encompassing both the Other and the Self; they are both *They* and *Us*; they bring together in one entity all that is familiar and all that is alien. Monstrous creatures are *almost* human, they create a necessary antithesis that is only apparent, they operate as a contrasting backdrop on which Western society may establish a cultural identity, and they are a container for Christian culture's repressed fears, anxieties, fantasies, and aspirations.

During the Hellenistic period, monstrous people were located just beyond the closest regions of Asia, lands with which the ancient world had come into closest contact for commercial and cultural interactions. During the Middle Ages the monsters continued to be placed in the East because of convention and habit; yet, *Wonders of the East* does not depict the actual geography of the mentioned places, such as Armenia, Persia, or Babylon. Just as monster races constitute the imagined construction of the Other, the East described in the treatise is the place of the Elsewhere, the only place where the monstrosities depicted might be born and survive, because the extreme frontier of known reality is a space imbued with moral connotations (M. Campbell, 47–69). The medieval Christian vision of the world implied a fundamental ethnocentrism, manifested in the concentric segmentation of the universe as depicted in maps and in ethnographic writings. The *mappae mundi* designated a space for monstrous creatures placed at the world's extremes, on the ocean's shores, to the north and south, as if the monsters themselves were the border's signal. According to the macrobian theory, the globe was divided into five climatic regions: two areas of freezing weather at the poles, two temperate zones, which are the only ones believed suitable for intelligent life, and an equatorial region of torrid climate. Because the middle section was thought to be impossible to cross, it was assumed that the southern hemisphere was unoccupied. Therefore, the only location reserved for humanity was the European continent, referred to as οἰκουμένη, 'the inhabited world', which expanded around the city of Jerusalem, seen as the ideal centre of the world. According to this purely ethnocentric approach, the Mediterranean region – precisely the places inhabited by the authors and cartographers who advocated this viewpoint – offered a natural world that appeared to be more benign, due to the temperate climate and lack of monstrosities. The more one moved away from the ideal centre, the less *human* the men were.

After the conversion to Christianity, Anglo-Saxon society adopts this worldview, which appears to relegate the island to the outskirts of civilization and impact the Anglo-Saxons' opinion of their own culture. Indeed, intellectuals situated in British territory have viewed their place in the world to be isolated and liminal since the early Middle Ages: Britain was the last solitary outpost before the unsurpassable ocean. The British Isles, as the last European region, were placed in the far north of the globe on the 'T-O' maps. Gildas, who laments the country's invasion by Germanic peoples, writes about its geographical location: 'Britannia insula in extremo ferme orbis limite circium': 'Britain is an island situated at the furthest boundary of the earth' (*De Excidio Britanniae*: III, 1); image echoed in the incipit of Bede's *Historia Ecclesiastica Gentis*

Anglorum: 'Britannia Oceani insula' ('Britain is an island in middle of the Ocean') (*Historia Ecclesiastica*: I, 1). Through the Mediterranean-centric vision, *Britannia* and *Hybernia*, surrounded only by the sea, were as distant from the centre of the Christian world as confused and mythical regions such as Scythia and Ethiopia.[244]

England has had a fairly diverse cultural and ethnic composition since its founding and throughout the Anglo-Saxon period. When, at the end of the sixth century, Christian doctrine extends its influence over lands originally occupied by British peoples but recently captured by Germanic tribes of Angles, Saxons, and Jutes, the Romano-Christian epistemological system overlaps the pre-existing traditions. The ecclesiastical hierarchies supported the grafting of a theological and cultural syncretism inside a society already marked by contacts and struggles between different political and ethnic identities by opting not to destroy the sites of worship previously consecrated to pagan divinities.[245] The Romano-British kingdoms, which were often markedly different from one another, were replaced and merged with equally heterogeneous Germanic kingdoms (fifth century) which over time were shaken firstly by the conversion to Christianity (sixth century), then by Viking invasions (ninth–tenth centuries), finally by the Norman conquest (eleventh century). The history of Anglo-Saxon England, and the core idea of an *English* nation, is built on fragments of disparate identities derived from many conceptions. As J. Cohen (*Of Giants*, 4) brilliantly puts it:

> The history of Anglo-Saxon England is a narrative of resistant hybridity, of small groups ingested into larger bodies without a full assimilation, without cultural homogeneity: thus the realms of Hwicce, Sussex, Kent, Lindsey, Surrey, Essex, East Anglia, Northumbria, Mercia, and Wessex were sutured over time into progressively larger kingdoms; but although they were eventually unified in political hegemony, these areas retained enough force of heterogeneity to remain dialect regions that persist to the present day.

---

244 For a study on how the geographical perception influenced the Anglo-Saxons' cultural identity, see Mittman, *Maps and Monsters*, 11–26.

245 In terms of the procedures used during the conversion of the Angles, the indications of Gregory the Great to the abbot Mellitus are well known, in the epistle recorded also by Bede, in *Historia Ecclesiastica*, I, 30. See Gregorius Magnus *Registrum epistolarum* (XI, 56).

The unique identity of an Anglo-Saxon community, the *Englishness* sought out by the monarchs of Wessex in the ninth and tenth centuries in ideal juxtaposition to the foreign and pagan *Dene*, was actually founded on many and contradictory sources. It is hardly unexpected, then, that between the liminal position in which the Anglo-Saxons placed their own culture and the experience of 'resistant hibridity' characterizing their community formation, the monstrous categories recur repeatedly throughout Anglo-Saxon cultural production.

In fact, the hybrid monster, like the Anglo-Saxon society's hybrid and contradictory character, defies categorization: the uncanny hybridity of the deformed body resists any attempt at systematic organization. The liminal being, with its dual nature, continuously threatens to collapse the barrier between Other and Self, nature and culture, exteriority and interiority, and demonstrates the frailty of categorical differences. The monstrous, as an absolute Other, illustrates the ambiguities of the concept of Otherness itself: the poles of any binary confrontation are never radically opposed to each other, but rather rely on and interact with one another; the boundary between what is considered Self and what is considered Other must have a dual state, because it is both a dividing line and a stretch of continuity (Uebel, 265).

'The monster is difference made flesh, come to dwell among us' J. Cohen ('Monster Culture', 7) writes, echoing the *Gospel of John* (1:14). In the treatise, the in-between-creatures populating the East embody everything that is rhetorically placed at a distance but actually arises from within: these extraordinary beings emerge in the imagination and reality of those who created them to provide a point of comparison through which to exorcise cultural anxieties about their identity as Anglo-Saxons and human beings.

Conclusions

'What is an animal, and what is its relationship to a human? Are animals distinctly separate creatures, or is humanity something that is readily lost into animality?' (Salisbury, 1). These questions introduce the main thematic argument in Joyce E. Salisbury's ground-breaking study on animal perception in the Middle Ages, *The Beast Within*. Since reflecting on how a society views animals is a way to study how that society sees itself, similar issues have been the driving force behind the composition of this book. What constituted an animal in the eyes of the Anglo-Saxons? How is the animal-human relationship depicted in the Anglo-Saxon literary record? From this starting point, the *Exeter Book* riddles and *Wonders of the East* offered a fruitful ground of research because they provided perspectives that might be viewed as complementary to one another. Together, *Riddles* and *Wonders* demonstrate the dynamic instability of human-animal relations in Early Medieval England and their animal and monstrous representations contribute to threaten any kind of categorical distinction: between nature and culture, between similar and dissimilar, between exteriority and interiority.

In the Old English riddles, the constant use of metaphor favours the depictions of the key subjects in an ambivalent way; the personalities that inhabit the *Exeter Book* collection have a double or metamorphic nature. Generally, enigmatic poems are based on contradictions and status changes: from being animated to inanimate item, from living being to working tool, from happy beginnings to an adult existence full of misery. The freedom of creativity provided to poetry in general, and to the enigmatic genre in particular, enables these poems to thoroughly explore the mutability of natural elements. Moreover, the rhetorical devices designated to confuse the riddlic game, such as anthropomorphizing strategies like prosopopoeia and personification, facilitate a process of mimesis and create an empathic connection between the main speaking subject and its human audience. These anthropomorphic strategies that have been perceived as a limitation of perspective on some occasions have proven to be useful tools to favour the autonomy of the animals in the

Exeter Book riddles: lending a human voice to animals helps to better understand them, while the riddle's focus is directed on similarities rather than differences. Furthermore, personification can occasionally permit a reversal in the reciprocal positions of man and animal; it, in fact, helps to recognize the creature as an entity separated from human, while also allowing humans to assume, and thus attempt to understand, the animal point of view. The collection, as a whole, appears to acknowledge animals as having a vital strength and an ability to endure negative condition associating them to humans.

Rising out of the comparison among the notions on animals, slaves and foreigners, the monstrous people depicted in the *Wonders of East* reveal the complexity of human-animal relations because of their intrinsic hybridity. In the text's structure, hybrids take on the key role of being the bridge between entirely animal creatures and completely human individuals. The ambiguities inherent in Plinian people, as well as the concerns they raise regarding the notion of humanity, have clearly surfaced in the treatise's portrayal. Despite being identified as belonging to one sort of mankind (*manncynn*), hybrid races bring together and confuse aspects of different categories: whether in outward appearance or in antisocial behaviours, liminal populations such as Cynocephali, ichthyophagi, and onocentaurs go beyond the definition of human. As a result, ichthyophagi and onocentaurs are categorized as ambiguous beings, beginning with the name ascribed to them, Homodubii; a designation that may, in fact, be applied to all monstrous populations. Similarly elusive is the definition of the lion-headed giants and the Donestres, two peoples that take their attested form out of an incessant process of modification in textual transmission: undergoing anthropomorphization, these figures rise out of the infinite possibilities of commixture in the spectrum between humanity and animality. The Donestre, an anthropophagous and deceiving beast that is both familiar and dangerous, aptly represents the threat posed by the hybrid monster. Similarly, in a context of detached and neutral narratives, the position of hybrid women eventually emerged as anomalous: they are the only monstrous race to face explicit moral censorship, because they are seen as perverse figures bringing the subject back to the distinction between male and female, as well as human and animal. Hybrid humans are created out of a psychological necessity. The monstrous function as a mark for difference: on one hand, it signals the boundaries of the Self and the limited space of society, on the other, Donestres and Homodubii reveal that the alien can also be found within. Hybrids are kristevian abject: they push towards a confrontation with the limits of the Self and the Other, while, at the same time, threaten to dissolve those boundaries.

In conclusion, it became clear that, while being anything but a faithful reproduction of natural conditions, the subjects depicted in the *Exeter Book* riddles and in *Wonders of the East* provide a complex and nuanced vision of non-human animals, a perspective that allows to explore both species' affinities and anxiety for the Other. In these depictions, animality became a *locus* for the Other, and the monstrous a distortion of the Self in which Anglo-Saxon cultural identity might be reflected.

References

Adams, James Noel. *The Latin Sexual Vocabulary*. London: Duckworth, 1982.
Adamson, Melitta Weiss. *Food in Medieval Times*. London: Greenwood Press, 2004.
Ælfric's Anglo-Saxon Versions of Alcuini Interrogaziones Sigeuuilfi Presbyteri in Genesin. Ed. G. E. MacLean. Halle: E. Karras, 1883.
Ælfric's Catholic Homilies: The First Series: Text. Ed. Peter Clemoes. London, New York: Oxford UP, 1997. Early English Text Society suppl. series 17.
Ælfric's Catholic Homilies. The Second Series: Text. Ed. Malcolm R. Godden. London: Oxford UP, 1979. Early English Texts Society suppl. series 5.
Ælfric's Colloquy. Ed. George Norman Garmonsway. London: Methuen's Old English Library, 1939. Rev. ed. Exeter: University of Exeter Press, 1991.
Ælfric's Lives of Saints. Ed. Walther W. Skeat. London, I ed. 1881–1900. Repr. 2 vols. 1966. Early English Texts Society orig. series 76, 82, 94, 114.
Ælfric's prefaces. Ed. Jonathan Wilcox. Durham: Durham Medieval Texts, 1994.
Ælfrics Grammatik und Glossar: Text und Varianten. Ed. Julius Zupitza and Helmut Gneuss. Berlin: Weidmann, 1880. Repr. 1966.
ALD = Lewis, Chaltron T. and Charles Short, editors. *A Latin Dictionary*. Oxford, 1879–1933.
Afros, Elena. '*Sindrum begrunden* in Exeter Book *Riddle 26*: The Enigmatic Dative Case'. *Note and Queries* 51.1 (March 2004): 7–9.
Aldhelm. *The Poetic Works*. Ed. Michael Lapidge and James Rosier. Cambridge: D. S. Brewer, 1985.
Ambrosius, Aurelius. *Opera: Pars VII*. Ed. Otto Faller. Wienn: Tempsky, 1955. Corpus Series Ecclesiastica Latina LXXIII.

Amodio, Mark C. *The Anglo-Saxon Literature Handbook*. Oxford: Wiley-Blackwell, 2014.
Aristotle. *Historia animalium*. Ed. David M. Balme and Allan Gotthelf. New York: Cambridge UP, 2002.
Aristotle. *Poetics*. Ed. Leonardo Tarán and Dimitr Goutas. Leiden, Boston: Brill, 2012. Mnemosyne Supplements 338.
Aristotle. *Retorica*. Ed. Silvia Gastaldi. Roma: Carocci Editore, 2014.
ASD = Bosworth, Joseph J. and T. Northcote Toller, editors. *An Anglo-Saxon Dictionary: Based on the Manuscript Collection of the Late Joseph Bosworth, Enlarged Addenda and Corrigenda by Alistair Campbell of the Supplement by T. Northcote Toller*. Oxford: Clarendon Press, 1898–1978.
Athenaeus. *I deipnosofisti. I dotti a banchetto*. 4 vols. Ed. Luciano Canfora and Christian Jacob. Roma: Salerno Editore, 2001.
Augustine of Hippo. *De Civitate Dei*. Ed. Bernhard Dombart and Alphons Kalb. Turnhout: Brepols, 1955. Corpus Christianorum Series Latina XLVII–XLVIII.
Augustine of Hippo. *Opera: Pars II.2*. Ed. William M. Green. Turnhout: Brepols, 1970. Corpus Christianorum Series Latina XXIX.
Augustine of Hippo. *Opera: De genesi contra manichaeos*. Ed. D. Weber. Wien: Österreichische Akademie der Wissenschaften, 1998. Corpus Series Ecclesiastica Latina XCI.
Aulus Gellius. *Noctes Atticae*. Ed. Peter K. Marshall. Oxford: Oxford UP, 1990.
Austin, Greta. 'Marvelous People or Marvelous Races? Race and the Anglo-Saxon *Wonders of the East*'. *Marvels, Monsters and Miracles*. Ed. Timothy S. Jones and David A. Sprunger. Kalamazoo: Western Michigan University, 2002.
Banham, Debbie and Rosamond Faith. *Anglo-Saxon Farms and Farming*. Oxford: Oxford UP, 2014.
Banham, Debbie, editor. *Monasteriales Indicia: The Anglo-Saxon Sign Language*. Middlesex: Anglo-Saxon Books, 1991.
Banham, Debbie. *Food and Drink in Anglo-Saxon England*. Stroud: Tempus, 2004.
Barajas, Courtney Catherine. 'Reframing the monstrous: Visions of desire and a unified Christendom in the Anglo-Saxon *Wonders of the*

East'. *East Meets West in the Middle Ages and Early Modern Times; Transcultural Experiences in the Premodern World*. Ed. Albrecht Classen. Berlin: De Gruyter, 2013.

Barley, Nigel F. 'Old English colour classification: Where do matters stand?'. *Anglo-Saxon England* 3 (December 1974): 15–28.

Barney, Stephen A. et al., editors. *The Etymologies of Isidore of Seville*. Cambridge: Cambridge UP, 2006.

Battles, Paul. 'Toward a theory of Old English poetic genres: Epic, elegy, wisdom poetry, and the "traditional opening"'. *Studies in Philology* 111.1 (Winter 2014): 1–33.

Bayless Martha and Michael Lapidge, editors. *Collectanea Pseudo-Bedae*. Dublin: Dublin Institute for Advanced Studies, 1998.

Bede. *Historia Ecclesiastica Gentis Anglorum – Storia degli inglesi*. Ed. Michael Lapidge. Trans. Paolo Chiesa. Milano: Fondazione Valla, 2008.

Bede. *Opera exegetica: Libri quatuor in principium Genesis usque ad nativitatem Isaac et eiectionem Ismahelis adnotationum*. Ed. C. W. Jones. Turnhout: Brepols, 1967. Corpus Christianorum Series Latina cxviiia.

Bergamin, Manuela, editor. *L'enigmistica medievale e gli indovinelli di Simposio*. Firenze: Edizioni del Galluzzo, 2017.

Biggam, Carole P. *Grey in Old English: An Interdisciplinary Semantic Study*. London: Runetree Press, 1998.

Biggam, Carole P. 'The ambiguity of brightness (with special reference to Old English) and a new model for color description in semantics'. *Anthropology of Color: Interdisciplinary Multilevel Modeling*. Ed. Robert E. MacLaury et al. Amsterdam: John Benjamins, 2007.

Biggam, Carole P. 'The development of the basic colour terms of English'. *Interfaces between Language and Culture in Medieval England A Festschrift for Matti Kilpiö*. Ed. Alaric Hall et al. Leiden: Brill, 2010.

Bitterli, Dieter. 'Exeter Book Riddle 15: Some points for Porcupine'. *Anglia* 120.4 (2003): 461–487.

Bitterli, Dieter. *Say What I am Called: The Old English Riddles of the Exeter Book and the Anglo-Latin Riddle Tradition*. Toronto: University of Toronto Press, 2009.

Black, Max. *Models and Metaphors*. Ithaca: Cornell UP, 1962.

Blauner, D. G. 'The early literary riddle'. *Folklore* 78.1 (Spring 1967): 49–58.

Borysławski, Rafał. *The Old English Riddles and the Riddlic Elements of Old English Poetry*. Frankfurt am Main: Peter Lang, 2004.

Bragg, Lois. 'Color words in Beowulf'. *Proceedings of the Patristic, Medieval and Renaissance Conference* 7 (1983): 47–55.

Bragg, Lois. *The Lyric Speaker of Old English Poetry*. London, Toronto: Associated University Presses, 1991.

Bremmer, Rolf H. Jr. 'Ælfric's downsized version of Alcuin's *Quaestiones in Genesim*: Enough is enough'. *Limits to Learning: The Transfer of Encyclopaedic Knowledge in the Early Middle Ages*. Ed. Concetta Giliberto and Loredana Teresi. Leuven, Paris, Walpole: Peeters, 2013.

Brett, Cyrill. 'Notes on Old and Middle English'. *The Modern Language Review* 22.3 (July 1927): 257–264

Bruce-Mitford, Rupert. *The Sutton Hoo Ship-Burial*. 3 vols. London: British Museum Press, 1975–1983.

Budiansky, Stephen. *If a lion could talk: Animal Intelligence and the Evolution of Consciousness*. New York: Free Press, 1998.

Bynum, Caroline W. *Metamorphosis and Identity*. New York: Zone Books, 2001.

Caillois, Roger and Jeffrey Mehlman. 'Riddles and Images'. *Yale French Studies* 41 (1968): 148–158.

Campbell, Mary. *The Witness and the Other World: Exotic European Travel Writing 400–1000*. Ithaca: Cornell UP, 1988.

Campbell, Jackson J. 'Knowledge of Rhetorical Figures in Anglo-Saxon England'. *Journal of English and Germanic Philology* 66.1 (January 1967): 1–20.

Carver, Martin et al. *Sutton Hoo: A Seventh Century Princely Burial Ground and Its Context*. London: British Museum Press, 2005.

Catullus, Gaius Valerius. *Il Liber e i frammenti dei 'Poeti Nuovi'*. Ed. Giovanni Battista Pighi. Torino: Utet, 2004. Collana Classici Latini.

Cavell, Megan. 'The Igil and Exeter Book Riddle 15'. *Notes and Queries* 64 (June 2017): 206–210.

Cavell, Megan. *Weaving Words and Binding Bodies: The Poetics of Human Experience in Old English Literature*. Toronto: University of Toronto Press, 2016.

Cavell, Megan. 'A poetics of empathy?: Non-human experience in the Anglo-Saxon Bovine Riddles'. *Medieval Ecocriticisms*. Ed. Heide Estes. Amsterdam: University of Amsterdam Press, forthcoming.

Cicero, Marcus Tullius. *Scripta quae manserunt omnia, fasc. 3. De Oratore*. Ed. Kazimierz Kumaniecki. Leipzig: Teubner, 1969. Bibliotheca scriptorum Graecorum et Romanorum Teubneriana.

Claudianus, Claudius. *Carmina*. Ed. John B. Hall. Leipzig: Teubner, 1985. Bibliotheca scriptorum Graecorum et Romanorum Teubneriana.

Claudius Aelianus. *De natura animalium*. Ed. Manuela Garcia Valdés et al. Berlin: De Gruyter, 2009.

Cockayne, Thomas Oswald, editor. *Narratiuncula anglice conscriptae: De Pergamenis Exscribebat Notis Illustrabat Eruditis Copiam*. London: Iohannem R Smith, 1861.

Cohen, Jeffrey Jerome. 'Monster culture (seven theses)'. *Monster Theory: Reading Culture*. Ed. Jeffrey Jerome Cohen. London, Minneapolis: University of Minnesota Press, 1996.

Cohen, Jeffrey Jerome. *Of Giants: Sex and Monsters in the Middle Ages*. London, Minneapolis: University of Minnesota Press, 1999.

Cohen, Jeffrey Jerome. *Hibridity, Identity and Monstrosity in Medieval Britain: On Difficult Middles*. New York: Palgrave Macmillan, 2006.

Cohen, Ralph. 'History and genre'. *Neohelicon* 13.2 (September 1986): 87–105.

Colli, Giorgio. *La nascita della filosofia*. Milano: Adelphi, 1975.

Cook, Eleanor. *Enigmas and Riddles in Literature*. Cambridge: Cambridge UP, 2006.

Crane, Susan. *Animal Encounters: Contacts and Concepts in Medieval Britain*. Philadelphia: University of Pennsylvania Press, 2013.

Cross, James E. and Thomas D. Hill, editors. *The Prose Solomon and Saturn and Adrian and Ritheus*. Toronto: University of Toronto Press, 1982.

Daily, Patricia. 'Riddles, wonder and responsiveness in Anglo-Saxon literature'. *The Cambridge History of Early Medieval English Literature*. Ed. Clare A. Lees. Cambridge: Cambridge UP, 2013.

Dale, Corinne. *The Natural World in the Exeter Book Riddles*. Cambridge: D. S. Brewer, 2017.

Daly, Lloyd William and Walther Suchier, editors. *Die Altercatio Hadriani Augusti et Epicteti Philosophi, nebst einigen verwandten Texten*. Urbana: University of Illinois Press, 1939.

Davidson, Arnold I. 'The horror of monsters'. *The Boundaries of Humanity: Humans, Animals, Machines*. Ed. James Jay Sheehan and Morton Sosna. Berkeley, Los Angeles: University of California Press, 1991.

Deitz, Klaus. 'Die Altenglischen Präfixbildungen und ihre Charakteristik'. *Anglia* 122.4 (2005): 561–613.

Dietrich, F. 'Die Räthsel des Exeterbuchs: Würdigung, Lösung und Herstellung'. *Zeitschrift für deutsches Altertum und deutsche Literatur* 11 (1859): 448–490.

Dietrich, F. 'Die Räthsel des Exeterbuchs: Verfasser; Weitere Lösungen'. *Zeitschrift für deutsches Altertum und deutsche Literatur* 12 (1865): 232–252.

Doane, A. N. 'Three Old English Implement Riddles: Reconsideration of Numbers 4, 49 and 73'. *Modern Philology* 84.3 (February 1987): 243–257.

DOE = Angus Cameron et al., editors. *Dictionary of Old English: A to I online*. Toronto: Dictionary of Old English Project, 2018. https://tapor.library.utoronto.ca/doe/

Dolcetti Corazza, Vittoria, editor. *Il Fisiologo nella tradizione germanica*. Alessandria: Edizioni dell'Orso, 1992.

DuBois, Page. *Centaurs and Amazons: Women and the Pre-History of the Great Chain of Being*. Ann Arbor: The University of Michigan Press, 1991.

Dutchak, Patricia. 'The Church and Slavery in Anglo-Saxon England'. *Past Imperfect* 9 (2001–2003): 25–42.

Ehwald, Rudolfus, editor. *Aldhelmi opera*. Auctorum antiquissorum xv, 1919. Monumenta Germaniae Historica.

Erbert, A. 'Die Rätselpoesie der Angelsachsen'. *Berichte über die Verhandlungen der Königlich Sächsischen gesellschaft der Wissenschaften zu Leipzig* 29 (1877): 20–56.

Ericksen, Janet S. 'Penitential nakedness and the Junius 11 *Genesis*'. *Naked before God: Uncovering the Body in Anglo-Saxon England*. Ed. Withers, Benjamin and Jonathan Wilcox. Morgantown: West Virginia UP, 2003.

Ernout, Alfred and Antoine Meillet, editors. *Dictionnaire étymologique de la langue latine*. Paris: Éditions Klincksieck, 1979.

Estes, Heide. *Anglo-Saxon Literary Landscapes: Ecotheory and the Environmental Imagination*. Amsterdam: Amsterdam UP, 2017.

Faral, Edmond. 'Une source latine de l'histoire d'Alexandre: la lettre sur les merveilles de l'Inde'. *Romania* 43.171 (1914): 199–215 and 353–370.

Fehr, Bernhard, editor. *Die Hirtenbriefe Ælfrics in altenglischer und lateinischer Fassung*. 1914. Repr. with a supplement by Peter Clemoes. Darmstadt: Wissenschaftliche Buchgesellschaft, 1966.

Forcellini Lex = Forcellini E. et al., *Lexicon totius latinitatis cum appendicibus* [online]. Patavii, 1940.

Ford, A. J. *Marvel and Artifacts:* The Wonders of the East *and Its Manuscript Context*. London: Brill, 2016.

Forman, Maurice B., editor. *The Letters of John Keats*. Oxford: Oxford UP, 1935.

Frank, Roberta. 'Some uses of Paronomasia in Old English scriptural verse'. *Speculum* 47.2 (April 1972): 207–226.

Frantzen, Allen J. *Anglo-Saxon Keywords*. Oxford: Wiley-Blackwell, 2012.

Frantzen, Allen J. *Food, Eating and Identity in Early Medieval England*. Woodbridge: The Boydell Press, 2014.

Friedman, John Block. 'The Marvels-of-the-East tradition in Anglo-Saxon art'. *Sources of Anglo-Saxon Culture*. Ed. Paul E. Szarmach. Kalamazoo: Western Michigan University, 1986.

Friedman, John Block. *The Monstrous Races in Medieval Art and Thought*. Harvard UP, 1981. Repr. Syracuse: Syracuse UP, 2000.

Fry, Donald K. 'Exeter Book Riddle solutions'. *Old English Newsletter* 15.1 (Fall 1981): 22–33.

Fudge, Erica. *Animal*. London: Reaktion Books, 2002.

Fulk, R. D., editor and translator. *The* Beowulf *Manuscript: Complete texts and the* Fight at Finnsburg. Cambridge, London: Harvard UP, 2010. Dumbarton Oaks Medieval Library 3.

Funk, Holger. 'How the Ancient "Krokottas" Evolved into the Modern Spotted Hyena "Crocuta Crocuta"'. *Quaderni Urbinati di Cultura Classica: New Series* 101.2 (January 2012): 145–166.

Gervase of Tilbury. *Otia imperialia: Recreation for an emperor*. Ed. S. E. Banks and J. W. Binns. Oxford: Clarendon Press, 2002.

Gibb, Paul A., editor. *Wonders of the East: A Critical Edition and Commentary*. Diss. Duke University, 1977.

Gildas. *La conquista della Britannia: De Excidio Britanniae*. Ed. Sabrina Giuriceo. Rimini: Il Cerchio, 2005.

Glorie, Francois, editor. *Variae Collectiones Aenigmatum Merovingicae Aetatis*. Turnout: Brepols, 1968. Corpus Christianorum Series Latina 133–133a.

Glosecki, Stephen O. 'Movable beasts: The manifold implications of early Germanic animal imagery'. *Animals in the Middle Ages*. Ed. Nora C. Flores. New York, London: Routledge, 2016.

Gneuss, Helmut. 'The study of language in Anglo-Saxon England'. *Bulletin of the John Rylands University Library of Manchester* 72.1 (1990): 1–32.

Godden, Malcolm R. and Susan Irvine, editor. *The Old English Boethius: An Edition of the Old English Versions of Boethius's De Consolatione Philosophiae*. 2 vols. Oxford, New York: Oxford UP, 2009.

Graff, Eberhard G. *Diutiska: Denkmäler deutscher Sprache und Literatur, aus älten Handschriften*. Stuttgart: Druckerei Anton Hain, 1827.

Greenfield, Stanley B. 'The formulaic expression of the theme of "exile" in Anglo-Saxon poetry'. *Hero and Exile: The Art of Old English Poetry*. Ed. George H. Brown. London, Ronceverte: The Hambledon Press, 1989.

Gregorius Magnus. *Opera. Registrum epistularum*. Ed. Dag Norberg. Turnhout: Brepols, 1982. Corpus Christianorum Series Latina CXL- CXLa.

Grein, C. W. M. *Sprachschatz der angelsächsischen Dichter*. Coll. Ferdinand Holthausen. Heidelberg: Carl Winter, 1912.

Guerrieri, Anna Maria. 'Per uno studio dell'arte retorica germanica: esempi di prosopopea'. *Nel segno del testo: edizioni, materiali e studi per Oronzo Pecere*. Ed. Lucio Del Corso et al. Firenze: Edizioni Gonnelli, 2015.

Hagen, Ann. *Anglo-Saxon Food and Drink: Production, Processing, Distribution and Consumption*. Hockwold cum Wilton: Anglo-Saxon Books, 2006.

Hall, J. R. 'Duality and the dual pronoun in *Genesis B*'. *Papers on Language and Literature* 17.2 (Spring 1981): 139–145.

Härke, Heinrich. 'Early Anglo-Saxon social structure'. *The Anglo-Saxons from the Migration Period to the Eighth Century: An Ethnographic Perspective*. Ed. John Hines. Woodbridge: Boydell Press, 1997.

Harpham, Geoffrey G. *On the Grotesque: Strategies of Contradiction in Art and Literature*. Princeton: Princeton UP, 1982.

Haslam, Nick. 'Dehumanization: An integrative review'. *Personality and Social Psychology Review* 10.3 (August 2006): 252–264.

Hayes, Mary. *Divine Ventriloquism in Medieval English Literature*. New York: Palgrave Macmillan, 2011.

Hessels, Jan Hendrick. *An Eighth-Century Latin-Anglo-Saxon Glossary*. Cambridge: Cambridge UP, 1890.

Hilka, A. 'Ein neuer (altfranzösischer) Text des Briefes über die Wunder Asiens'. *Zeitschrift für französische Sprache und Literatur* 46.1/2 (1923): 92–103.

Historia Apolloniis regis Tyri. Ed. Gareth Schmelling. Leipzig: Teubner, 1988.

Holsinger, Bruce. 'Of pigs and parchment: Medieval studies and the coming of the animal'. *Publications of the Modern Language Associations* 124.2 (March 2009): 616–623.

Holtz, Louis, editor. *Donat et la tradition de l'enseignement grammatical: étude sur l'Ars Donati et sa diffusion (IVe-IXe siècle) et édition critique*. Paris: Centre National de la Recherche Scientifique, 1981.

Homilies of Ælfric. A Supplementary Collection, 2 vols. Ed. John C. Pope. London: Oxford UP, 1967–1968. Early English Texts Society orig. series 259–260.

Honegeer, Thomas. *From Phoenix to Chauntecleer: Medieval English Animal Poetry*. Tübingen, Basel: Francke, 1996.

Howe, Nicholas. *Writing the Map of Anglo-Saxon England: Essays in Cultural Geography*. New Haven, London: Yale UP, 2008.

Irving, Edward B. Jr. 'Heroic experience in the Old English Riddles'. *Old English Shorter Poems: basic readings*. Ed. Katherine O'Brien-O'Keeffe. New York: Garland, 1994.

Jacoby, Felix, editor. *Die Fragmente der griechischen Historiker*. Vol. C. Leiden: Brill, 1958.

James, Montague Rhodes, editor. *Marvels of the East. A Full Reproduction of the Three Known Copies with Introduction and Notes*. Oxford: Oxford UP, 1929.

Jember, Gregory K., translator. *The Old English Riddles*. Denver: Society for New Language Study, 1976.

Joy, Eileen. 'The signs and location of a flight (or return?) of time: The Old English *Wonders of the East* and the Gujarat massacre'. *Cultural Diversity in the British Middle Ages: Archipelago, Island, England*. Ed. Jeffrey Jerome Cohen. New York: Palgrave Macmillan, 2008.

Kay, Sarah. 'Legible skin: Animal and the ethics of medieval reading'. *Postmedieval: A Journal of Medieval Cultural Studies* 2 (2011): 13–32.

Kay, Sarah. *Animal Skin and the Reading of the Self in Medieval Latin and French Bestiaries*. Chicago, London: The University of Chicago Press, 2017.

Keil, Heinrich and Theodore Mommsen, editors. *Grammatici Latini: Probi, Donati, Servii qui feruntur De arte grammatica libri, et Notarum laterculi*. Vol. 4. I ed. 1864. Repr. Cambridge: Cambridge UP, 2009.

Kennedy, Charles W. *The Earliest English Poetry*. Oxford: Oxford UP, 1943.

Ker, Neil R. *Catalogue of Manuscripts Containing Anglo-Saxon*. 215–216. Oxford: Clarendon Press, 1975. Repr. 1990.

Kim, Susan. 'Man-eating monsters and ants as big as dogs'. *Animals and the Symbolic in Mediaeval Art and Literature*. Ed. L. A. J. R. Houwen. Groningen: Egbert Forsten, 1997.

Kim, Susan. 'The Donestre and the person of both sexes'. *Naked before God: Uncovering the Body in Anglo-Saxon England*. Ed. Benjamin Withers and Jonathan Wilcox. Morgantown: West Virginia UP, 2003.

King Alfred's West Saxon Version of Gregory's Pastoral Care. Ed. Henry Sweet. London, 1871–1872. Early English Text Society orig. series 45–50.

Klaeber's Beowulf and the Fight at Finnsburg. Ed. R. D. Fulk et al. Toronto: University of Toronto Press, 2008.

Klein, Thomas. 'Resolving Exeter Book Riddles 74 and 33: Stormy allomorphs of water'. *Quidditas* 35 (2014): 29–47.

Klinck, Anne L., editor. *The Old English Elegies: A Critical Edition and Genre Study*. Montreal: McGill-Queen's UP, 2001.

Klingender, Francis. *Animals in Art and Thought to the End of the Middle Ages*. Cambridge: The MIT Press, 1971.

Knappe, Gabriele. 'Classical rhetoric in Anglo-Saxon England'. *Anglo-Saxon England* 27 (1998): 5–29. https://doi.org/10.1017/S02636 75100004774

Knappe, Gabriele. *Traditionen der klassischen Rhetorik im angelsächsischen England*. Heidelberg: Carl Winter, 1996.

Knock, Ann, editor. *Wonders of the East: A Synoptic Edition of the Letter of Pharasmenes and the Old English and Old Picard Translations*. Diss. University of London, 1982.

Krapp, George P. and Elliot V. K. Dobbie, editors. *The Anglo-Saxon Poetic Records: A Collective Edition*. 6 vols. New York: Columbia UP, 1931–1953.

Kristeva, Julia. *Powers of Horror: An Essay on Abjection*. Trans. Leon S. Roudiez. New York: Columbia UP, 1982.

Lapidge, Michael. *The Anglo-Saxon Library*. Oxford: Oxford UP, 2006.

Leach, Edmund. 'Anthropological aspects of languages: Animal categories and verbal abuse'. *New Directions in the Study of Language*. Ed. Eric Lenneberg. Cambridge: The MIT Press, 1964.

Lehr, Amanda. 'Sexing the cannibal in the *Wonders of the East* and *Beowulf*'. *Postmedieval: A Journal of Medieval Cultural Studies* 9 (2018): 179–195. https://doi.org/10.1057/s41280-018-0082-6

Lendinara, Patrizia. 'Aspetti della società germanica negli Enigmi del Codice Exoniense'. *Antichità germaniche I: Parte I Seminario avanzato di filologia germanica*. Ed. Vittoria Dolcetti Corazza and Renato Gendre. Alessandria: Edizioni dell'Orso, 2001.

Lendinara, Patrizia. 'Di meraviglia in meraviglia'. *Circolazione di uomini, di idee e di testi nel Medioevo germanico. Atti del xxv Convegno dell'Associazione Italiana di Filologia Germanica*. Ed. Franco De Vivo. Cassino: Edizioni dell'Università di Cassino, 2002.

Lendinara, Patrizia. 'I donestri, pericolosi indovini delle *Meraviglie dell'Oriente*'. ... *un tuo serto di fiori in man recando. Scritti in onore di Maria Amalia D'Aronco*. 2 vols. Ed. Silvana Serafin and Patrizia Lendinara. Udine: Forum, 2008.

Lendinara, Patrizia. 'Mostruosità femminili/ -e nel *Liber monstrorum* e nelle *Meraviglie dell'Oriente*'. *Mostri, animali, macchine: Figure e controfigure dell'umano*. Ed. Francesca Maria Dovetto and Rodrigo Frías Urrea. Roma: Aracne Editrice, 2019.

Lenfant, Dominique. 'Monsters in Greek ethnography and society'. *From Myth to Reason?* Ed. Richard Buxton. New York: Oxford UP, 1999.

Lester, Godfrey Allen. '*Sindrum Begrunden* in Exeter Book Riddle No. 26'. *Notes and Queries* 38 (1991): 13–15.

Lévi-Strauss, Claude. *Le cru et le cuit*. Paris: Plon, 1964.

Liberman, Anatoly. 'Berserks in history and legend'. *Russian History* 32 (2005): 401–411.

Liebermann, Felix, editor. *Die Gesetze der Angelsachsen*. 3 vols. Halle: Max Niemeyer, 1903.

Lindelöf, Uno Lorenz, editor. *Rituale Ecclesiae Dunelmensis. The Durham Collectar. A New and Revised Edition of the Latin Text with the Interlinear Anglo-Saxon Version*. Durham: Andrews & Co., 1927.

Lloyd, H. G. *The Red Fox*. London: Batsford, 1980.

LSJ = Liddell, Henry et al., editors. *A Greek-English Lexicon: With a Revised Supplement*. Oxford: Clarendon Press, 1843–1996.

Maag, Victor. 'Das Tier in den Religionen'. *Das Tier in der menschlichen Kultur*. Ed. Josef Frewein. Zurich: Artemis, 1983.

Mackie, William S., editor. *The Exeter Book, Part II: Poems IX–XXXII*. London, New York: Oxford UP, 1958.

Magennis, Hugh. *Anglo-Saxon Appetites: Food and Drink and Their Consumption in Old English and Related Literature*. Dublin: Four Court Press, 1999.

Malcolm Shaner, D. and Kent A. Vliet. 'Crocodile tears: And thei eten hem wepynge'. *BioScience* 57.7 (July/August 2007): 615–617.

Malone, Kempt, editor. *The Nowell Codex: British Museum Cotton Vitellius A. xv, second ms.* Copenhagen: Rosenkilde and Bagger, 1963. Early English Manuscripts in Facsimile 12.

Manganella, Gemma. 'Gli animali nella poesia anglosassone'. *Annali dell'Istituto Orientale di Napoli, Sezione Germanica* 8 (1965): 261–284.

Marino, Matthew. 'The literariness of the "Exeter Book" Riddles'. *Neuphilologische Mitteilunge* 79.3 (1978): 258–265.

Marsden, Richard. 'Ask what I am called: The Anglo-Saxons and their Bibles'. *The Bible as Book: The Manuscript Tradition.* Ed. John L. Sharpe III and Kimberly Van Kampen. London: British Library, 1998.

Martial. *Epigrams.* 3 vols. Ed. and trans. D. R. Shackleton Bailey. Cambridge, London: Harvard UP, 1993. Loeb Classical Library.

Masters, Roger D. 'From duality to complexity in the study of human nature'. *Politics and the Life Sciences* 13.1 (1994): 112–115.

McGurk, Patrick et al., editors. *An Eleventh-Century Anglo-Saxon Illustrated Miscellany (British Library Cotton Tiberius B. v part 1).* Copenhagen: Rosenkilde and Bagger, 1983. Early English Manuscripts in Facsimile 21.

Meadows, Ian. *The Pioneer Burial: A High Status Anglian Warrior Burial from Wollaston Northamptonshire.* Oxford: Archaeopress Archaeology, 2019.

Meli, Marcello. 'Enigmi nella sapienza e sapienza negli enigmi'. *L'immagine Riflessa* 19 (2010): 37–65.

Meritt, Herbert Dean, editor. *Old English Glosses: A Collection.* New York: Modern Language Association General Series, 1945. Repr. 1971.

Merkelbach, Rebecca. '*Eigi í mannligu eðli*: Shape, Monstrosity and Berserkism in the *Íslendingasögur*'. *Shapeshifters in Medieval North Atlantic Literature.* Ed. Santiago Barreiro and Luciana Cordo Russo. Amsterdam: Amsterdam UP, 2019.

Miller, Rowland S. *Embarrassment: Poise and Peril in Everyday Life.* New York: Guilford, 1996.

Mittman, Asa Simon and Susan Kim, editors. *Inconceivable Beasts: The Wonders of the East in the* Beowulf *Manuscript.* Tempe: The Arizona Center for Medieval and Renaissance Studies, 2013.

Mittman, Asa Simon. *Maps and Monsters in Medieval England*. New York, London: Routledge, 2006.

Muir, Bernard, editor. *The Exeter Anthology of Old English Poetry*. 2 vols. Exeter: University of Exeter Press, 2000.

Muratori, Antonio Ludovico. *Antiquitates Italicae Medii Aevi*. 6 vols. Mediolani, ex Typographia Societatis Palatinae in Regia Curia, I ed. 1738–1742. Repr. Bologna: Forni, 1965.

Murphy, Patrick J. *Unriddling the Exeter Riddles*. University Park: Penn State UP, 2011.

Nalesini, Oscar. 'History and use of an ethnonym: *Ichthyophágoi*'. *Connected Hinterlands: Proceedings of Red Sea Project IV*. Ed. Lucy Blue et al. Oxford: Archaeopress, 2009.

Napier, Arthur Sampson. *Old English Glosses.* Oxford: Clarendon Press, 1900. Repr. Hildesheim, 1969. Anecdota Oxoniensia, Mediaeval and Modern Series 11.

Nelson, Marie. 'Old English Riddle 15: The "badger" an early example of mock heroic'. *Neophilologus* 59.3 (July 1975): 447–450.

Nelson, Marie. 'The rhetoric of the Exeter Book Riddles'. *Speculum* 49 (1974): 421–440.

Neville, Jennifer. *Representation of the Natural World in Old English Poetry*. Cambridge: Cambridge UP, 1999.

Niles, John D. *Old English Enigmatic Poems and the Play of the Texts*. Turnhout: Brepols, 2006.

Niles, John D. *Old English Literature: A Guide to Criticism with Selected Readings*. Chichester, Walden: Wiley Blackwell, 2016.

North, Richard. 'You sexy beast: The pig in a villa in Vandalic North Africa and boar-cults in Old Germanic heathendom'. *Representing Beasts in Early Medieval England and Scandinavia*. Ed. Michael Bintley and Thomas Williams. Woodbridge: Boydell & Brewer, 2015.

O'Loughlin, Thomas. *Teachers and Code-Breakers: The Latin Genesis Tradition, 430–800*. Turnhout: Brepols, 1999.

The Old English Dialogues of Solomon and Saturn. Ed. Daniel Anlezark. Cambridge: D. S. Brewer, 2009.

The Old English Heptateuch and Ælfric's 'Libellus de veteri testamento et novo'. Ed. Richard Marsden. Oxford: Oxford UP, 2008. Early English Text Society orig. series 330.

Oppianus Apameensis. *Cynegetica, Eutecnius Sophistes: Paraphrasis Metro Soluta*. Ed. Manolis Papathomopoulos. München, Leipzig: K. G. Saur, 2003. Bibliotheca Scriptorum Graecorum et Latinorum Teubneriana.

Orchard, Andy. *Pride and Prodigies: Studies in the monsters of the Beowulf-Manuscript*. Cambridge: D. S. Brewer, 1995.

Orchard, Andy. 'Enigma variations: The Anglo-Saxon Riddle-Tradition'. *Latin Learning and English Lore: Studies in Anglo-Saxon Literature for Michael Lapidge*. 2 vols. Ed. Andy Orchard and Katherine O'Brien O'Keeffe. Toronto: University of Toronto Press, 2005.

Orchard, Andy. 'Reconstructing The Ruin'. *Intertexts: Studies in Anglo-Saxon Culture Presented to Paul E. Szarmach*. Ed. Virginia Blanton and Helene Scheck. Tempe: Brepols, 2008.

Orchard, Andy. 'Performing writing and singing silence in the Anglo-Saxon Riddle Tradition'. *Or Words to that Effect: Orality and the Writing of Literary History*. Ed. Daniel F. Chamberlain and J. Edward Chamberlain. Philadelphia: John Benjamins, 2016.

Orchard, Andy, editor and translator. *The Old English and Anglo-Latin Riddle Tradition*. Cambridge, London: Harvard UP, 2021. Dumbarton Oaks Medieval Library 69.

Orchard, Andy. *A Commentary on The Old English and Anglo-Latin Riddle Tradition: Supplement to Dumbarton Oaks Medieval Library 69*. Cambridge: Harvard UP, 2021.

Orel, Vladimir, editor. *A Handbook of Germanic Etymology*. Leiden, Boston: Brill, 2003.

Ortner, Sherry B. 'Is female to male as nature is to culture?' *Woman, Culture, and Society*. Ed. Michelle Z. Rosaldo and Louise Lamphere. Stanford: Stanford UP, 1974.

Orton, Peter. 'The technique of object-personification in *The Dream of the Rood* and a comparison with the Old English *Riddles*'. *Leeds Studies in English* 11 (January 1980): 1–15.

Osborn, Marijane. 'Vixen as hero: Solving Exeter Book Riddle 15'. *The Hero Recovered: Essays on Medieval Heroism in Honor of George Clark*. Ed. Robin Waugh and James Weldon. Kalamazoo: Western Michigan University, 2010.

Oswald, Dana. 'Unnatural women, invisible mothers: Monstrous female bodies in the *Wonders of the East*'. *Different Visions: A Journal of New Perspectives on Medieval Art* 2 (June 2010): 1–33.

Oswald, Dana. *Monsters, Gender and Sexuality in Medieval English Literature*. Cambridge: D. S. Brewer, 2010.

Page, Raymond Ian, *Anglo-Saxon Aptitudes: An Inaugural Lecture Delivered before the University of Cambridge on 6 March 1985*. Cambridge: Cambridge UP, 1985.

Palatine Anthology = *Antologia Palatina*. 3 vols. Ed. Fabrizio Conca et al. Torino: Utet, 2005–2011.

Parkes, M. B. 'The manuscript of the Leiden Riddle'. *Anglo-Saxon England* 1 (January 1972): 207–217. https://doi.org/10.1017/S0263675100000168

Paz, James. *Non-Human Voices in Anglo-Saxon Literature and Material Culture*. Manchester: Manchester UP, 2017.

Pelteret, David. *Slavery in Early Medieval England*. New York: Boydell, 1995.

Petronius. *Satyricon*. Ed. and trans. Gareth Schmeling. Cambridge, MA: Harvard UP, 2020. Loeb Classical Library 15.

Pinsker, Hans and Waltraud Ziegler. *Die altenglischen Rätsel des Exeterbuchs*. Heidelberg: Carl Winter, 1985.

Pitra, Jean Baptiste. *Analecta Sacra Spicilegio Solesmensi Parata*. Vol. II. Typis Tusculanis, 1884.

Plautus. *Bacchides*. Ed. John Barsby. Liverpool UP, 1986.

Plinius, Caius Secundus. *Naturalis historia*. 6 vols. Ed. Ludwig Ian and Karl Mayhoff. Leipzig: Teubner, 1892–1909.

Plumwood, Val. *Feminism and the Mastery of Nature*. London, New York: Routledge, 1993.

Pope, John C. 'An unsuspected Lacuna in the Exeter Book: Divorce proceedings for an ill-matched couple in the Old English Riddles'. *Speculum* 49 (October 1974): 615–622.

Porsia, Franco, editor. *Liber Monstrorum (secolo IX)*. Napoli: Liguori, 2012.

Powell, Kathryn. *The Anglo-Saxon Imagery of the East: A Psychoanalytic Exploration of the Image of the East in Old English Literature*. Diss. University of Notre Dame, 2001.

Preston, Todd. 'An Alternative Solution to *Exeter Book* riddle 77'. *Viator* 42.1 (2011): 25–34.
Quintilian. *Institutio oratoria*. Ed. Tobias Reinhardt and Michael Winterbottom. Oxford, New York: Oxford UP, 2006.
Ramazzina, Elisa. 'Le Meraviglie d'Oriente: due Versioni a Confronto'. *Medioevi Moderni – Modernità del Medioevo*. Ed. Marina Buzzoni. Venezia: Ca' Foscari – Digital Publishing, 2013.
Rauer, Christine, editor. *The Old English Martirology*. Cambridge: D. S. Brewer, 2013.
Richards, I. A. *The Philosophy of Rhetoric*. Oxford: Oxford UP, 1936.
Richards, Mary P., editor. *The Old English Poem Seasons for Fasting: A Critical Edition*. Morgantown: West Virginia UP, 2014.
Robinson, Fred. *Beowulf and the appositive style*. Knoxville: University of Tennessee Press, 1985.
Roby, Matthew. 'Eating people and feeling sorry: Cannibals, contrition, and the didactic Donestre in the Old English *Wonders of the East* and Latin *Mirabilia*'. *Darkness, Depression and Descent in Anglo-Saxon England*. Ed. Ruth Wehlau. Kalamazoo: Medieval Institute Publications, 2019.
Rypins, Stanley, editor. *Three Old English Prose Text in MS Cotton Vitellius A. XV*. London, 1924. Early English Text Society orig. series 161.
Salisbury, Joyce. *The Beast Within: Animals in the Middle Ages*. London, New York: Routledge, 2011.
Salvador-Bello, Mercedes. 'Direct and indirect clues: Exeter Riddle No. 74 reconsidered'. *Neuphilologische Mitteilungen* 99.1 (1998): 17–29.
Salvador-Bello, Mercedes. *Isidorean Perception of Order: The Exeter Book Riddles and Medieval Latin Enigmata*. Morgantown: West Virginia UP, 2015.
Saunders, Roselyn. 'Becoming undone: Monstrosity, *leaslicum wordum*, and the strange case of the Donestre'. *Different Visions: A Journal of New Perspectives on Medieval Art* 2 (June 2010): 1–36.
Schlauch, Margaret. 'The dream of the Rood' as Prosopopoeia'. *Essays and studies in Honour of Carleton Brown*. Ed. P. W. Long. New York: New York UP, 1940.

Schneider, André, editor. *Le premier Livre* Ad Nationes *de Tertullian: Introduction, texte, traduction et commentaire*. Rome: Institut Suisse de Rome, 1968.

Schröer, Arnold, editor. *Die angelsächsischen Prosabearbeitungen der Benediktinerregel*. Kassel, 1885. Repr. Darmstadt: Wissenschaftliche Buchgesellschaft, 1964.

Senderovich, Savely. *The Riddle of the Riddle: A Study of the Folk Riddle's Figurative Nature*. London: Kegan Paul, 2005.

Shook, Laurence Kennedy. 'Riddles relating to the Anglo-Saxon scriptorium'. *Essays in Honour of A. C. Pegis*, Ed. J. Reginald O'Donnell. Toronto: Pontifical Institute of Medieval Studies, 1974.

Sisam, Kenneth. *Studies in the History of Old English Literature*. Oxford: Clarendon Press, 1953.

Snorri Sturluson. *Heimskringla I. The beginnings to Óláfr Tryggvason*. Trans. Alison Finlay and Anthony Faulkes. London: Viking Society for Northern Research, University College London, 2011.

Solinus. *Wunder der Welt*. Ed. Kai Brodersen. Darmstadt: Wissenschaftliche Buchgesellschaft, 2014.

Soper, Harriet. 'Reading the *Exeter Book* Riddles as life writing'. *The Review of English Studies: New Series* 68.287 (November 2017): 841–865.

Stallybrass, Peter and Allon White. *The Politics and Poetics of Transgression*. Ithaca: Cornell UP, 1986.

Steel, Karl. 'How to make a human'. *Exemplaria* 20.1 (2008): 3–27.

Steel, Karl. *How Not to Make a Human: Pets, Feral Children, Worms, Sky Burial, Oysters*. University of Minnesota Press, 2019.

Steen, Janie. *Verse and Virtuosity: The Adaptation of Latin Rhetoric in Old English Poetry*. Toronto, Buffalo, London: University of Toronto Press, 2008.

Stryker, William G., editor. *The Latin-Old English Glossary in MS. Cotton Cleopatra A.III*. Diss. Stanford University, 1951.

Swanton, Michael, editor. *The Dream of the Rood*. Exeter: Exeter UP, 1987.

Tally Lionarons, Joyce. 'From monster to martyr: The Old English legend of Saint Christopher'. *Marvels, Monsters and Miracles*. Ed. Timothy

S. Jones and David A. Sprunger. Kalamazoo: Western Michigan University, 2002.

Taylor, Archer. 'The Riddle'. *California Folklore Quarterly* 2.2 (1943): 129–147. https://doi.org/10.2307/1495557

Terence. *The woman of Andros; The self-tormentor; The eunuch*. Ed. and trans. John Barsby. Cambridge, London: Harvard UP, 2001.

Thompson, Stith. *Motif-Index of Folk-Literature: A Classification of Narrative Elements in Folktales, Ballads, Myths, Fables, Medieval Romances, Exempla, Fabliaux, Jest-books, and Local Legends*. Bloomington: Indiana UP, 1955–1958.

Tigges, Wim. 'Snakes and ladders: Ambiguity and coherence in the Exeter Book Riddles and Maxims'. *Companion to Old English Poetry*. Ed. Henk Aertsen and Rolf H. Bremmer. Amsterdam: VU UP, 1994.

Tilley, Maureen A. 'Martyrs, monks, insects and animals'. *The Medieval World of Nature*. Ed. Joyce E. Salisbury. New York: Garland, 1993.

Torre Alonso, Roberto. *Morphological Process Feeding in the Formation of Old English Nouns: Zero-Derivation, Affixation and Compounding*. Diss. Universidad de la Rioja, 2011.

Trautmann, Moritz, editor. *Die Altenenglischen Rätsel (die Rätsel des Exeterbuchs)*. Heidelberg, New York: Carl Winter, 1915.

Tupper, Frederick, editor. *The Riddles of the Exeter Book*. Boston: Ginn & Co., 1910.

Uebel, Michael. 'Unthinking the monster'. *Monster Theory: Reading Culture*. Ed. Jeffrey Jerome Cohen. Minneapolis, London: University of Minnesota Press, 1996.

Vegetti, Mario. *Il coltello e lo stilo*. Milano: Il Saggiatore, 1996.

Volpato, Chiara. *Deumanizzazione: Come si legittima la violenza*. Roma, Bari: Editori Laterza, E-book ed., 2014.

Walz, John A. 'Notes on the Anglo-Saxon Riddles'. *Harvard Studies and Notes* 5 (1896): 261–268.

Webster, Leslie. *Anglo-Saxon Art: A New History*. London: British Museum Press, 2012.

Whitelock, Dorothy. *The Beginnings of English Society*. Baltimore: Penguin Books, 1954.

Whitman, Frank H. 'Medieval riddling: Factors underlying its development'. *Neuphilologische Mitteilungen* 71 (1970): 177–185.

Wilcox, Jonathan. '"Tell Me What I Am": The Old English Riddles'. *Readings in Medieval Texts: Interpreting Old and Middle English Literature*. Ed. David Johnson and Elaine Treharne. Oxford: Oxford UP, 2005.

Wilcox, Jonathan. 'Naked in Old English: The embarrassed and the shamed'. *Naked before God: Uncovering the Body in Anglo-Saxon England*. Ed. Benjamin Withers and Jonathan Wilcox. Morgantown: West Virginia UP, 2003.

Williams, David. *Deformed Discourse: The Function of the Monster in Medieval Thought and Literature*. Montreal, Kingston: Mc Gill-Queen's UP, 1996.

Williamson, Craig, editor. *The Old English Riddles of the Exeter Book*. Chapel Hill: University of North Carolina Press, 1977.

Williamson, Craig. *A Feast of Creatures: Anglo-Saxon Riddle-Songs*. Philadelphia: University of Pennsylvania Press, 1982.

Wittkower, Rudolf. 'Marvel of the East: A study in the history of monsters'. *Journal of the Warburg and Courthauld Institutes* 5 (1942): 159–197.

Wulfstan. *Sammlung der ihm zugeschriebenen Homilien nebst Untersuchungen über ihre Echtheit, Erste Abteilung; Text und Varianten*. Ed. Arthur Sampson Napier. 1883. Repr. Berlin: Weidmann, 1967.

Wyatt, Alfred John, editor. *Old English Riddles*. Boston: D. C. Heath, 1912.

Wyatt, David. *Slaves and Warriors in Medieval Britain and Ireland, 800–1200*. Leiden, Boston: Brill, 2009.

Yamamoto, Dorothy. *The Boundaries of the Human in Medieval English Literature*. Oxford: Oxford UP, 2000.

Young, Jean I. 'Riddle 15 of the Exeter Book'. *Review of English Studies* 20.80 (October 1944): 304–306. https://doi.org/10.1093/res/os-XX.80.304

Zaki, Jamil and Kevin N. Ochsner. 'Empathy'. *Handbook of Emotions*. Ed. Lisa Feldman Barrett et al. New York: Guilford, 2016.

Zambon, Francesco, editor. *Il fisiologo*. Milano: Adelphi, 1975.

Ziolkowski, Jan M. 'Literary genre and animal symbolism'. *Animals and the Symbolic in Mediaeval Art and Literature.* Ed. L. A. J. R. Houwen. Groningen: Egbert Forsten, 1997.

Zweck, Jordan. 'Silence in the Exeter Book Riddles'. *Exemplaria: Medieval, Early Modern, Theory* 28 (October 2016): 319–336.

SITOGRAPHY

British Library: Digitized Manuscripts: Cotton MS Tiberius B V/1. <http://www.bl.uk/manuscripts/Viewer.aspx?ref=cotton_ms_tiberius_b_v!1_f002r>.

British Library: Digitized Manuscripts: Cotton MS Vitellius A XV. <http://www.bl.uk/manuscripts/Viewer.aspx?ref=cotton_ms_vitellius_a_xv_f094r0>.

Leahy, K., 'The contents of the hoard'. *Portable Antiquities Scheme.* <https://finds.org.uk/staffshoardsymposium/papers/kevinleahy>.

Migne, J. P., editor. *De bestiis et aliis rebus, Patrologia latina cursus completus 177*, Paris. I ed. 1854, dig. ed. *Corpus Corporum:repositoriumoperumLatinorumapuduniversitatemTuricensem.* <http://mlat.uzh.ch/?c=2&w=AuInHuD.DeBeEtA>.

Digital Bodleian: Oxford, Bodleian Library MS. Bodl. 614. <https://digital.bodleian.ox.ac.uk/objects/a43be554-c5b0-42f0-94e0-70222bb2a964/>.

University of Nottingham: Manuscripts and Special Collections. <https://www.nottingham.ac.uk/manuscriptsandspecialcollections/researchguidance/medievalbooks/materials.aspx>.

Critical Perspectives on English and American Literature, Communication and Culture

Edited by
María José Álvarez-Faedo, Andrew Monnickendam &
Beatriz Penas-Ibáñez

The peer-reviewed series provides a forum for first-class scholarship in the field of English and American Studies and focuses on English and American literature, drama, film, theatre and communication. The series welcomes critical perspectives on the reading and writing of texts, the production and consumption of high and low culture, the aesthetic and social implications of texts and communicative practices. It publishes monographs, collected papers, conference proceedings and critical editions. The languages of publication are both English and Spanish. Scholars are invited to submit their manuscripts to the editors or to the publisher.

Vol. 1   Juan Jesús Zaro
         Shakespeare y sus traductores. Análisis crítico de siete traducciones españolas de obras de Shakespeare.
         2007, 176 p. ISBN 978-3-03911-454-2

Vol. 2   María José Chivite de León
         Echoes of History, Shadowed Identities.
         Rewriting Alterity in J. M. Coetzee's *Foe* and Marina Warner's *Indigo*.
         2010, XVI, 241 p. ISBN 978-3-0343-0070-4

Vol. 3   Nela Bureu Ramos (ed.)
         Flaming Embers.
         Literary Testimonies on Ageing and Desire.
         2010, 361 p. ISBN 978-3-0343-0438-2

| Vol. | 4 | Manuel Brito
Means Matter.
Market Fructification of Innovative American Poetry in the Late 20th Century.
2010, XII, 170 p. ISBN 978-3-0343-0444-3 |

| Vol. | 5 | José Ruiz Mas
Guardias civiles, bandoleros, gitanos, guerrilleros, contrabandistas, carabineros y turistas en la literatura inglesa contemporánea (1844–1994).
2010, 395 p. ISBN 978-3-0343-0506-8 |

| Vol. | 6 | Juan Ignacio Oliva (ed.)
The Painful Chrysalis.
Essays on Contemporary Cultural and Literary Identity.
2011, 282 p. ISBN 978-3-0343-0666-9 |

| Vol. | 7 | Celia M. Wallhead (ed.)
Writers of the Spanish Civil War.
The Testimony of their Auto/Biographies.
2011, 329 p. ISBN 978-3-0343-0696-6 |

| Vol. | 8 | Laura Ma Lojo Rodríguez
Moving across a Century.
Women's Short Fiction from Virginia Woolf to Ali Smith.
2012, 131 p. ISBN 978-3-0343-1064-2 |

| Vol. | 9 | Marta Sofía López
Ginealogías sáficas.
De Katherine Philips a Jeanette Winterson.
2012, 167 p. ISBN 978-3-0343-1125-0 |

| Vol. | 10 | Marta Fernández Morales (ed.)
La década del miedo.
Dramaturgias audiovisuales post-11 de septiembre.
2013, 398 p. ISBN 978-3-0343-1311-7 |

| Vol. | 11 | Michele Bottalico (ed.)
No! In Whispers
The Rhetoric of Dissent in American Writing
2018, 240 p. ISBN 978-3-0343-2001-6 |

Vol. 12   José María Mesa Villar
           Women in Dante Gabriel Rossetti's Arthurian
           Renditions (1854-1867).
           2014, 482 p. ISBN 978-3-0343-1298-1

Vol. 13   Martin Simonson & Raúl Montero Gilete
           El Héroe del Oeste en *Las Crónicas de Narnia*.
           2014, 173 p. ISBN 978-3-0343-1601-9

Vol. 14   Nailya Garipova & Juan José Torres Núñez (eds)
           Women in Nabokov's Life and Art.
           2016, 272 p. ISBN 978-3-0343-2056-6

Vol. 15   Núria Casado-Gual, Emma Domínguez-Rué &
           Brian Worsfold (eds)
           Literary Creativity and the Older Woman Writer.
           A Collection of Critical Essays.
           2016, 299 p. ISBN 978-3-0343-2199-0

Vol. 16   Beatriz Penas-Ibáñez & Akiko Manabe (eds)
           Cultural Hybrids of (Post)Modernism.
           Japanese and Western Literature, Art and Philosophy.
           2016, 234 p. ISBN 978-3-0343-2136-5

Vol. 17   Masako Nasu
           From Individual to Collective.
           Virginia Woolf's Developing Concept of Consciousness.
           2017, 226 p. ISBN 978-3-0343-2121-1

Vol. 18   Elsa Cavalié & Laurent Mellet (eds)
           Only Connect.
           E. M. Forster's Legacies in British Fiction.
           2017, 348 p. ISBN 978-3-0343-2599-8

Vol. 19   Martin Simonson
           El Western fantástico de Stephen King.
           Hibridización y desencantamiento de la tradición
           literaria europea en *El Pistolero*
           2018, 160 p. ISBN 978-3-0343-3232-3

| Vol. | 20 | Celia M. Wallhead (ed.)
More Writers of the Spanish Civil War.
Experience Put to Use
2018, 372 p. ISBN 978-3-0343-3209-5 |
|---|---|---|
| Vol. | 21 | Elena Ungari
Voss: An Australian Geographical and Literary Exploration
History and Travelling in the Fiction of Patrick White
2018, 356 p ISBN 978-3-0343-3544-7 |
| Vol. | 22 | Martin Simonson
El Oeste recuperado.
La literatura del pasado y la construcción
de personajes en *El Señor de los Anillos*
2018, 206 p. ISBN 978-3-0343-3731-1 |
| Vol. | 23 | Maurizio Ascari, Serena Baiesi
& David Levente Palatinus (eds.)
Gothic Metamorphoses across the Centuries
Contexts, Legacies, Media
2019, 242 p. ISBN 978-3-0343-3228-6 |
| Vol. | 24 | Irene Pérez-Fernández and Carmen Pérez Ríu (eds.)
Romantic Escapes. Post-Millennial Trends in
Contemporary Popular Romance Fiction
2021, 330 p. ISBN 978-3-0343-4212-4 |
| Vol. | 25 | Laura Martínez-García & María José Álvarez Faedo (eds.)
(Re)defining gender in early modern English drama.
Power, sexualities and ideologies in text and performance
2020, 258 p. ISBN 978-3-0343-4252-0 |
| Vol. | 26 | María Luisa Candau Chacón (ed.)
Viajeras de Élite.
Experiencias, recorridos, textos.Siglos XIX y XX.
2021, 284 p. ISBN 978-3-0343-4183-7 |
| Vol. | 27 | Martin Simonson & Jon Alkorta Martiartu
From East to West
The Portrayal of Nature in British Fantasy and
its Projection in Ursula K. Le Guin's Western American
Earthsea
2021, 160 p. ISBN 978-3-0343-4250-6 |

| Vol. 28 | Juan de Dios Torralbo Caballero
Fugitive Papers
Orinda's Literary Career
2023, 210 p. ISBN 978-3-0343-4622-1 |

| Vol. 29 | Raúl Montero Gilete & Aitor Seijas Conde
Visión ambiental del hogar en la británica La Comunidad del Anillo de J. R. R. Tolkien frente al Lejano Oeste americano de Mago y Cristal de Stephen King
2023, 200 p. ISBN 978-3-0343-4675-7 |

| Vol. 30 | Bruno Echauri-Galván
Polvo eres y en cine te convertirás
Valoraciones y relevancia de la fidelidad
en la recepción de la adaptación
cinematográfica de *Ask the Dust*
2023, 184 p. ISBN 978-3-0343-4681-8 |

| Vol. 31 | Jasmine Bria
Riddles and Wonders: Defining Humanity in Anglo-Saxon England 2023, 196 p. ISBN 978-3-0343-4504-0 |

www.ingramcontent.com/pod-product-compliance
Lightning Source LLC
Chambersburg PA
CBHW020110020526
44112CB00033B/1127